SCRATCHING

the HORIZON

Izzy Paskowitz

with Daniel Paisner

SCRATCHING the HORIZON

A Surfing Life

St. Martin's Press
New York

www.stmartins.com

Design by Kathryn Parise

ISBN 978-1-250-00600-4 (hardcover)
ISBN 978-1-250-02399-5 (e-book)

First Edition: August 2012

10   9   8   7   6   5   4   3   2   1

To Eli . . .
thanks for putting up with
all of our crazy shit.
I love you.

CONTENTS

There is a wisdom in the wave,

highborn and beautiful,

for those who would but paddle out.

—Hawaiian proverb, pinched from the author's father,
Dorian "Doc" Paskowitz, who's been passing it off as his
own for just about forever

SCRATCHING
the HORIZON

PROLOGUE

A Good Day

June 29, 2011.

Wasn't really thinking of this day as anything different, anything *other* than all the rest. Wasn't really thinking much at all, except to do what I had to do, get where I was going. Feed the horses. Load a bunch of boards and wet suits in the truck. Hug my kids. Grab a change of clothes for later. Get to work.

Just another stretch of daylight on a long string of many.

The focus, heading out, was the Surfers Healing event I was running with my wife, Danielle, together with a couple dozen big-hearted surfer pals and assorted friends and family members. Surfers Healing is a foundation Danielle and I started in 1999 after we discovered our autistic son, Isaiah, did a whole lot better in the water than on dry land. Seemed like it was our own little discovery at first, just a way to calm our own kid; Isaiah was small enough I could grab him by the scruff of his life vest and get him up on a board, and for a few moments he was like any other kid on the beach. Riding waves. Laughing. Folks took notice, and soon they were asking me to help their kids catch some of the same, so what started as something for us became something for everybody; families with kids on the autism spectrum, covering the whole range of pervasive developmental disorders, filled the beach, and I was stoked to help out.

These days, Isaiah is six-three, three hundred pounds, and way too big for me to get up on a board, but he still loves the water. We've found some giant bully boards, made for big ol' Hawaiians like Isaiah, and he lolls about on one of them for hours at a time, bear-hugging the shoreline. These days, too, Surfers Healing is way too big for Danielle and me to handle on our own. We've grown into a full-fledged non-profit, with free one-day camps for autistic children, which we run up and down both coasts, as well as in Hawaii, Puerto Rico, and Mexico—and, next year for the first time, in Canada. In a typical year, we'll surf with over twenty-five hundred kids. We're not so full of ourselves to think we're delivering any kind of cure-all or washing away a lifetime of hassle and heartache, but we are giving families a bright spot on their calendars, something to look forward to. Even better, something to remember. For an afternoon, at least, these kids are able to run and laugh and splash and shout on a whole other spectrum, and I've come to think of this as a great good thing.

Yep, it's pretty cool. Don't mind saying.

The drill, whenever we run one of these camps, is to bring together all these moving parts and make it seem like we're a well-oiled machine—when, really, the only things well oiled are our faces, to keep clear of the sun. Oh, we have our shit together, at this point; been at it so long we can't help but have it down. But sometimes it feels like it all comes together on its own. Chasing permits, from all the different town beaches. Reaching out to our sponsors, who turn up with food and drink and giveaway items for our campers. Signing up all these families and getting their paperwork in order. Coordinating the itineraries of the world-class surfers, who carve out time in their busy schedules to fly in from Hawaii or Cabo or wherever the hell they're doing their world-class surfing to help out. Making sure we have enough boards and vests and wet suits.

On this day, we're running the event at Doheny State Beach, in Dana Point, California. Been surfing this beach as far back as I can remember. Place gets a bad rap, if you ask me. Way back when, it rated a mention in that Beach Boys song "Surfin' USA," but that was a long time ago. It's since been called one of the most polluted beaches on the West Coast, and for a time it was just that. A lot of hard-core surfers I know won't come anywhere near this beach, although on some days it still draws a crowd. On some days the wave breaks just right and the beach is fine and clean and you get why the place was once a big deal. It's not the easiest spot for us to do our thing, though. The park rangers have us on a tight head count. Most times, we run one of these events, we get a hundred and twenty kids in the water, maybe more, but these guys at Doheny have us capped at eighty. Means we've had to turn away a lot of good people. Means we can't have more than eight boards in the water at any one time. Sucks, but what can you do? Rules are rules…it's just that, here, there are a few too many of them.

The good thing about Doheny is it's in our own backyard, closest thing we've got to home sand. Gives the event a hometown spin. We run these things up and down the California coast—Malibu, Pacific Beach, Tourmaline—but this one's local, personal. Folks here, they know us. And we know them. And this, too, is a great good thing.

Okay, so that's the backdrop when I hop into Danielle's white Ford pickup for the seven-mile zigzag down the mountain from our ranch to civilization. Feels to me like I'm running late, but I'm making good time. Pull into the old part of San Juan Capistrano, right behind the legendary Swallows Inn. Check my watch and see I've got a couple minutes, so I duck into Starbucks for a cup of chai tea. Call ahead to a couple of my volunteer surfers, to see if they want something. Bullshit with some of the locals.

Finally pull in to the beach at Dana Point and start unloading. It's just after nine in the morning; event doesn't start until eleven. And I'm not even the first one here. Far from it. Jennifer Tracy, our volunteer-in-chief, has been at it a good long while, along with a fistful of folks to help out. They've already unloaded a mess of gear, pitched our few sun tents, got our registration desk all set up.

Jennifer's on top of it, so I don't have to be.

From here, the day goes like it's supposed to. Perfect weather. Perfect surf. Perfect vibe. *This part's easy,* I tell myself. *This part's why we bother.* To hang with these families, these special kids, to give them something they can't grab at themselves. It's like a blessing.

Danielle arrives with our own kids, just before we hit the water. Actually, she arrives with Isaiah and our younger son, Eli, fifteen going on Level 93 of whatever video game he's been playing. Our oldest, Elah, arrives separately, in her own car. She lives on her own these days, does her own thing, but Surfers Healing is a full-on family affair, so whenever she can, wherever she is, she drops whatever she's doing to help out. Next, my in-laws check in, along with old friends and new. Everywhere I look, there's a familiar face and a helping hand. I move along the beach between hugs and fist pumps and back claps, and I can't go two feet in any one direction without finding a happy, grateful, nostalgic distraction. I end up making all kinds of small talk with folks I can't quite place. Families we surfed with last summer, or the summer before that. Pose for a ton of pictures. Wonder at the *wonder* of what we're doing.

I'm anxious to get in the water, so I paddle out with my first kid of the day and look to lose myself in the moment. Soon, as we get out past the break, I think to chill. Already the heat and haste of the morning seem to want to drag me down, distract me from why we're here in the first place, so I straddle my board and clear my head. Out here in the water, on the outside, time doesn't mean all that much. When you're competing, you're watching the clock, trying to grab as many waves as you can in the allotted time, but when you're just surfing you're just surfing. There's no rush. You're alone with your own thoughts and a bunch of other surfers alone with their own thoughts. You're all alone together. You're thinking and not thinking, waiting and not waiting. It's like a deep breath. I can hang here with this sweet-faced kid, who seems to be about eight or nine. Doesn't talk much, but he's smiling. A bit anxious, but happy. A lot of times, you paddle out with one of these special kids, they're all coiled up and nervous. You're taking them way away from their comfort zone, and you can see it in their bodies. Some of them, they tense up or shut down. Some of them, they start to cry. But this kid is cool, like he's just waiting for something to happen. Something big.

I ask his name. He tells me. I ask if he likes school. He tells me. I ask if he thinks he can spot his mom on the beach, from all the way out here, and he gives it a long, hard look but comes back blank. He really, really tries but can't even guess. Finally, I ask him if he's ready to catch a wave and head on in and he nods that he is, but it's like a part of him isn't. It's not because he's scared or tentative. It's more like he wants to stay lost in this deep breath moment, this pocket of calm, same as me, because he knows once he gets back to the beach his world will switch back on and he'll be back to how he's always been. He'll find his mom and she'll be on him like she always is, like she has to be, collecting him in a giant towel-hug. Out here he's just like any other kid on the planet, chasing thrills, waiting for something he can't yet know, but back on the beach he'll be special, different.

But then I catch myself and realize, *Hey, this is just me, projecting,* and as I do I see a good-size wave rolling in over my shoulder. Wave feels like it's shaping up just right. Not too big, not to small . . . just right. Feels like one we should take, so we do, and then I repeat the scene a couple times more, with a couple more kids. When I'm on the beach, there's so much warmth and good feeling I don't want to get back in the water, but when I'm out past the break, waiting on the just right wave, chilling with one kid after another, there's such a sweet point of pause I don't want to head back in.

Being out here with these kids, surfing, it's a way to keep their world from spinning. Mine, too. "Extreme special ed"...that's the phrase I use when I tell folks what we're up to with Surfers Healing. Whatever we call it, it's not for the faint of heart—it can get pretty hairy out in the water, so it takes a certain kind of kid to throw in on this kind of adventure. A certain kind of parent, too.

The day unravels like this to where I lose all sense of time. Don't even stop to eat. There are food and energy drinks, donated by some great local sponsors, but it doesn't occur to me to refuel. My dad has come by, like he always does when he's feeling up to it, but I don't have time to hang with him. Not the way I'd like. Not the way we used to. He's ninety years old, and for the past couple years I've been catching myself thinking we can probably count the days in the sun we have left together, so I count this one and file it away while he's off doing his thing. Holding court. Spinning stories. Receiving the warm hellos and glad tidings of the surf set like he's the mayor of the beach, like he has them coming. And he is, he surely is; he does, he surely does.

At some point, I notice that the crowd on the beach has thinned, that the line of kids waiting their turn has disappeared. The sun, I see, is no longer so damn high.

I can't think where the hours have gone, where all these families have gone. We've been so damn knee-deep in doing our thing we don't even look up until the thing is done. It's not until we're cleaning up the beach, hauling our gear back to our trucks and vans, bagging our recyclables, checking the cell phone I'd left in the glove box for messages, that I remember the change of clothes for later. *Oh yeah,* I think. *That.* There's some place I need to be, I'm reminded—downtown San Clemente, for an event honoring a bunch of local surfing legends, past and present. One of those Chamber of Commerce–type deals, to stir up interest in our community, maybe put San Clemente on the map as a happening, legendary surf spot. This, too, is a great good thing—a necessary thing, even, far as our sagging-flagging local economy goes. Since the late 1960s, San Clemente has been known as the home of Richard Nixon's Western White House, but folks who live here know it as a vibrant, Spanish-flavored village with fantastic ocean and mountain views and a rich surfing history. Makes sense to call attention to it, maybe drag some tourists down to see what we're all about.

It just so happens my family is among the group of honorees, together with a mess of good people with giant surfing pedigrees, although it's not really clear if the honor is mostly for my dad, Dorian "Doc" Paskowitz, or for the whole lot of us. Either way, we're grouped with local legends like Dale Velzy, one of my first heroes, a visionary guy who did more to change the shape and vibe of surfboard design than anyone else in the history of our sport; Tubesteak Tracy, the original "Big Kahuna," who was like an uncle to me and my siblings as we grew up on the beach at San Onofre; Corky Carroll, a true surfing pioneer, considered by many to be the sport's first "professional," winner of more than one hundred big-time competitions; and on and on.

Somewhere in there the organizers thought to find room for us Paskowitzes, who came to be known around these parts over forty years ago when my father decided to pack it in on a life of convention and routine and pile all of us kids into a twenty-four-foot camper. We'd live out the American dream—*his* version of it, anyway. We'd come and go as we pleased, unbound by convention. No work. No school. Just an endless, open stretch of days, set against an endless, open stretch of shoreline. There were nine of us before long, and we all surfed, some of us professionally. All of us passionately, purposefully. My parents surfed, too. My father still surfs, when the water's warm enough and the waves don't threaten his old bones.

We spent most of my childhood hopscotching from beach to beach, down into Mexico, along the Gulf coast, and up the Atlantic, with a couple side trips to Israel because it seemed to my quirky, Zionist father that this was something we should do. We never quite knew where we were going, where we'd just been, where our next meal was coming from, or even where we'd park the camper for the night, but at the end of the day—at the end of *every* day!—we were at home with each other, on some beach or other. Between waves and side trips and assorted misadventures, we collected this vast network of great surfing friends. Somehow, our vagabonding, bohemian, fucked-up lifestyle tapped into some of the same currents that moved the workaday worlds of these other kindred spirits, who for the most part had real jobs, real homes, real responsibilities away from the water. And somehow, too, we kept coming back to these beaches in and around San Clemente, where most of us have now settled and continue to surf, so it feels a little bit validating, a little bit thrilling, to be included among this group of surfing honorees.

Folks here, they know us. And we know them. Same deal as before.

Here's the thing you need to know about "local surfing legends": we tend not to think of ourselves as local surfing legends. Hell, we're no more legendary than the scratches on our boards, the scrapes and bruises we wear like badges, the stories we tell over beers. But some of us have made a kind of mark on the sport, on surf culture, and around here I guess that gets us our picture on a big old street banner on what they're calling Surfer's Row, in downtown San Clemente.

Shit, us Paskowitzes pretty much perfected the live-on-the-beach, surf-all-day, party-all-night way of life that came to symbolize the California surfing scene in the sixties and seventies. We *owned* it, lived it. All these years later, we're still going at it in a lot of the same ways, so we're proud to be included among this group. Humbled, too. And, in some ways, a little self-conscious, because whenever these Chamber of Commerce types line you up and get you to pose for pictures it usually means you've been at it a too-long while.

Back of my mind, all day long, I've been planning to go to the OC Tavern for the festivities. It comes up, with folks on the beach, in a *hey, will I see you later?* sort of way. Danielle has been planning to join me, too. It's kind of a big deal, and we want to be there. (Hell, yeah, we want to be there!) But then, as the day runs away from us, the back of my mind gets cluttered up with a whole mess of other stuff, and I put the ceremony out of my head. With all this other shit going on, there's just no room for it. Danielle, too, gets caught up with the boys back at the ranch, and it starts to look to her like she won't be able to drive back down our big-ass hill to make it to town. Isaiah is a little fried and frazzled, from hanging all day on the beach at Doheny; Danielle doesn't think he's up for another outing, and Eli's made plans with some of his buddies, and I catch myself thinking I'm a little fried and frazzled myself, and that a night at home with Danielle and Isaiah is sounding pretty good right now.

Finally, as I'm fitting the last of the boards back onto the bed of Danielle's pickup, I notice a text message reminding me to pick up my father at his apartment and drive him to the OC Tavern. A part of me thinks how cool it is, that we walk around with these hand-held devices that remind us of shit we don't even remember knowing in the first place. I set the phone on the dashboard and guess this means I'm going, after all.

Don't have time for the change of clothes, though, so I slip out of my wet suit and throw on a pair of shorts and a clean-enough-looking Maui Jim T-shirt and point the truck towards my parent's apartment. The event is called for five o'clock, and already it's a quarter past, but we'll get there when we get there.

Dad is dressed for the occasion. Doesn't quite dress to the nines, my old man, but he hits those sixes and sevens. He's wearing a loose-fitting corduroy blazer, some throwback shade of green, over a button-down surf shirt and a pair of jeans. Next to me, he looks like he's in formal attire, but it doesn't much matter what we're wearing, not with this crowd. Only matters that we're here, and soon as we arrive it's like the tide rolls out to clear a path for us. Of course, I realize the welcome is mostly for my old man, but I'm happy to follow in his wake. Been that way my whole life, just about, and by now I'm happy to soak up some of the smiles I know are meant for him. My siblings are the same way, for the most part. We've reached a place where we can celebrate the lives our parents built for us, the opportunities that stretch before us, the legacy we're still finding ways to inhabit.

Place is packed with smiling, familiar faces, just like the beach was packed earlier this morning, only here my dad stands at the center of attention. Something about the unconventional, romantic, vagabonding, bohemian, fucked-up lifestyle he's embraced, the laid-back California surfer ethos he helped to create . . . guess it embodies what this event is all about. What surf culture is all about. He's like the *surf whisperer,* a spirit guide with stories to tell, stories these good people seem to want to hear, and he moves about the room like he owns the place. And he does; in his own way, he does.

There he is, huddled with his old pal Mary Lou Drummy, another local legend, one of California's first female surfers, going all the way back to the pre-*Gidget* days. And there he is with Fran Velzy, Dale's widow, and Paul Strauch, Jr., one of the sport's first genius artists who used to ride with the Duke Kahanamoku Surf Team. And there, finally, he's huddled with his great friend Tubesteak, their backs to the wall, soaking in the scene, reaching past the years for some shared memory or other.

I stand at the bar, sucking back Guinness drafts, collecting congratulations and reminiscences from people I've known my whole life, surfed with my whole life, made trouble with my whole life. I think, *Well, Izzy, this doesn't suck.* And, really, it doesn't. To see your life unfurl in front of good people you care about, to celebrate each other, to *be* celebrated in return . . . yep, it's pretty damn cool. Still don't mind saying.

At some point, our friend Steve Pezman takes the stage and sets the scene. Steve is probably the most influential surf journalist on the planet. He used to be the editor and publisher of *Surfer* magazine. He knows us better than we know ourselves. And he's got a little something to say about each of the twenty-one Surfer's Row honorees. A personal memory. A bit of context or history. Something. I start to listen to what Steve is saying about all these great surfers, about the contributions they've made to our sport, our culture, our lifestyle. The contributions they're making still. And for a couple beats I forget all about my family and our place in the mix. I forget how brave and crazy it must have been for my father, and my mother alongside him, to drop off the grid the way they did and raise a bunch of surf rats in a crappy, run-down camper. As Steve talks, I slip into a sweet, dull fog—kind of like that deep breath that finds me when I'm out past the break, waiting on a wave. Time doesn't matter. Work doesn't matter. Everything is just put on a kind of temporary hold, and a minute feels like an hour, and an hour feels like a minute, and you step outside yourself, a little bit. It's quiet, but not really. I'm listening to Steve, and I'm not listening to Steve. I'm waiting to hear what he's got to say about us and the way we've lived, the way we staked out our own territory on the surfing scene, and I'm not waiting to hear. And next thing I know he's shot right past us, and he's finishing up his remarks about the event, the moment, whatever.

Underneath whatever nice things Steve Pezman has to say about us, whatever ribbon he's tied around this sweet, fine moment, I catch myself thinking, *It's been a good day.* Thinking, *It's been a good life, an interesting life.* And, *Where do I sign on for more of the same?* Yeah, it's been a rich, wild ride, and here, surrounded by these good people, my dad, my daughter, Elah, and a bunch of her friends, my brother Abraham and his family…it feels like it's meant something. Like it continues to *mean* something.

So what do I do with this sweet, fine revelation? Well, I take it in…in what ways I can. I down another couple pints of Guinness. Talk shit for a while longer with some of my pals, pose for a couple more pictures. Hang with Elah for a bit, enjoying the way my baby girl moves about in the life she's managed to make for herself, alongside the life I've managed to make for myself, alongside the life my father had wanted for all of us.

Finally, I check my watch and decide it's time to head back up the hill and make for home. On the way, I stop to pick up some takeout schnitzel at this new German place, Barth's, just opened up on Ortega Highway, figuring Danielle and I can eat a little something when I get home.

Been meaning to check the place out, and this seems as good a time as any, so I park the truck in front of the restaurant's big storefront window and bounce inside, where I'm met by an attractive young waitress, looks to be about my daughter's age. She motions towards a table for me to sit down, but I tell her I only want takeout. She goes to get me a menu, and when she returns with it she points through the storefront window.

"You are a surfer?" she asks, in a thick German accent.

I follow her gaze and see she is looking at my truck, with the eight or nine boards fitted onto the bed. "I am a surfer," I say back, and we fall into talking.

She brings me a beer, to fill the waiting. Soon, she asks about the tattoos that spill from my T-shirt and run all along my left arm. She's never seen anything like them, she says. She shows me hers—a simple star, on her belly. Unadorned. Me, I'm adorned as hell. The German waitress, she is curious as hell. She says, "The design, it is almost tribal, yes?"

I say, "Some of it. And some is just a tribute to my family, to my children." And then I tell her about the markings on my arm. The names of my kids. A portrait of Danielle from when we first met. The Surfers Healing logo. The tribal designs on my fingers—native shark teeth, pointing away from my body, which is meant to indicate energy and the spirit of aloha flowing out into the world. I tell her how in Hawaii a tattoo tells a story, how the symbols you wear are meant to announce who you are. I say, "This way, when you meet someone, it's like they already know you."

The waitress disappears to collect my food and returns with the restaurant's owner—also German, also struggling to fill the holes in his English. He looks to be in his thirties. The waitress is anxious to show her boss my tattoos, to introduce him to her new customer.

"It is very beautiful," the owner says, after looking at my arm. "Very interesting."

"It tells a story," the waitress says. And then, turning to me: "Someday, you must come back and tell it to us."

1

The Start of Something

My story begins in Texas, of all places.

That's where my father was born in 1921, in Galveston. His parents, Rose and Lewis, were also born in Texas, so it's not like they were just passing through. There was actually a small, close-knit Jewish community in and around Galveston, which was a popular port for Jews entering the country from Russia. My grandfather ran a dry-goods store, although from what I hear he didn't do such a good job of it. He ended up as a door-to-door salesman—shoes, mostly, but he sold a bunch of stuff. Basically, he hustled his way all through the Depression. Whatever he could buy on the cheap and flip for a quick profit, that's what he was into.

My father, Dorian, was the oldest of three. Behind him were his brother, Adrian, and his sister, Sonia—both characters, same as my dad. (Some quirk in our gene pool, I guess.) My dad and his sibs would all veer off in their own separate directions. Doing their own thing, their own way... that's what they had in common. Uncle

Adrian became a knockabout musician. He played the violin, here and there, off and on. Everyone always said how gifted he was, what an incredible teacher he was, what an incredible talent, but to us he was just crazy Uncle Adrian. Very creative, very artsy … but, also, very crazy. When I was a kid, he lived for a time in a big house in Hollywood Hills, but other than that he never seemed to have a steady job or stay in a relationship for too, too long. He did have a couple kids—our cousins Nina and Yoab—and we got together with them from time to time, but there was a lot we never figured out about Uncle Adrian. All we knew was that he played the violin. As a gift, he offered to play for my wedding, which is getting ahead of the story, I know, but as long as I'm on it I'll hit these few notes. I happened to duck into the bathroom during the reception, and there was Uncle Adrian, completely naked. Surprised the crap out of me. He'd taken off all his clothes and was splashing water under his arm-pits, getting ready for his performance, and I remember thinking he was cut just like my dad. Whacky. Out there. Different. Yeah, he could play the violin like a dream, but he'd go at it his own way.

Aunt Sonia was on her own wavelength, too. As a young woman she was beautiful—stunning, really. After the family moved to California, she found her way to Hollywood and started working as an actress, during the last gasp of the old studio system. She's probably best known for her role as Agnes Lowzier in the 1946 Howard Hawks classic, *The Big Sleep*, opposite Humphrey Bogart and Lauren Bacall. She acted under the name Sonia Darrin, but she was never credited for her most famous role, even though her character's on-screen more than anyone other than Bogey or Bacall.

She bounced around Hollywood for a time, appeared in a bunch of pictures, but then the gigs stopped coming, which I guess is what happens to a lot of stunning young actresses, eventually. Everything is entirely and wildly possible … until one day it isn't. By the time I was born, Aunt Sonia's acting career had come and gone; she'd married a set designer named Bill Reese and started adopting a bunch of kids—my first cousins Mason, Suky, Lanny, and Mark. (Yep, that's Mason Reese, of Underwood Deviled Ham fame, one of the first true child stars of the advertising age—and a good, good guy.) We saw a lot of them, too, back when we were kids, which I guess left us with the message that family was important. Also with the message that actually working for a living, in a traditional nine-to-five way, was for other families.

Here again I'm getting ahead of my story, or at least a little off to the side, so let me just head back to Texas for a bit. It was there, in the Gulf of Mexico, that my father rode his first wave. A lot of folks don't think of Galveston as any kind of surf spot, but these days there's a thriving surf community down there. Okay, so maybe it's not thriving in the same way surfing is thriving in California or Hawaii or Australia, but everything's relative, right? The waves along the Gulf coast in popular surf spots like Stewart Beach can be small and choppy, but if you time it right you can catch a good surf day. There wasn't a whole lot of surfing going on back in the late 1920s, though. Wasn't even called surfing, what there was of it, but my father saw a picture in the newspaper of a guy riding a wave off the coast of San Diego and thought this was something he'd like to try.

I've heard so many different versions of this story over the years, it's tough keeping them straight. Every time my father tells it, he sprinkles in a couple new details and tosses out some old ones. Here are the nuts and bolts of it: When my father was seven or eight years old, he found some old strips of rubber tire and crimped and bound them together like a raft. Then he covered the whole deal in canvas and set off to do his thing. Guess you'd say he was a resourceful kid, the way he made something out of nothing, the way he'd seen a picture of something that captured his imagination and went out and grabbed at it for himself. Damn near amazing, when you think about it—only it wasn't a very satisfying experience, he says, in almost every version of the story. Says it was more like white-water rafting than actually standing up on a hard surface and riding a wave into shore. But it was something. A germ, a seed, a kernel. A place to start.

And it wasn't just a one-off with him, surfing. Once he tasted it, he wanted more. And more.

Soon, my father got to reading whatever he could about the legendary wave riders out in California or on the beaches of Hawaii. He'd cut surfing pictures from newspapers and magazines and tack them to his wall. He became almost fanatical about it, maybe even a little evangelical. Got it in his head that the only place he could be happy, truly happy, was out in San Diego, so he put it out there that the California sea air would help his asthma. Almost forgot that part: my father suffered from a serious case of childhood asthma; at least, he *claims* he was asthmatic, although I never once heard the man wheeze or cough. Not once, not ever. But somehow he convinced his parents the flats of Texas were debilitating to a young boy in his condition, and eventually they packed up their house and moved the whole family out to San Diego in the early 1930s.

Now, I've got no real idea if this is how things truly went down. All I know is that this is the story my father has told, for years and years. If I had to bet, I'd say there's probably a grain of truth in it. I'd say there probably was a diagnosis of asthma, at some point, and a suggestion that my father might do better in a different climate. But there was also the pull of the ocean, the romance of surfing, so I'm sure he went all out to make his case to his parents. He could be very persuasive, my old man—even as a young man. When he sets his mind to a thing, he's all over it, and he won't back off until he gets his way. And he's charming about it, make no mistake. He can be completely full of shit, but he'll make such a strong case for whatever it is he wants or needs you'll never know he's completely full of shit until much, much later. And you won't really mind when you finally figure out that he's been jerking your chain to get his way. That's probably how it happened back in Texas, when he was pushing for that move to California. Truth was, San Diego at the time was all mudflats, so I can't imagine it was a healthy environment for a young asthma sufferer. It couldn't have been good for him to breathe all that sulfur percolating through that mud. But that didn't keep my father from pushing hard for what he wanted.

Story of his life—and, soon enough, it would be the story of mine.

As a young teenager, my father hit the beach. Wasn't much more of a surfing community in San Diego than there'd been in Texas, but in California at least you could find a good few like-minded souls. The other kids on the beach started calling my father Tex, which I guess must be the default nickname for every transplanted Texan in recorded history, and he was quick to make friends. That's another key trait of my dad's that would play a big part in our family history. He was an accomplished social animal, and a real pro at getting other folks to throw in with him on whatever it was he had in mind. All through high school, he tells, most afternoons he'd find his way to the beach and ride as many waves as the sun would allow. Weekends, more of the same. He'd meet up with his new friends on the beach and together they'd work those waves for all they were worth, and after a while he was as good as anyone else.

The deal back then was you had to make your own board. Weren't enough surfers to support any kind of commercially made boards, so you had to have a do-it-yourself mentality. There was no other option—even if you had money, you couldn't buy a board. Had to just figure it out, you know, and if you weren't handy or clever in this way you found a way to trade for someone else's board.

Early on, my father got a job as a lifeguard on Mission Beach, where he worked with a one-eyed lifeguard captain, Emil Sigler.

This guy had made a bunch of heroic saves, so everyone on the beach knew him. Everyone in town knew him. All the other surfers, all the other lifeguards, they wanted to be just like Emil; if Emil rode a really giant board, that's what everyone else decided to ride.

The Mission Beach lifeguards got the wood for their surfboards from Pacific Homes, a local building supply outfit. The boards weren't shaped, curved, or beveled. They were just big planks of choice wood, which Tex and his pals would cut down into a basic surfboard shape and laminate. Their boards were long—about ten to eleven feet. And heavy—well over one hundred pounds. At night, they'd just leave their boards on the beach, because they were too big, too heavy to steal. No one else had any use for them, really, although I suspect a few of them ended up as firewood.

All through high school, surfing was my dad's main interest. His only interest, really. He did well enough in school, but he did as much riding as he could. For years, he'd tell us his parents never minded if he ditched school when the surf was up. Don't know if that's entirely true, but that's how he remembers it. True or not, surfing was his priority; same went for his friends; it filled their days. And when my father finally graduated from Point Loma High School he joined the navy—I guess under the thinking that he'd be on, around, or near enough to the water to continue with his surfing. Didn't exactly work out to the good, in terms of surfing. All of a sudden, my father's time was no longer his own. He didn't have his fellow lifeguards to keep him company. He'd built up all these great friendships on the beach, and then he'd had to leave those friendships behind, and I don't think he found too many surfers among his new navy buddies. He was assigned to a medical ship that operated in the Pacific; after the war, he went to Stanford University Medical School, on the G.I. Bill, earning his degree in 1946.

Up until this time, even with the way he'd skipped out on school when the surf was up, my father was very much a by-the-book kind of guy. By that I mean he always did what was expected of him—or he did just enough of it so he could go through the same motions as everyone else. His parents wanted him to at least make the effort to finish school, so he made the effort. His friends were all enlisting, so he enlisted. And then the thing to do was go back to school and pursue some sort of profession, so he did that, too. But I don't think his heart was ever in it. High school, the navy, medical school... these grand institutions seemed to suck the life out of him. His heart was on the beach, in the water.

Once he got his medical degree, he took a job in Hawaii. The waves were calling to him, he said. It would be a chance to live in paradise. He worked in a hospital, in the state medical office, wherever there was a need or an opportunity. He wasn't much interested in private practice, because he didn't want to be tied down. He resented the idea of taking money from people in exchange for his services; he preferred working in a clinic or hospital or agency setting. Whenever he had to charge a patient some kind of fee, he tried to barter instead; he was forever coming home with crap he didn't need, crap he didn't even want, because he took it in trade for some medical service or other. A plate of home-cooked food. An old bicycle. A rusted-out car that had seen way better days. A lot of times, he took whatever his patients had to offer, just because they'd taken the time to think what the young doctor from the mainland might need or enjoy. It's not that he didn't appreciate the value of a dollar, or that he rejected the idea of material possessions; it's just that he wasn't sure he saw the need for either; he helped people because they needed his help, not because they paid him for it.

For the first time in his life he found himself thinking like a free spirit—not just in his professional life, but in his personal life as well. He actually got married during this period, to a nice Jewish girl he met in Hawaii; he even had two daughters, but underneath his day-to-day he started to realize he wasn't happy. To his friends, he seemed to have it all; to his parents and siblings back home, he appeared to be living like a prince in paradise; but deep down he believed there was something missing in his life. More and more, he was feeling tied down—by work, but also by the demands of raising a young family. More and more, he was becoming conventional. And, also more and more, he *hated* that he was becoming conventional.

Dad never really talked about this time in his life except to suggest that he and his first wife wanted different things and seemed to drift apart. In the end, they got a divorce. As I understand it, the divorce was amicable, but my father wasn't really a part of his daughters' lives after that. Growing up, we never knew them. We knew *of* them, but that was it, and even this was a little weird. I mean, by the time I was old enough to know what was going on, I had four or five brothers, and it was strange to think there were two sisters (or *half* sisters) out there in the world I'd never even met, but we never really talked about it. Whenever the subject came up, Dad found a way to paddle past it, although I imagine it must have been painful for him, to make such a clean break with his young family. But something wasn't working in that relationship, something wasn't right, so he set it aside and moved on. That was his way, we'd all learn. He'd push past a difficulty or set it aside and after a while it was like there'd never been any trouble at all. He even got married a second time, but that didn't work out, either, and here again he was reluctant to share too many details. It's like he wanted us all to believe his life didn't really begin until he met our mother.

Through it all, he surfed. Whenever he could, he surfed. He hung with all these pioneers of Hawaiian surfing, guys like Duke Kahanamoku, Rabbit Kekai, Blue Makua, Wally Froiseth, George Downing, Chubby Mitchell, Buffalo Keaulana—legends, even then. Duke Kahanomoku was the granddaddy of them all; he was like the Hawaiian Jim Thorpe, a world-class athlete who excelled in every sport. He was an Olympic swimmer, a champion beach volleyball player, a decorated lifeguard…but mostly he was a surfer. He had more than twenty years on my father, but for some reason they hit it off—and once you were in with the Duke, you were in with that whole crowd.

Hawaiian surf culture was a whole lot different from California surf culture: it was all about being serious watermen, rather than just surfers; it was about being at home in, on, and around the water, which was very much in keeping with the spirit of the islands. Back home in California, even the best surfers were mere mortals: they had plain, workaday jobs; they scrambled to pay their rent. In Hawaii, it's like the great watermen were immortal, like they operated on some higher plane, removed from the day-to-day concerns that moved the rest of the world. Surfing was all. My father was part of that scene, fit himself right in. By this time, they all knew him as Doc, another default nickname—this one probably got tagged on anyone who'd gone to medical school and hung around with folks who'd done no such thing. They found something to like about this eccentric doctor. To the locals, my father was a haole—the Hawaiian word for an outsider, a newcomer, a pale-white mainland American— but they made him feel welcome. At first he was dividing his time between work and the beach, but after a while the split began to bother him. In his own mind, at least, he stood apart from the local surfing gods, who were in truth just a bunch of pals from the beach. To Doc, though, there was a key distinction. His buddies lived to surf—but Doc, he only *worked* to surf.

Oh, there was a real difference. You could even see it in the way he moved on a board. There's some 16mm footage that's survived from that period, and you can see that my father then was more of a weekend warrior. These other guys, they were real surfers; my father, he wasn't a real surfer, not yet. Now, I don't know exactly what it takes to be a *real* surfer. That's tough to pin down, but basically you have to have talent, to start. That part's a given, and to my father's great credit, he was talented . . . to a degree. By Texas standards, he was more than talented; by California standards, he was talented enough; by Hawaii standards, he was only getting there.

But it goes deeper than talent. You've got to live and breathe the sport; you've got to take it all in, all at once; you've got to give yourself over to it, and let it wash over you, and here young Doc was falling short. He couldn't help it, and he hated that he couldn't help it; he wanted to change things up, but he couldn't think how. With his responsibilities as a doctor, he'd boxed himself out of *really* developing as a surfer. The one didn't fit with the other. In that old film footage, you could see he looked kind of pasty compared with all the other riders. Kind of soft. You could see his balance was a little *off.* It was subtle, almost imperceptible, but after a lifetime spent watching this man surf, I almost can't recognize him in these shots. In one shot in particular, he's riding a wave and he seems to be leaning the wrong way, his body tense and maybe a little off-balance, like he's waiting for the wave to tell him what to do, instead of the other way around. Like I say, it's a subtle distinction, but I could see it whenever we looked at those old films; my brothers could see it. And my father, I'm sure he could see it, too. He could feel it, absolutely. At the time, he knew better than anyone that he wasn't keeping up with these other guys.

Finally, he went and did something about it. You see, my father's not the sort of guy who can go at something in a half-assed way. He's all or nothing—and as a young doctor in Hawaii, only *playing* at surfing, he must have felt like nothing, especially if he dared to measure himself against the Duke or those other great watermen. And so, basically on a whim, he quit whatever job he was working at the time and decided to go to Israel. Just like that. Wasn't so easy, to just drop everything and go. Wasn't so easy to leave a well-paying job on a whim, without giving any notice, and expect to be able to return to another one like it. Wasn't so easy to scrabble together enough money for a plane ticket, but he found a way; he was determined; he got rid of his few things and moved out of his apartment and made a clean, swift break. He didn't have any kind of timetable in mind, any kind of plan. He just up and went. When he tells the story now, he makes it seem like he was on some kind of mission—and I guess he was.

He got it in his head that he was going to bring the sport of surfing to Israel, and in the end he did just that, but what he also did was find himself. Don't know what it was that got him thinking like some sort of surfing messiah, but this was his plan, and at the other end, once he got to Israel, halfway around the world, I believe he found the balance he didn't fully know he was seeking. He went to Israel in the middle 1950s, around the time of the Kadesh operation, a period of intense fighting around the Sinai Peninsula. It was a difficult, uncertain time. What the hell my father was thinking, bringing a quiver of ten-foot balsa Hobie longboards to Israel, into the middle of such conflict, I'll never know. Every time he tells the story, he offers a different explanation, but in every version he has his four or five or six boards, all decorated with the Star of David or the Israeli flag. Traveling with all those boards fell somewhere between a bitch and a hassle, he says. Israeli authorities had never seen such things; they had no idea what to make of them. It took a while for the boards to get through customs; my father claims they were quarantined for weeks and weeks, but knowing my dad it was more likely days and days. (Hey, it's tough to tell a good story without *a little* exaggeration!) Custom officials ended up drilling holes in the boards, thinking my father was trying to smuggle weapons. When they were finally satisfied that the boards weren't a threat, they released them to my father's custody, and he plugged the holes and made the best of it.

Anyway, my father found his way to the beach. Soon, he had a network of Israeli friends—lifeguards, mostly. He dedicated himself to a natural, vigorous lifestyle: he learned to spearfish, and he slept on the beach, as often as not. He ate healthy, and tried to clear his head of unhealthy thoughts, which in his mind had mostly to do with money. He started hanging around with a guy named Shamai "Topsi" Kanzapolski, on Frishman Beach outside Tel Aviv, and they struck up a great friendship. Actually, it was Topsi's wife, Naomi, who was the first Israeli to get up on a board. She was the most curious, the most enthusiastic, so my father took her out past the break and showed her what to do. Topsi learned next, and then the two of them, together with my father, started teaching all the other lifeguards and Israeli beach bums how to surf.

At that time, the Tel Aviv beaches were wide open. There were no piers or jetties to break the surf, so the waves could be extremely high. They'd break right on the beach, which forced all these rookie surfers to get it going double-quick. Waves like that, they can be difficult to navigate, but after a while the first-timers got the hang of it, and soon after that the sport seemed to catch on. Today, you can walk up and down the beaches of Tel Aviv and see a vibrant, thriving surf culture. There are popular breaks and surf spots. There are shops and cafés, catering to surfers. There are even a bunch of surf rental shacks and schools—including one run by Topsi's kids. But back in the 1950s the scene was just coming into focus, as Topsi and his lifeguard pals soaked up Doc's stories of life in Hawaii and California like manna from heaven. They'd lived by the sea their entire lives, made their livings by the sea, but they'd never dared to dance across those waters the way Doc would dance across those waters.

At night, over bonfires—Doc taught them how to make those, too!—my father dreamed of forming an Israeli surfing team, to compete in the world championships.

I've seen pictures of my father from this period, and he looks more like himself, more like the young man I remember from growing up. He was tan and fit. He carried himself like an Adonis. He was no longer the weekend warrior surfer he'd been back in Hawaii.

He was at home in Tel Aviv, more like himself than he'd ever been before, transformed.

After living in Israel for about a year, he volunteered for the Israeli Army during the Suez Crisis, hoping to defend his adopted country against Egypt, but he was turned down. At first he couldn't believe the Army didn't want him, but then he took the rejection as a sign that he should perhaps return to the United States, only this time he would do so on his own terms. He would not be bound by convention. He would live by the sea, by his wits. His days would spread out before him like an endless possibility.

The thing about Israel, my father always said, was that it was mostly a place to refresh, recharge, and replenish his energy, more than it was a place to live. As much as he loved the place, and the people, he couldn't see himself living there in any kind of open-ended way. For one thing, the surfing wasn't nearly what it was on the beaches of the Pacific. For another, he couldn't really practice medicine, even though he wasn't much interested in practicing medicine in the states, either. The part about helping people when they were sick, that part he liked, but he came to believe that the American medical model was more about making a profit than keeping people healthy, and he didn't want to be a part of a system where the rich got a certain level of care and the poor got a lesser level of care. He wasn't foolish enough to walk away from his medical training entirely, however; he knew there'd be times when the fact that he was a doctor would come in handy; he liked *being* a doctor, but he didn't really like the responsibilities that came with actually *working* as a doctor, if that makes any sense.

First job he took when he got back to the United States was at a small hospital in Catalina. He hated the job, he said, same way he'd hate every job we knew him to have, because it was all tied up in getting and spending. Because it kept him from the water. But the job did come with one enormous fringe benefit: it set it up so that he could meet my mother.

Juliette Paez was a tall Mexican beauty who'd been born and raised in Long Beach, California, and she just happened to be at a bar in Catalina on the same night as my father. Dad used to tell us that the place where he met our mother was a godforsaken watering hole on a godforsaken rock, but it wasn't so bad. I actually like Catalina. I've met a lot of good people who've made a good life there. And the bar wasn't so bad, either. I've been there myself a couple times, and I always have a good time there. But my father remembers it as a wretched place, probably because he'd just come from this idyllic existence in Israel and had to take a job he didn't want in order to buy himself the freedom he now desperately craved. His wants and his needs didn't exactly fit, not just yet.

My mother was sitting with a girlfriend, having drinks. At the time, she was working as a switchboard operator, although her passion was the opera. She sang opera in high school, and after graduating she sang with an opera company in Long Beach. Opera, to her, was like surfing to my father; it was the sweet engine that moved her days. There was no good way to make a living from it—same as surfing—but her idea was to work during the week and sing in the evenings and on weekends. Her job was just a job; her *thing* was opera. And she had a lovely voice. Really. One of the first memories I have as a little kid is of my mother singing. She used to teach us all these different arias, from all these different operas. *La Bohème. Rigoletto. Aida.* Sometimes, she'd be off by herself, just singing, singing, singing, and her voice would reach us and fill our campsite with joy and wonder. We'd hear little bits and snatches from these classic operas all day long, without really realizing what they were, and to this day I can hear a piece of music from one of the great nineteenth-century operas and seem to know it by heart. And it wasn't just opera; she had us listening to all the great classics. (She loved Bach, and played us his concertos over and over.) The style of music didn't exactly fit with the California surf scene we inhabited, but none of us really noticed or cared. We were big into doing our own thing— and I think we got this from my mother, who was every bit the free spirit my father was. They were an unlikely but perfect match, and the combination only added to the odd picture we must have made as we tooled around in our ratty old camper. A surf-mad Jewish doctor from Texas. An opera-loving Mexican beauty. And, soon enough, a passel of sun-drenched Mex-ish kids, running around the beach, making noise, making trouble, making waves.

I can close my eyes and see the scene: me and my older brothers and possibly a younger brother or two, playing in the sand, watching my father ride one of Hawaii's big waves while my mother's sweet music fills the air.

My mother had eight brothers and sisters—she was one of the youngest. Some had been born in Durango, Mexico, where her parents had been born; the youngest, like my mom, were born in Long Beach. Her father, Salvador, was a heavy smoker and died young, from a heart attack, in his middle forties. Her mother, Amelia, managed to find enough work to keep a roof over her family's head; the older kids were able to pitch in with jobs of their own, while my mom and some of the younger kids helped out by being independent and learning to take care of themselves. The thing about my mother's family is that they didn't look like most Mexicans. They were tall and skinny; they looked more Aztec than Mexican. And my mother... well, she was stunning and graceful and unlike any woman my father had ever seen. And her voice! My father always told us she had the most beautiful contralto voice he'd ever heard, and none of us kids had any idea what the word "contralto" meant. She used to sing to him, when they first got together. Not on that first night, in Catalina—but soon, and ever after.

My father caught sight of my mother across the crowded cantina. He was drawn to her, he always said. Certainly, she stood out. She was tall, dark, lovely. She looked nothing at all like the California beach blondes he was used to seeing, but it wasn't just her looks that caught my father's attention. It was the way she carried herself, he always said. It reminded him of the way he carried himself, the way he looked out at the world. At this point in his life, he moved with great confidence. His time in Israel left him feeling like he could accomplish anything. That's what surfing had done for him, he said. It wasn't joining the navy or going to medical school; it was surfing, to where all he needed to do was picture a situation and will it so—and here he willed himself across the room to a meeting with my mother. He introduced himself, said he was a doctor working in the local hospital. Said he was a surfer, too. Said he was just back from a year in Israel.

None of these things seemed to make an impression on my mother, but there was something about this assertive young doctor that caught her interest. At some point, my mother's girlfriend disappeared into the crowd, and my father sat talking with my mother for the longest time. When he learned she was from a big family, he turned to her and said, "Someday, you will be the mother of my eight sons."

It was a bold prediction, a killer come-on line, but that was the kind of confidence my father had started to carry; that was his way; and it must have struck something in my young mother. Maybe it was the way he'd just come out with it, plain as day. Maybe she admired his brass. That's what they called it back then, brass. These days, it'd be "balls." He said whatever popped into his head. There was no filter.

They looked into each other's eyes and saw something of themselves. (Sounds kind of cornpone, I know, but that's how they always told the story.) Physically, they could not have looked more unalike—a tall, Mexican opera singer and a chiseled Jewish surfer. But it turned out they were more alike on the inside than different on the outside. Soon, they were spending all of their time together— talking, planning, dreaming. After just a couple weeks, before they had time to think things through, they quit their jobs and piled into my mother's shit-box of a car, an old Studebaker, and drove to Mexico—towards the Gulf coast, at first. My father taught my mother to surf. They fished, spent what little savings they had, and dreamed of a life without responsibility to anyone or anything but each other. For months, they managed to get by. They lived out of my mother's car, just parked it right on the beach, where they caught lobsters and crabs and whatever fish came in close to shore. My father was happier than he'd ever been, and my mother was happier than she thought she'd had any right to expect; she'd never once imagined that a man would come along and lift her from the sameness of her life and collect her in such a great adventure. It felt to her like the kind of epic love stories they wrote operas about.

It was while they were down in Mexico living out of that old Studebaker that my father proposed to my mother. This was the woman of his dreams, he thought. A woman who shared his ideals and his idealism. A woman who wouldn't throw back any crazy notion he'd throw at her. At that point, his only crazy notion was fathering seven sons—he wanted to do his part to repopulate the Jewish state of Israel, he said—but that was crazy enough for the time being. As far as my mother was concerned, I don't know that my father was the man of her dreams. A nice Jewish surfer (who happened to also be a nice Jewish doctor) wasn't exactly high on the fantasy list for most young Mexican women. But he was smart and handsome and strong and confident. He made her smile, she said.

And, it was down in Mexico that my oldest brother, David, was probably conceived. My parents didn't get married until they moved back to California, but by that point their adventure had already begun—and my father's big, bold come-on line had already started to come true. My mother would deliver many, many children—many, many sons. (She would end up going his prediction one better, giving him eight sons and my baby sister, Navah.) My parents would live a life of purpose and meaning. No one day would look like another. They would not be tied to routine or to anyone's expectations but their own.

What this might mean, what their lives might look like...they had no idea. But they would see.

2

Surfing by Osmosis

One thing I need to make clear straightaway: there's no such thing as an official record in my family. Sorry, folks, but there's no paper trail of documents or school records to track our comings and goings. No travel itinerary or gas receipts to help retrace our steps. We moved from here to there, up and back, around and around, without writing anything down or thinking there was any reason to remember any of the details.

Not the best way to start in on this memoir-writing business, but I want to tell it straight. You see, the deal in my family was to focus on the present. We didn't care so much about where we'd been or where we were going, only where we were and what we were doing, just then. We lived in the moment, long before the phrase became something you'd see on a bumper sticker.

We rode whatever wave we were on at the time. (Hey, that'd look sweet on a bumper sticker, too!)

My father always jokes that we have a good collective memory, only it's no joke. There are eleven of us, and I'm afraid no single one of us remembers everything; some of us don't remember shit—but at least one of us remembers a little something about almost everything, and there are enough bits and snatches of memory among us to tell a couple good stories. That's always been our thing; poll the family, and you'll eventually find someone who gets it right; put together enough of our bits and snatches and you'll get at least a fuzzy version of a clear picture. The trick comes in knowing who to believe and who's completely full of shit.

My earliest memories are of my parents—and as memories go they're all positive and pleasant and perfect. I was a happy baby. This is what I've been told, but it's also what I remember. Whatever early memories I've held on to are pumped with feelings of warmth and well-being. I remember thinking my father could do no wrong. He was so big, so strong, so handsome...he filled the room with his presence, his personality. First time I ever heard the Greek legend of Zeus, it made me think of my father. My older brothers all had a similar take. Like me, as little kids they remember feeling completely safe and taken care of by my father—and a little bit in awe of him. The man cast a kick-ass shadow. (Still does!) My mother, too, but my father was the dominant personality in our little lives. He ran the show—and, once we were a little older, we also got that it was definitely a show. The more we surfed and bounced around the planet, the more I got that he liked being the center of attention; he liked what our family came to represent to surfers and beach-goers, the free-spirited, anything goes–type mind-set that attached to our lifestyle.

For my younger siblings—meaning the ones born after me—I'm guessing their experiences were different. By the time they came along, there were a bunch of older, rambunctious brothers on the scene, and we might have been the more dominant personalities in their lives; we might have set the tone of their childhoods.

But for the oldest, including me, it was definitely my father. He was like Superman, to us. He was our Zeus, our God. Whatever he said, we listened. Whatever he did, we wanted to do. We moved to his rhythms.

First house I remember living in was in Hawaii, on the southeastern side of Oahu, in a place called Koko Head. I was about three or four years old—which meant there were just five or six of us kids. Don't remember much about the house, apart from pictures and family stories, but I do remember it was in a neighborhood of tract houses that all looked the same. Even the people who spilled from those houses looked the same—dark-skinned, dark-haired Hawaiians all, except for us. Weren't a whole lot of Mexican Jews in the tract houses of Koko Head, I guess.

I also remember that our Koko Head house was tiny, just a couple rooms, and that it sat on a beautiful hill, and that my paternal grandparents came to stay with us there for a stretch, and that when they did we were crowded on top of crowded. Also, it's where I first went to school—barefoot, which was more of a Hawaii thing than a Paskowitz thing. A lot of the kids went to school barefoot in those days. It's like shoes and sneakers were optional, which in our family worked out great because we probably couldn't afford them anyway; we had too many damn feet.

There was another house in Hawaii, before Koko Head, this one on the western side of Honolulu County, in a little place called Makaha. The bay behind that house is a world-famous surf spot. That's where we were living when I was born, and the house came to us on the back of one of my father's stories. For all I know, this one might have even been true. The way my father always told it, he'd been living on the Big Island of Hawaii. He'd given up medicine to become a fish photographer. This was part of his plan to pare down his existence and live more honestly, more purposefully. Somehow, in his head, this translated as having nothing to do with money—or, at least, as little to do with money as was practical, or possible. Wasn't exactly the best idea in the world, to try to carve a bare-bones living by taking pictures of fish, but my father couldn't always separate his pie-in-the-sky ideas from his workable schemes; this one might have fallen somewhere in between. My oldest brother, David, had already been born, and it's possible the next in line, Jonathan, had also arrived. My mother was pregnant—although this wasn't any kind of telling marker. My mother was *always* pregnant. She used to tell people she was pregnant or nursing for more than ten years straight, without letup, and if you look at our birth certificates and do the math you'll see she's about five years short. There were about fourteen years between my oldest brother, David, and my youngest brother, Joshua, so it was almost fifteen years, really, if you count from the time she was pregnant with David to when she was finished nursing Joshua.

(In all that time, we must have sucked all the calcium right out of her, but she never lost a step; she had as much energy as any of us.)

Anyway, my father got it in his head to quit being a doctor. He liked that he understood about the human body and was in a position to help people, but he didn't like all the hassle and paperwork that came with it, so he bought a used camera and tried to make a living taking pictures of fish. After a while, he got the idea to take pictures of people. One idea followed from the other.

"What's the greatest photograph in the world?" he used to ask us, whenever he told this story. Even though we'd heard the answer a dozen times, we'd still stumble over the question. It was like an old vaudeville routine. We all knew our parts, and my father played the lead.

"What's the greatest photograph in the world?" he'd ask again—sometimes clapping his hands together, like he was about to share some ancient piece of wisdom. "I'll tell you. It's one that you're in. A picture of yourself, that's what people want. After that, the second-greatest picture in the world is a picture of a fish, and if you can find a way to put the person and the fish in the same picture... well, then maybe you've got something."

So this was his big idea, his grand plan to support his young family, and after trying it out on the Big Island for a year or so he realized he'd probably have better success on Oahu, where there'd be more people to photograph. Maybe not more fish, but more people. So he and my mother threw their few possessions (and their few kids!) together and made their way to Oahu, where my father soon talked his way into an extended stay in a small hotel on the beach, probably in exchange for some photographs and free medical advice. Like I wrote earlier, he was big into bartering, my old man. It's like he was living in the Wild, Wild West, swapping and trading for everything. Bottom line: if he was living in a hotel room on the beach with his wife and small children, you can bet he wasn't paying for it.

They couldn't stay in that hotel room forever, of course. My father had to find a way to get established, to provide for his family, so he started asking around. One thing about my father, he was great with people. He could talk his way into or out of pretty much anything, and here he fell in with a local Chinese man who had some sort of connection to Henry J. Kaiser, the great shipbuilder and steel magnate, who had settled in Honolulu and become a real estate developer. The connection to Kaiser was always a little vague to us kids, but my father set it out like an important part of the story, and maybe it was. In later years, my father claimed he'd even met old man Kaiser a time or two, although the circumstances of those meetings were never entirely clear—and never quite the same, from one story to the next. My father remembers that they were friends. Who knows, maybe they were. My guess is they were more like acquaintances—and by "acquaintances" I might mean they shook hands, once or twice. Either way, Kaiser had built a new development on the western side of the island, in Makaha, and my father learned from his new Chinese friend that they were having trouble selling the houses. This part checks out. Back then, Makaha was fairly remote and only the true die-hard surfers were willing to live that far from town, but the true die-hard surfers didn't have any money. My father must have seen all these empty houses as an opportunity, because he put it out that he would very much like to see this development and possibly consider buying a home there.

Only problem was that my father was like every other surfer in Makaha Bay; he had no money and not a whole lot of prospects. This would become the running theme of his life—of *all* of our lives. Same goes for almost any other die-hard surfer, then as now. Surf long enough, hard enough, and there won't be a whole lot of time left for mundane, workaday realities like earning a living or building a savings account. Spend too much time worrying work or long-term security and you'll cut into your time in the water.

Either way, you're screwed.

Back then, all Doc had were his medical degree and his used camera, so he and his new friend got to talking. My father told him his story. He told him about his plans to step away from medicine and become a photographer. He told him of his time in Israel, and his determination to live a simple, healthy life. He told him of his plans to have eight sons, and announced proudly that he was well on his way. He told him of his love of surfing. And he didn't just talk about himself, my father. He pumped his friend for details on *his* story, *his* worldview, *his* passions ... and he listened with great interest, another one of my father's great gifts.

After a few days, the Chinese man took such a liking to my father he told him he'd like to sell him one of his houses in Makaha. It turned out he'd invested in Kaiser's development and all he had to show for it were some empty houses. He figured he would do well to help this interesting young doctor and his family get established on Oahu. He probably also figured it would be easier to sell his other houses if he could show people some nice, young families living in the neighborhood, so he turned to my father and said, "What can you afford as a down payment?"

My father gave this some serious thought. He said, "Well, what's the smallest amount you'd take?"

Now it was the other guy's turn for some serious thought. He was a businessman, after all. And yet there must have been something in my father's tale of dreams and woe that sparked something in his new friend, because it got this guy thinking he wanted to help my father out, even if it would be a losing proposition on paper. He finally said, "Whatever you think is fair. Whatever you can afford."

This was my father's favorite part of the story to tell. Usually, he dressed it up by reaching into his pocket, the way he said he'd done when he was sitting with his friend. In most versions of the story, they were sitting in the lobby of the hotel where my parents were staying and my father reached into his pocket and came out with a dime. That's it, just one dime. It was all he had on him, ten lousy cents.

With great fanfare and showmanship, he slapped the dime on the table between them and said, "That's all I have."

The great kicker to the story was the Chinese gentleman saying, "I'll take it."

Probably, the truth was a whole lot less dramatic. My father didn't end up buying the house, but my family did end up living there, with that one dime as a deposit. There'd be another few "last dime" stories that would become part of our family history, and I'll share them as I move along with my story, but I like this one for the way it shows my father as a bold, adventurous, likable young man, willing to abandon his worldly possessions (and even his *profession*) for a half-baked ideal—namely, that he could find a way to get by on a good heart and the best intentions. I always thought it was kind of amazing, kind of remarkable, the way he could get others to throw in with him. Like his surfer pals, who made a place for him as one of their own. Like the lifeguards on the beaches of Tel Aviv, who took to surfing like they'd been born to it. Like the Chinese guy, who put my parents into their first house.

Like my mother, most of all.

Just to be clear, my mother was a strong-willed, talented, fiercely proud Mexican-American woman. Still is. A lot of folks we met over the years seemed to think she'd taken a kind of backseat to my father in the way we were raised, the choices we made as a family, but that wasn't at all the case. Yeah, my father was the dominant personality, the front person, but my mother was with him all the way. We might have moved to his rhythms, his whims, but she accepted them as her own. That's how much she loved my dad, I always believed. So much that she was willing to drink whatever batch of Kool-Aid he was pouring at the time. If he believed in a thing wholeheartedly, then she did as well, even if it cut against whatever ideas about family and parenting she might have come to on her own. And it's not like she ever resented my father for having to set aside her dreams for his. It wasn't like that, with them. She was so crazy in love with him that nothing else mattered.

We filled that first house, before long. And the one after that. (And the one after that.) I was born in 1963, fourth in line after David, Jonathan, and Abraham, and I was quickly followed by Moses and Adam. Basically, we kind of burst onto the scene one after the other. We were our own little population explosion. We all slept in one big room—the living room, I think—almost like a litter of puppies. My parents threw a bunch of mats down on the floor and that was it. If we were tired, we'd just drop off to sleep, wherever we happened to be. In the morning, we'd stow the mats and clear the room for whatever else was going on.

During the day, we went to the beach. All day, every day. My father would surf. Maybe David and Jonathan were starting to find their way on a board at four or five or six. The rest of us just splashed around in the shorebreak, learning to swim, getting comfortable in the water. We were like tadpoles—just a bunch of brown, big-bellied boys. In later years, we'd be leaned out and wiry, but when we lived in Makaha and in Koko Head we were like fat little calves, all plump and happy. One of the highlights of those days for me was going to the market with my mother. She shopped at a place where they gave free samples of poi. They had a bunch of tiny tasting spoons and you were only supposed to take a small amount, but I'd really get into that poi bowl and eat my fill. My brothers, too.

Eventually, my father gave up on photography and went back to being a doctor. It went against what he'd decided was his nature, but he had no choice, really. There were too many mouths to feed, too many bills to pay, so he moved from one hospital to another, one clinic to another. He worked in a local VD clinic for a while, and then for another while in the state medical office. He'd stay at one place long enough to figure out what he didn't like about it, and then he'd go off looking for another gig. The one thing he wouldn't do was work in private practice. He didn't want to be tied down like that. He'd rather fix the dings in his buddy's surfboards, or hang out on the set of *Gunsmoke,* where he worked for a stretch as a doctor for the cast and crew. That's where he met the actor James Arness, who my father quickly added to his growing collection of pals and acquaintances.

I keep a picture in my head of the first five or six of us, standing in front of the Koko Head house. If it's a real picture, I haven't seen it in years, but it's just as likely one of those freeze-frame snapshots we all carry of some special moment or memory; we set up the shot so we can look back at how we were. In the picture, we're all wearing these crappy, hand-me-down, Salvation Army–type clothes.

Even David, the oldest, wore hand-me-downs—so our hand-me-downs were already hand-me-downs. By the time they were handed down to me or Moses or whoever was the youngest at the time, they were pretty threadbare and hideous, but we never wasted anything. Probably, my father was making enough money to buy us new clothes, but he didn't like the idea of buying new clothes, so we went to the thrift store, came out looking like well-fed ragamuffins.

There were a lot of other kids in our Koko Head neighborhood, but this didn't really mean all that much. We had a kind of pack mentality, us Paskowitz kids. We moved about the neighborhood together. There were so many of us, we were self-sufficient. We didn't need any of those other kids; we had each other; we brothers were constant companions—running through the neighborhood, playing on the beach, making our share of little-kid trouble. And we had a blast. That's the one great takeaway from our time on Oahu—how much we all laughed, all the time. Don't remember what the hell we were laughing about, but we all remember laughing—uncontrollably, at times. Really, we enjoyed the crap out of each other. (I supposed we beat the crap out of each other, too, but it was never anything more than good-natured roughhousing.) As we got older, we paired off in little sub-sets, by age, and had our own mini-adventures. David and Jonathan were a great twosome. Abraham and I hung out a lot together. Eventually, Moses and Adam were best buddies. And then we'd mix it up from there.

If I went to school while we were living in that Koko Head house, that means David, Jonathan, and Abraham all went ahead of me, which bumps into a line we'd hear from my mother later on, when we were living in the camper. Whenever we'd meet someone new, they'd want to know about us kids and school. That was always the first question we'd get, when folks came to know us; they'd want to know how we managed to avoid the truant officer. My mother always said that if you don't put your kids in the system they'll never know about your kids. The "they" in my mother's mind were the government, the authorities, the man. My parents never had a whole lot of faith in authority, but for a brief time back in Koko Head they sent us to the local school, same as everyone else. After a couple years, I guess they decided we were no better off in school than we would have been on the beach, so they changed things up and went at it a different way.

I don't believe this change happened all at once. There wasn't one day when my parents decided we'd no longer be going to school. My father didn't clap his hands, like he did when he told one of his stories, and announce any kind of big, sudden change. We just sort of stopped going, gradually. Maybe we'd all ditch school as a family one day, if the surf was up and the sun was out, and maybe the next day would check in just as good so we'd skip school again. School just wasn't important, just then. Don't think it was ever any kind of big deal to my folks. We would learn on our own—not in a traditional homeschooling sort of way, but in a scattershot, spontaneous sort of way. We'd learn what we needed to know, and if something grabbed our interest we'd learn a little bit more about that one thing. Or not.

Soon, by the time I was five or six, our days seemed to have more to do with going to the beach and being at the beach than with anything else. Eventually, our days at the beach were all about surfing, but that took a while to set in. Like I said, David and Jonathan took to it first. The rest of us were at the baby beaches, just getting used to the water, and we took to it one by one. Wasn't anything my father ever forced. If you ask him about it now, he'll say he wanted us to come to surfing on our own, when we were good and ready, each of us in our own way, but that always sounds to me like a pile of crap. The way I remember it, it's more like he was off doing his thing, surfing, hanging with his surf buddies, and we were hanging back with my mother, doing our thing, and after a while those separate things just kind of bumped into each other—and by that I mean he probably looked up one day and noticed one or another of us itching to paddle out and he got to thinking, *What the hell...*

Don't think he ever put any more thought into it than that.

My first specific memory of surfing didn't happen until we'd moved to California, to a little house in a remote part of San Marcos. It would be our last house for a while. I went back to school for a short stretch in San Marcos, together with my older brothers, I guess because my parents wanted to give the California schools a chance to screw us up like the Hawaii schools had screwed us up. Only here, too, we went in a half-assed, halfhearted way. One day, might have even been a school day, we drove down to Tourmaline Beach in San Diego, which had always been one of my father's favorite surf spots, going back to when he was a kid, lifeguarding just down the beach from Tourmaline Canyon. Even now, more than forty years later, we still surf that beach. It's where we've run our family surf camp, since 1972, but this was a couple years before that. I was about six years old, and for some reason I was sitting still on the beach long enough to watch my father in the water. For a good long time, I watched him. Oh, I'd seen him surf before. I'd seen him out there and thought he was absolutely bigger than life, strong as a mule, fearless on top of fearless. But this was the first time I really *watched* him surf. The first time I considered what he was doing out there, against what my older brothers were doing, what the other surfers were doing. Don't know that I'd go so far as to say I was *studying* my father as he rode those big waves, but I was certainly checking him out. Taking notes.

You learn to surf by osmosis. By hanging on the beach, hanging with other surfers. And this was me, starting to pay attention. Starting to soak in what it meant to be up on a board, dancing across the waves.

Here's what I noticed, that day on the beach. My father was a throwback kind of surfer. Old-school. Even at six years old, I could see there was something different about the way he rode. He was doing these ancient maneuvers that even in 1969 were seriously dated. The way he turned, he did an exaggerated drop-knee turn, which looked a whole lot different from the way other surfers carved their turns. But my father had grown up on such big, heavy boards that was what he knew. He'd put his foot back and his knee would almost touch the deck of the board, almost like one of those Olympic ski jumpers trying to stick a big-ass landing. From that position, he'd basically stall—meaning he'd lean back in such a way that the front end would pop out of the water, slowing his momentum—and then bring the board around, almost in a pivot. It might have been state-of-the-art in the 1930s, but by the time I was a kid it looked weird and old-fashioned.

And it wasn't just because he rode his big old wooden boards that my father surfed this way. In the years since he'd started surfing, boards had gotten shorter and lighter. There was more shape to them. They were made of foam and fiberglass, instead of wood. They were much more maneuverable. You could do things on these newer, shorter, lighter boards that my father and his old Mission Beach lifeguard pals could never have imagined. But my father rode those new boards in his antique, old-fashioned way. It was in his bones. He didn't mean to, but he couldn't help himself. Stingers, swallowtails... whatever was new at the time, he'd be out there on one ripping it—really, really ripping it—but I'd catch him trying to carve a more graceful turn and underneath it you could still see the clunky, drop-knee pivot. It was what he knew, and it stuck to him, and this was the first time I really noticed he had his own style out there on the waves.

So there I was sitting off by myself, watching my father do his thing, and I caught myself thinking I wanted to be out there, doing my version of the same thing. I'd been on a belly board before. I'd paddled around on the inside with my brothers, but I'd never gone out past the break. It had never occurred to me, until just that moment, and as I watched my father—so strong, so big, so full of life—I wanted to be just like him.

When he finally came in, I went right up to him and said, "I want to surf."

So he paddled me out, right then and there. It's like he didn't want to give me a chance to think too hard about it, to talk myself out of it. He just threw me on his board and I lay out on my belly, while he knelt behind me and paddled out. It's a lot harder than it looks, paddling out on your knees with a kid in tow, but my father had no trouble with it. He was big and lean and muscular. He even paddled in an old-school way, supertraditional, with both hands reaching for the water at the same time, like a two-sided stroke.

I wish I could remember what we talked about, as we paddled out, if we even talked at all. I'm sure we did. We must have. I do remember that I wasn't afraid. I felt completely safe in my father's care, completely without worry. The waves were high, even for Tourmaline, and we had to get past some giant sets that knocked us around pretty good, but I was completely without fear. I was with my father, on a great adventure. Nothing bad could happen.

Soon as we got out there, my father turned us around and grabbed a wave and rode it back to shore. I stayed on my belly, up front. God, it was fast! In my little-kid head, it felt like we were going a hundred miles an hour. I gripped the rails tight. It was exhilarating. Years later, first time I ever heard that word, "exhilarating," I thought back to this moment with my father, and this first-ever wave.

We went right back out, of course. Wasn't even a question. And this time I wanted to ride in standing up. I said, "I want to ride like you, Dad. I want to stand."

He said, "We'll see about that, Israel. We'll see."

And we did. If that first ride was exhilarating, this second one was the absolute shit—another term I did not yet grasp. But it fit. Hell, yeah, it fit. My dad held my hand and helped to stand me up and as I did I had a quick case of nerves. For a tiny, quick-shot moment I fixed on the idea that I would slip and fall and maybe hit my head on the rail, but as soon as I got up and found my balance and felt certain in my father's grip those nerves were gone. I was washed over by that same sense of security from the first ride on my belly. I felt like nothing could go wrong. Like nothing could *ever* go wrong. And with it came this giant adrenaline rush of pure excitement. Still felt like we were going a hundred miles an hour. Maybe even a million miles an hour. Couldn't think of a bigger number or a faster speed. But on top of that it was such a giant thrill.

I didn't want it to end.

And there was also this: as I rode, I realized I was standing in the goofy position. I knew my dad rode goofy—meaning right foot forward—and I'd been wondering if I would ride goofy, too. I'd stand on a board on the beach, and I'd try it every which way, trying to figure it out. The thing is, you can't really know until you're up on a board which way is more comfortable. And so, as I stood up, I had no real idea what my stance would be, but I set myself right foot forward, just like him. Instinctively. It's like being left-handed or right-handed, only it doesn't match up. You can be right-handed and ride goofy, or you can be right-handed and ride regular—left foot forward. It just comes naturally, and whatever your stance that first time you get up on a board, that tends to be your stance forever. Like it or not, plan on it or not, you're stuck with it. And here I was, riding like my dad. Moving like my dad. Imagining myself like my dad.

Cool.

That one ride standing up was enough. I was hooked, stoked, gone...whatever words express how absolutely sold I was on the sport of surfing, that's what I was. But that was it for me, that first time. Just those two rides—one on my belly and one on foot. After that, I started to feel cold, shivering cold. My father could see that I was almost shaking. He said, "That's enough for today, Israel. There'll be more waves tomorrow."

◎

My father had a thing about working past his fears, which he told us in the form of a story. Over and over, he told us this story. Never the same way twice. But always with dramatic pauses and prompts and questions built in, so he could make double sure we'd been listening the last bunch of times.

The story went like this: As a young man, in the early 1960s, he was surfing the point at Makaha, where you could find some of the hairiest, gnarliest, bitchin'est waves on the island. One of our Makaha neighbors was a great big-wave surfer named Buzzy Trent. My father had seen Buzzy surf these giant, killer waves, up to twenty feet. Waves like that scared the crap out of my old man, who preferred to ride waves about half that height. That was his comfort zone. Maybe he could psych himself up to try a twelve-footer, maybe fourteen-, but twenty feet was way out of his reach.

For some reason, Buzzy kept trying to help him ride bigger and bigger waves, but something in my father kept holding him back. At the same time, there was another something that told him he had to try. Something that told him if he stayed in his comfort zone he'd become soft. So he started working on his stamina, by running the hills around our house. He worked on his wind, by skin-diving and learning to hold his breath for a minute and more. He worked on his approach, by studying the big-wave surfers and trying to mimic their technique.

Finally, one winter day, the northern swells reached to our little point and my father decided he was ready. And as he made to paddle out he realized he'd worked on his endurance, his wind, his approach, but he still hadn't tackled his fears. In fact, the closer he came to trying to ride these monsters, the more terrified he became, and he realized this was one part of his conditioning he couldn't control. He also realized that if he couldn't control his fears, he could at least get to where his fears couldn't control him. But this was no easy thing; didn't exactly work the way he told it to. Each day, the waves would get a little bigger, and he'd grow a little more fearful. It was an impossible equation. He'd see his pals getting more and more juiced about the tides and the weather, and then he'd see these same pals getting slapped around and wonder how the hell he was going to ride that kind of surf. These guys weren't just his friends, they were his heroes, and my father started to think that if big-wave legends like Buzzy Trent and Bud Morrissey were struggling he'd be a fool to even attempt those giant sets. He hung back, and he hated himself for hanging back, so he pushed himself to paddle out.

It was one of those one-step-forward/two-steps-back-type deals, because once my father was past the break, on the outside, he couldn't imagine riding one of those giant waves back to shore. He'd psych himself up for it; then he'd psych himself right back down. Up close, the waves were even more terrifying than they'd been at a distance. So what did he do? Basically, he froze, but as he did he realized something about himself, something important, and it was at this point in the story that he always asked us kids if we knew what that something was. We'd always wait for him to answer his own question. He'd say, "I am who I am. I don't have anything to prove."

And so he never surfed those twenty-foot waves. Not then, not later. Not if he could avoid them. The lesson, for him, was to take your own measure. To know the difference between being soft and being reasonable. To know your own limits.

Only I never thought this was a lesson he wanted for his sons, because the story came with a punch line—and the punch line came, he said, from an old World War II movie, where an officer finds a lowly paratrooper shivering in fear before attempting a jump. The officer can't understand why this young man keeps jumping, since by this point he has completed a great many practice jumps and still appears to be paralyzed by fear.

"Why do you keep jumping if you're so scared?" the officer asks the paratrooper.

"Because, sir," the paratrooper replies. "I love to be around men who aren't scared."

That young paratrooper was like my father, who loved to be around men who weren't scared. Men like Buzzy Trent and Bud Morrissey and all the other great big-wave surfers of the day—the fearless giants of the sport who went looking to surf the giant waves, typically twenty feet and taller. That's why he pushed himself past those killer sets, to at least think about attempting to surf a giant well, to soak in the fearlessness of his friends. It's not like he was out of his element, my old man, or in over his head as a surfer. No way. He could keep up with a lot of these guys, when the waves were in reach, but when things got a little hairy he pulled back. He drew off their fearlessness, but only to a point. And looking back, I can't shake thinking my father was raising us to be like those balls-to-the-wall surfers in Makaha Bay. It's like he was breeding this band of tiny surf warriors. Like we could somehow stand in for him when it came time to surf those giants. Like we could become those men without fear.

Anyway, that was my take. My brothers might have seen it another way. And my father, he'd wonder what the hell I was talking about. But why else would my old man make us march around our house each morning to the blare of Chairman Mao's wake-up call? This went on for a long stretch. My father had this scratchy old record he'd play at full volume, and he had us march to Chinese military music and do calisthenics and all these bizarre drills. And he had us do them in all seriousness. He'd line us up and put us through our paces, while the music blared on and on. It almost had a *Captain America*, cartoony feel to it; I'd hear the horns of Chairman Mao's march and think we were in a cartoon all our own. But we couldn't smile or goof around or not take it seriously because then we'd have to go at it again.

He was big into rituals, my father. They framed our days. They made us stronger, he always said. He'd start each day with his morning prayers, and when we were old enough we'd join him. When he sang the Shema blessing on Friday nights he'd have us stand and sing along, like we were saying the Pledge of Allegiance at school. He'd say the evening prayers at the end of the day, too.

At night, we'd have to be home by sundown. That was our dinner bell. Even when we were living in the camper, spending all our time on the beach and in the cliffs along the coast, we'd know that when the sun started sinking low and dipping past the horizon we'd better hustle on home. We'd eat as a family, and every night my father would ask us what we did that day, what we learned, what we enjoyed. He'd start with the oldest and work his way down, and I was filled with dread as David, Jonathan, and then Abraham took their turns. Either I'd have no idea what I was going to say or I worried I wouldn't be able to find the words or that one of my brothers would steal what I was going to say, because of course a lot of what happened to me each day happened to my older brothers as well. It was a whole lot of worry, every night, so I usually ended up stammering and never quite making my point or even uttering a full sentence.

My brothers used to tease me and for a while my nickname was Wha Wha Wha, because that was the sound I made when I was fumbling. I don't think the nickname bothered me; I just heard it like an inside joke. But it fit: I stuttered as a kid. I shrank from any kind of public speaking, so most of my contributions to my father's evening ritual started out with, "Wha Wha Wha." When I finally spit out something intelligible—it could have been something I learned about surfing, or about people, or about how maybe the mussels we'd used for bait that day when we were out fishing weren't as good as when we'd used the live baby crab—I'd hang back and wait for my father's approval. If I managed to say something smart or insightful or helpful to the other brothers, he'd reward me with a big smile or a clap of his hands or a pat on the head. That'd be like getting an A. If I could only shrug and mumble, "Wha Wha Wha," he'd leave me to sit and fidget for a minute or so before moving on to Moses. That'd be like getting an F.

Soon, even our diets were regimented. My mother used to feed us this dreadful morning gruel for breakfast, made from millet, raw wheat, corn, and who knows what the hell else. We were always told it was made with seven different grains, but I don't think there's a single one of us (my mother included!) who could name them. The stuff would congeal the moment my mother dished it out. If you were hungry, it tasted okay; if you weren't hungry, it was awful. We were sometimes allowed to sweeten it with a bit of honey and a pinch of raisins, which didn't help it go down that much easier.

They used to feed us this super-ultraorganic healthy bread, from a local bakery. It was kind of nasty, actually. They'd cut us these big, thick slices and stand over us to make sure we ate them. Sometimes, my mother would bake her own bread—and I hate to say it, but it was also nasty. It's not that my mom couldn't bake; it's that she couldn't put anything *good* into whatever she was baking.

Throughout the day, whatever we ate was carefully monitored. We couldn't eat anything that had been processed or refined or manufactured in any way. We couldn't have any butter. We couldn't have any sugar—not even brown sugar. And our portions seemed to get smaller and smaller as we got bigger and bigger.

Our portions shrank because my father believed we should be thin and lean. (In later years, when there were more and more of us, and less and less work for my father, portions were small for an entirely different reason, but by then we were used to it.) We never complained about the small portions, because there was only so much of this stuff we could take, but after a while the big bellies the oldest four or five of us had carried as little kids began to melt away. After a while my parents had us looking like the leanest, fittest, healthiest kids on the beach—which we were, I guess.

Telling it now, a lot of their ideas on diet and fitness leaned a little on the wrong side of crazy, but my brothers and I were so full of energy and confidence...it had to have at least *something* to do with the way we were being raised. We were strong, fearless, healthy beyond measure—and by the time the oldest of us were teenagers, we started to feel invincible.

In some way, our energy and confidence spilled over into how we surfed, just as how we surfed spilled back over into how we lived. It was all tied together. Like I wrote earlier, we mostly learned to surf by hanging around and watching other surfers. By thinking about surfing, all day long, and soaking in the mood and movements of others. Even when I was way little, I understood the cycle of the waves. I got that they came in sets and that in between the sets there'd be lulls and gaps and that this was when you were supposed to paddle out. Nobody had to explain this to me; you watch something for so long, you figure it out. By the time I was six or seven and starting to ride myself, I'd seen so many people surf I could identify them from a couple hundred yards away. I could tell by their stance, their style, their foot placement. How they held their hands. And by the paddle, too. They might have one foot in the air, or they might paddle with two hands at once, like my father. So I watched all these surfers, all these waves, over and over and over, and eventually I carried a picture of myself in my head, of the way I wanted to surf. It's like I was holding a mirror to the scene on the beach and finding myself in the reflection.

My father had some particular ideas about surfing, and he passed these on to us as well. Not so much in terms of style or approach, but more in terms of philosophy. As kids, we were taught not to waste anything. This applied to the food we ate, the clothes we wore...all the way down to the waves we chose to ride. A lot of times, you'll see surfers hanging on the outside, sitting on their boards, waiting and waiting on the perfect wave, but that wasn't the Paskowitz way. My father's idea was to catch every wave you can, and to ride it all the way in, as far as you can. It was the same as telling me not just to eat the center of the watermelon but to eat the whole thing, right down to the rind. He'd say, "Ride that wave as long as you can, Israel. If you ride it in longer, you'll be a better surfer than the other guy. He'll just ride in the sweet spot and then kick out at first chance. He'll be done, and you'll still be surfing."

This made sense to me, as a kid. Still does. To this day, when I'm out surfing for a couple hours I'll grab every wave that comes my way. It's different when you're competing, when you've got a certain amount of time to do your thing for the judges. When you're competing, you have to pick your spots, but when you're just playing, you have to surf. A lot of folks don't get this. Serious, kick-ass surfers—some of them just don't get this. They'll see me point for a nothing-special wave, and they'll call out to me. They'll say, "Hey, Izzy, there's a much bigger set coming."

But in my head I'm gone. In my head I know there's no such thing as a better wave than the one I'm on.

3

Israel to Israel

Our adventures in the Pacific were interrupted by a couple trips to Israel, although I guess "interrupted" is probably not the best word in this case. Doesn't do these trips justice. Probably better to just say it straight: my parents found a cheap way to re-imagine our days and expose us to another part of the world, so they jumped on it.

Twice.

The first of these trips came just after the Six-Day War, in 1967. We were still living in a house back then, so pulling up stakes and traveling overseas represented a major change in our day-to-day. The plan was for us to stay on an *ulpan*, which was a little bit like a kibbutz, only we wouldn't work or farm or live in any kind of communal way. It was more like an intense school, so us kids could learn Hebrew and study our Jewish heritage. (Wasn't much chance of *that* happening—the studying part—but it must have seemed like a good idea at the time.)

The *ulpan* was located in a small village just north of Tel Aviv and was run by the Israeli government, which explains why my father moved us there—because he wouldn't have to pay for anything. Oh, he took it seriously, but the emphasis was on the *taking*. The idea behind these *ulpans* was to help immigrants assimilate after the state of Israel was founded in 1948. I don't think my parents ever planned to make aliyah and move us to Israel permanently; we were more like long-term tourists or guests who overstay their welcome. Clearly, the program didn't apply to us Paskowitzes, but that didn't stop us Paskowitzes from applying to the program. There were so many Jews from all over the world who wanted to move to their new homeland that the government had to put these *ulpans* in place to help with the transition. Even observant Jews didn't know the language, the traditions. My father was a big supporter of Israel, and I believe he really and truly and passionately expected to single-handedly repopulate the Jewish population with his (mostly) biblically named sons, but he wasn't above getting a free ride, or taking full advantage of a government subsidy. So he quit his job in Hawaii and made plans to ship the whole bunch of us to the Middle East, together with a couple surfboards and a puke-yellow Dodge Caravan with one of those camper pop-tops.

My father made us all kiss the tarmac when we got off the plane—as much for show as to demonstrate that this was a holy place. It was pretty embarrassing; that's how it registered at the time. At four or five, I didn't know what Israel was or what it meant. All I knew was that we had the same name and I had to kiss the ground when we got there.

My father remembers that we didn't stay very long on this first trip, and that we were probably the first Jewish family in the history of Israel to be asked to leave the country. I think he might be exaggerating on this one, but it's possible we were the first family to get kicked out of this one *ulpan*. Not only were we asked to leave, he

says, but the Israeli government paid for our airline tickets home—
another first, probably. The whole trip was essentially a struggle,
from start to finish. My older brothers kept getting into all kinds of
trouble; I joined them in some of that trouble, although I was still
a little young for some of the bigger-kid, starting-fires-in-Porta-
Potties-type messes they made. Jonathan was our chief trouble-
maker; he commandeered a tank and came home with a live grenade
he found in the hills with Abraham one afternoon. But the biggest
problem was we couldn't sit still in our classes, which my parents
could have predicted the first time they saw the words "intense" and
"school" used in the same sentence.

There's a story that goes with my brothers finding that live
grenade. Actually, there are two. The first one started innocently
enough. I was wandering the hills with my brothers and came across
a fence with a skull-and-crossbones sign, with Hebrew lettering. I
couldn't read Hebrew, but I knew what the skull and crossbones
meant. My brothers, too. To us it meant, "Hey, let's see what's on the
other side of this fence." So we snuck under the fence and started
looking around. There was a lot of neat stuff in there. Some abandoned, bombed-out buildings. Exploded grenade fragments and cas-
ings. We stuffed our pockets with our most interesting finds. I just
had a bunch of shells, but Jonathan grabbed something that looked
like a tin plate with some wiring coming out of it.

To us it just looked like a bunch of bitchin' stuff—way cool. So we
started heading home with it, back to the *ulpan,* and I guess someone
must have seen us eyeballing our prizes as we walked, because all of
a sudden there were sirens going off and all these military types forc-
ing us to empty our pockets. There were even a couple bomb squad
guys sent to dismantle Jonathan's cool tin plate, which turned out to
be a live grenade, set out like a land mine.

Oh, man, was my father pissed! We got spanked hard that night—
really hard. Mostly, I think he was pissed because we embarrassed

him in our adopted homeland. It wasn't the trouble we made so much as where we made it. He hated that his boys had made him look bad in the eyes of his Israeli fellows, so he lit into us pretty good.

Didn't exactly teach us a lesson, except that it probably wasn't a smart idea to piss him off.

The second live ammo story came around almost forty years later—at the Camp Pendleton base in San Clemente. I was a rookie member of a local riding group called the Tortugas. My wife, Danielle, and I were living at our ranch in the hills of San Juan Capistrano, where we'd moved so she could tend and ride her horses, and I'd taken to riding as well. I'd dragged Danielle to the beach for so many years and she'd been such a great good sport about it, I figured it was the least I could do to embrace her passion, same way she'd made a go at mine, and after I'd been riding awhile I fell in with this great group of local riders—my Tortuga brothers.

There are over a hundred of us, and we dress ourselves out like serious cowboys and head for the hills on long treks. But we do it in style. We're trailed by a gorgeous RV that serves as a kind of deluxe chuck wagon, dishing out great food and a bottomless supply of beer and cocktails. Every hour, we stop for beer breaks—because, hey, it's pretty gosh darn grueling out there on the open trail.

I was riding my horse True—a dark bay gelding who was always true to his name. He *was* True. Always took good care of me, even when I had no idea what the hell I was doing, like on this one ride through Camp Pendleton. I was a decent-enough trail rider by this point, but to my Tortuga brothers I was still something of an oddball. They were a bunch of ex-marines and retired executives, so they didn't know what to make of my long hair and tattoos. But I fit myself in, eventually. I wore them down. Didn't help, though, that I pulled up on this one ride in a beautiful stand of trees, on our way to our second or third beer stop of the day. We rode in a kind of string that stretched to almost a mile, but True and I got kind of sidetracked by a sweet little stream, so I pulled off the trail and had a look around. I was drawn to a shiny object that had kind of nosed itself into the ground. Kind of brassy in color. So I reached for it and saw that it was a giant bullet. A giant, heavy bullet. Thought it would look pretty cool in my house. So I dug it out of the earth with my trusty bowie knife. Felt like it weighed about eighty pounds, but I slung it on my shoulder and started walking back with True towards the group.

Well, I must have looked like a damn fool, trudging towards the gang with my boots, my spurs, my weekend cowboy gear. We really dress the part on these long trek rides, and there I was, humping down the hill with this big ole bullet on my shoulder.

When I reached camp, I leaned away from the weight on my shoulder as if I was about to drop the bullet to the ground at our feet, but just as I made to do so one of the guys screamed. He said, "What the fuck is that?" And it wasn't just a straight-out question; it was filled with alarm and panic and disbelief.

I froze, afraid to move.

Then another one of my Tortuga brothers came up alongside me to inspect my find and said, "You dumb motherfucker."

There was a whole bunch of mayhem and confusion at this point. And general disgust, towards me, because apparently I'd un-earthed a live 105 howitzer round. The ex-marines in our group knew what it was immediately, knew how much damage that thing would have done if it went off. Probably, it would have blown us all to bits—and wasted all that good food and drink. And here I'd been pounding on it with my knife to get it out of the ground, and slug-ging it back to camp, and treating it like a harmless piece of dis-carded ammo.

My guys cussed me out pretty good. Took a long, long while for me to recover whatever credibility I'd built up to that point. Took longer still for them to forgive and forget, which is about what happened back on the *ulpan* when we were kids, when we brought home that live grenade.

Must be something about us Paskowitz boys and shiny artillery.

◎

Back to Israel.

Wasn't exactly Club Med, where we were, but I think my father thought of it as a kind of vacation. A loophole. A way in. He'd slip us through the cracks of the system, and we could live and eat at relatively little expense, and get a good cultural education besides—only it didn't take long for the folks running the *ulpan* to figure we might be getting the better end of it. My poor mother would go out every day to a little market that was set up in the middle of the compound and collect whatever food she thought we needed. That's how it worked; you'd receive according to need, so she'd stand in line behind one woman who'd ask for one pear. Then there'd be another woman, who maybe asked for two pears. Then when it was my mother's turn, she'd ask for nine pears, because there were only seven of us kids at that point. (My next-to-youngest brother, Salvador, had just been born, so even though he was a long way from eating solid food my math might be a little off.) Whatever these other good people needed, to put together a subsistence-type meal, we'd have to multiply by nine, so the folks in charge started to see it cost a small fortune just to feed us.

Basically, we were a huge pain in the *tuchus*.

We went back a couple years later—this time just after the Yom Kippur War of 1973. This time I had a better idea what it meant, what we were in for. This time, we had Navah and Joshua in tow, so there were eleven of us, and we were probably an even bigger pain in the butt. That first trip we'd stayed just a couple months, but on this second pass we stayed a little longer—about six months. We lived on the beach, just south of Tel Aviv, and when my father wasn't working in a local clinic or lifeguarding or helping out on a kibbutz we'd pile into the van and tour the desert, the countryside, the cities. He wanted us to experience some of what he'd experienced on his first trip to Israel as a young man; most of us were old enough at this point to understand his deep and profound connection to the place and to its people—and, he was hoping, to feel some of that connection for ourselves.

Just before we left for this second trip to Israel, my dad had been working in Los Angeles, and he'd managed to save a lot of money. The reason I remember this is because we'd had a great Christmas that year. Oh yeah, I forgot to mention we also celebrated Christmas. We kissed the tarmac when we landed at the airport in Israel, we sang the Shema and lit the candles on Friday nights, and we also celebrated Christmas. We were a tough bunch to figure, but that year Santa came up huge for the Paskowitzes. That year we each got our own Schwinn bicycles, the ones with the big banana seats and the high bars, and we actually shipped a few of them over to Israel, so the oldest of us could get around. I was ten years old by this point, so the idea was I'd be able to ride with my older brothers all over the place.

One of my father's ideas for this trip was to have his oldest son become bar mitzvah. David had just turned thirteen, and my father let it be known that it was a great big deal for him to take this sacred rite of passage in Israel. And it was, I guess. Kind of, sort of. Didn't mean a whole lot to any of us in any kind of religious way, other than my father, but we could see that it meant a lot to him, so this was reason enough to go through the motions. Don't think David had any idea what he was doing or saying when he chanted his prayers and read from the Torah, but I remember thinking the whole thing was pretty cool. Looking back, I have to believe the ceremony made David one of the first kids in modern Jewish history to get a bike for Christmas and to have a bar mitzvah in Israel in the same year.

Once again, my father shipped everything over in our Dodge

conversion van. Bikes, boards, clothes, cooking supplies...he even snuck a .22-caliber revolver into the door panel, just in case. (He later said there was also a rifle stowed in there, just in double case, but I never saw any rifle.) He didn't tell any of us what he was doing, especially my mother; if she knew he was trying to smuggle in a gun, just after the Yom Kippur War, she'd have had a fit.

Once there, he found work as a lifeguard, through some pals he'd made back in the 1950s, so there was some money coming in, and there was food, too. He had it set up so he could get us fed at this little shack on the beach. Wasn't the kind of healthy food he insisted on feeding us back home, but it was free, so it kind of evened out. That's another thing you need to know about my father in order to understand how we lived; he had his ideals, but he also had his price. If he could find a way to live by principle, that's the way he'd go, but if he could find a shortcut he'd be all over that, too.

Turned out there was a big need for lifeguards on this one beach, because the wind used to kick up and you'd get these dangerous undertows. There were some waves, and on some days the surfing was halfway decent, but the undertows were a real and constant problem. That's how it is on some beaches; you can't surf for shit, but the riptides can drag you down, down, down. Every year, a bunch of people would drown, so the Israelis were happy to have a guy like my father on the lifeguard tower. He knew his stuff, and the folks who ran the beach knew that he knew his stuff, so they treated us pretty well.

We stayed on a beautiful stretch of beach, in our small pop-top camper van. Actually, there wasn't enough room for all of us in the van, so we set up a tent on the beach for the oldest kids; my mother and father stayed in the van with the little ones. There was a guard assigned to watch over us at night, because there was still a lot of tension among the Israelis and the Egyptians and the Syrians, but we kids tended not to notice any of that stuff. We lived in our own little world.

After a while, my mother set up a small cooktop in the van, which she used to prepare our meals; best she could, she'd match what she made for us back in the states; there'd be seven-grain gruel for breakfast, healthy breads, boiled chicken...the same damn menu, the same small portions. We'd usually eat as a family, on a small picnic-type table they'd set up on the beach; wasn't room for all of us around the table, either, but the little kids would sit on the big kids' laps, or some of us would sit on the ground, or maybe we'd eat in shifts.

As always, Juliette was a great good sport, only too happy to step in and make my dad's crazy schemes a reality. It's kind of remarkable, looking back, but she was completely devoted to my father, and absolutely and wholeheartedly willing to throw in with him on whatever he had in mind. His hopes and dreams became hers—although I don't recall it ever working the other way around. I mean, it's not like they piled us all into the camper and had us driving around to the world's great opera houses. Mom wasn't any kind of passionate or die-hard surfer; she'd grab a board from time to time and do a decent enough job of it in the water, but it's not like she lived and breathed surfing. And she certainly wasn't a Jew—but there we were, halfway around the world, trying on the one piece of our family history she couldn't exactly share.

Like I said, kind of remarkable.

Our days in Israel ran together and the time fairly flew. I remember walking the bluffs above the beach with my brothers and coming across a bunch of ancient artifacts. At least we thought they were ancient artifacts. For all I know, they were just artifacts. Just *stuff.* Anyway, from the bluffs you could see the archeology of the seawalls, and the elevated aqueducts. You could see the comings and goings of the locals. The place just reeked of history, and at the same time the country was very current, very contemporary. Every once in a while, we'd meet up with a group of Israeli kids about our age—maybe brothers, maybe not—and they'd show us around. Weren't too many other kids bouncing around during the week, so we mostly found our own distractions.

The beach was packed on the weekends, but during the week we had the place to ourselves. We got in the habit of looking for money and other valuables the weekenders might have left behind. The winds would blow the top layer of sand over whatever people might have lost or dropped, so we'd sift through the sands looking for shekels, which in those days were actually liroth. Didn't much matter to us what you called them. Money was money. We'd find a shitload of coins, and we ended up spending them on ice cream. In those days, on this one beach, there was a guy who walked up and down with a dry-ice cooler, selling ice cream. He was like the Pied Piper of the beach, the way all the little kids would follow him around. He sold this banana-chocolate thing that was so crazy good we'd scarf those suckers back until we ran out of coins. Man, I can still taste it. The chocolate was incredible, and the frozen banana underneath just popped with this delicious flavor—crazy good. I'd sit with my older brothers on the beach, and we'd be like pigs in shit, inhaling these great treats, which came with the additional benefit of going completely against the strict dietary laws of our parents.

We were regular little rebels, and this was our rebellion.

On weekends, when the beach was crowded, we'd zig and zag among the blankets and chairs, past people playing *matkot,* a beach tennis game that's so wildly popular you'd think it was the Israeli national sport. We'd help ourselves to whatever people were stupid enough to leave behind on their beach blankets when they went into the water—sandwiches, half-empty sodas, chips. Mostly, we'd pinch cigarette butts and finish them off, so despite my father's best efforts and strict code we were like any other group of no-good, surf bum teenagers you might have found on the beaches of California, except that we weren't exactly teenagers (other than David, the bar mitzvah boy) and we were a long, long way from California. We only had to make sure before heading back to our campsite that we jumped into the water to wash off the cigarette stink, so our folks didn't notice.

(We might have been rebels, but we weren't stupid; my father would have kicked the living shit out of us if he caught us smoking.)

We didn't surf much. Some, but not much. We didn't have enough boards to go around, so we couldn't all go at once, and in those days we liked to move around in a pack, especially us older kids. Also, the waves weren't so hot. On some days they were decent, but on most days they were small, sucky, nothing special. Mostly, we swam, and splashed around, and ran up into the hills above the beach looking for cactus apples. That was another great treat, not quite up there with the banana-chocolate but way closer to my parents' ideas on what we should be eating. The locals would put cactus apples on ice, so that's what we did. And they were good. Not crazy good, just pretty good.

One day, we were all on the beach, some of us swimming, some of us surfing, some of us just laying around. I was out in the water— way out in the water, actually—and I heard a sick, scary scream. Back home, you'd hear somebody cry out like that, it usually meant they'd been bitten by a stinger or a jellyfish. This was just around the time of *Jaws*—the book, not the movie—so people were afraid of sharks, although I don't think there were too many sharks in the Mediterranean. Anyway, I heard this scream, and my first thought was to get the hell out of the water. I swam back to shore, together with a couple brothers, and when we got there we saw little Salvador being attacked by a German shepherd in the shallows. It was horrible, terrifying. David got to him first. Poor Sal was being rag-dolled by this beast. The dog had him by the thigh, and David kind of pounced on the dog and tried to force his mouth open.

The whole time, there was a group of Israeli soldiers on the beach, and they were ridiculously slow to react. We'd been all the way out past the break and we were just a bunch of stupid kids, but we managed to get to Sal before they did. Don't know what the fuck those soldiers were doing, but eventually they got to Sal and helped to free his leg from the dog's mouth. There was blood everywhere. The dog had bitten all the way down through the muscle. Poor Sal was screaming and screaming his little head off, and the rest of us were screaming and screaming our little heads off, and it was just a mad, frantic scene. Someone ran to get my father, who raced Sal off to the hospital. He was just about four years old at the time, ended up with about a hundred stitches, and a rabies shot, and they had to put the dog down, and we were all so deeply traumatized, to have to see little Salvador getting mauled like that by this big, big dog. To this day, I'm still afraid of dogs, and it goes back to this day on the beach. And Sal's still got some pretty gnarly scars on his thigh.

He also got a nickname out of the deal—Sigmund. For a while, that's what we all called him (Sig, Siggy, Sigmund), although all these years later I'm not exactly sure why it came up on the back of this accident. It had something to do with a crappy Saturday morning kids show that ran at the time, called *Sigmund and the Sea Monsters,* but we didn't watch that many crappy Saturday morning kids shows, especially in Israel. It also had something to do with the fact that Salvador had a big, big mouth and he was always putting all kinds of shit into it. His fist, a sick amount of food . . . whatever. Guess maybe he was screaming so much, his mouth opened so damn wide, it reminded us of those bigmouthed puppets from those H. R. Pufnstuf–type shows. Anyway, the name stuck; Salvador still answers to it, from time to time, and whenever it comes up we're all taken back to that terrible scene on the beach.

◎

There was another hairy moment from our second trip to Israel that also shook us up pretty good. This one involved my father's .22-caliber revolver. (Hey, you didn't think I'd mention that my father had smuggled a gun into the country if I wasn't planning to come back to it, did you?) It also involved a kind of moral dilemma that put some of my father's free spirit–type values to the test.

We were on a deserted road, middle of nowhere. Doesn't exactly narrow it down or pinpoint our location, but stay with me. It was my father's day off, and we came upon a hitchhiker by the side of the road. Hitchhikers were fairly common back in California and all across the United States, but you didn't see too many in the Israeli desert. My father was in the habit of picking them up, wherever we traveled, so he pulled over and offered the guy a ride. Soon as he did, he regretted it. He didn't like the look of this guy. Something about him was off. Not right. He might have been a soldier; with our luck, he might have been an Arab soldier. Up close, inside the van, the man looked haggard, like he was in distress. I don't think he spoke any English, and the few words he managed to say sounded like they were in Arabic; our Hebrew was lousy, but we could usually figure out the basics, only with this guy there was no good way to communicate.

Very quickly, my father decided he didn't trust this Arab-looking hitchhiker who may or may not have been a soldier, but at the same time he couldn't bring himself to kick him back to the curb and leave him to fend for himself in the middle of nowhere. My father wanted to do the right thing, although I don't think he had even the first clue what "the right thing" might have been, in this case. Also, he didn't want to put his family in danger, so he hit upon a half-baked, half-assed solution. He reached for his revolver and motioned for the guy to lie down on his belly in the back of the van. It ran so completely counter to how things usually went in our family— which usually had nothing to do with being held at gunpoint. I almost didn't recognize my father underneath this bizarre act. Yeah, it was a defensive move, but Doc was the one with the weapon, which he then handed to David, his deputy, and told him to keep it pointed at the hitchhiker, who of course wasn't too happy about this latest turn. Either he was a good guy facing down a patch of bad luck, being held at gunpoint on the floor of a van by a bunch of brown-skinned beach urchins, or he was a bad guy who'd met his match. He could have been unhinged, this guy. He could have been violent. He could have been drunk or stoned.

Anyway, he was pissed. And the rest of us were completely freaking out. It was a small van to begin with, and now there was this full-grown, disheveled-looking, possibly crazy, possibly Arab soldier lying flat on his belly. We were all huddled against the walls of the van, trying to put as much room between us and this big, unfolding drama as the confines of the cab would allow. It was such a weird, tense moment, and the whole time my father just kept driving. Don't know what the hell he was thinking. Don't know where the hell he was going. Just know that he kept looking back—one eye on the road, one eye on our prisoner—making sure we were all okay.

The hitchhiker was probably wondering why the hell he'd gotten into *this* van, with *these* crazy people, these bag-of-bones boys.

It was a winding, bumpy road, and every time we'd hit a pothole or a twist or turn the guy would move or shake, and whenever he did my father would shout, "Sit down! Stay down!" That was all anybody said, once the guy was facedown on the floor. He might have mumbled a few words in protest, but after my father had him lying the way he wanted nobody talked. Just my father, every couple miles, shouting, "Sit down! Stay down!" Or, turning to David, saying, "Tell him to keep down! Tell him not to move!"

None of us can remember if David actually had his hand on the trigger or if he was just holding on to the handle, but he was doing his best to keep this guy still and to appear at least somewhat calm and in control. Inside, he must have been thinking, *Oh shit! Oh shit! Oh shit!* But on the outside he was a regular thirteen-year-old badass.

For a half hour, we rode in this way, and it felt to me like the longest fucking half hour of my life. I wondered where the hell my father was going, what was taking so long, how this standoff would end, why Dad hadn't just opened the door and kicked the guy out if he was so worried about him. It made no sense, but there it was.

Finally, we came to the outskirts of the next town and my father let the guy out. Grabbed him by the back of his shirt and pushed him to the street without a word. And that was that, except the whole exchange left me feeling uncertain, uneasy. We were all a little uncertain, uneasy—even my father. We drove on in silence for a while after that. We were all too stunned to speak, and as we drove I tried to understand what had just happened, what my father'd just put us through. At ten years old, I tried to understand it—and now, almost forty years later, I'm still working on it.

Best I can figure is my father was caught between his nature and his instincts. He wanted to do right by this guy, to help him out with a ride, but his gut told him to be careful about it. You have to realize, my father was always giving people rides back home in California. It was the most natural thing in the world to him. He'd pull up at a red light and notice some bum on the corner and jump out of the car to see if the guy needed anything; we'd be in the middle of the intersection, and the light would be green, and he'd be chasing the guy down with a twenty. But this was a whole other part of the world; this was essentially a war zone; this was a place where tourists like us couldn't always tell the good guys from the bad guys. And what this meant, for my father, was that his world-view was now on tilt. Whatever he needed, my father was always willing to touch up someone else, so they could share with him. Even if they had no interest in sharing, he'd bring them around. The flip side of that was that whatever he had my father was always willing to share. That was just his way, which I guess explains why he pulled over to give this nut job Israeli a lift in the first place, even though it doesn't explain why my father continued to give him that lift when the guy appeared to be bad news.

Maybe Doc wanted to put his best self on display for us kids, to model caring, compassionate behavior, even when the guy on the receiving end of his care and compassion looked like he wanted to do us dirt. Even if my father's idea of "care" meant he had to hold the guy at gunpoint in order to do him a solid. Or maybe my father was just stubbornly determined to do what he thought was the right thing, to not abandon this guy in the desert, whether or not it made sense to pick him up and give him a ride. Because, hey, we were in Israel. Just a bunch of scruffy, vagabonding Mexican-American Jews, roaming the beaches of our ancestral homeland, connecting to the people in what ways we could.

4

Establishment

Can't say for sure which came first, the camper or the call of the open road. It's our version of the classic *chicken vs. egg* question. No one in my family can agree if my father hit on the idea of living full-time in the camper because he got his hands on a quality used rig or if he decided to quit his job and move us out of our house and then went looking for a vehicle. So which came first? I've heard Doc tell the story both ways and each version seems plausible, reasonable. And my mother's no help; she backs up my dad whatever way he's telling it, whatever sounds good, and by this point they've both told the story so many times they can no longer separate the facts from the fictions.

Does it even matter? Probably not, except to me and my siblings. Everything we were, everything we would become…it all turned on this right here, and I guess it'd be nice to know it turned from some proactive, willful decision by my parents. If they'd given it some real, clearheaded thought. And if it happened in a more *what the hell* sort of way it'd be nice to know that, too.

Anyway, what I get from my parents is that it probably happened in fits and starts. Maybe our first trip to Israel as a family lit something in my father, same way his own first trip to Israel set him off on a whole new path. All of us on the road like that, living in such close quarters, relying only on each other... maybe it got him thinking. Or thinking back to conversations he'd had with my mother, all along. Remember, they'd started out living together in her Studebaker, on the beach in Mexico. I've seen pictures of that car and it looks like something for the scrap heap, but they were happy. They had what they needed. They camped; they fished; they fucked; they surfed. It was all *right there.* So it's possible this idea of living on the road, of just picking up and being completely untethered and free, had been a part of their plan since they first got together. It's possible they were just waiting until Mom stopped spitting out all us kids, one after the other.

Waiting until it made sense—that is, assuming it ever made sense.

The way I remember it, the way we picked up and hit the road, it was almost like a sleight of hand. Like it came about on its own. There was no big announcement or kickoff ceremony. We'd moved around the previous few years, from one small house to another; it was no big thing. We'd gotten used to my father quitting or getting chased from one job or other, and to the downtime that sometimes found him between jobs—downtime that conveniently fell in the summer and left him free to hang with us and his surfing buddies at the beach... until the money ran out and he had to go looking for another gig.

So when the money ran out yet again and it came time for us to move from our little house on La Moree Road in San Marcos, a small suburb outside San Diego, we just kind of stumbled into a twenty-four-foot camper we'd had in our yard the past while. That first rig was a Ford Establishment—a cab-over, Class C camper. It had some miles on it, by the time my father got his hands on it, some wear and tear, but it was in decent-enough condition. Wasn't the most comfortable ride, but it was reliable. When I think back on it, it seems kind of ironic that it was called the Establishment, because the rig represented our escape from all these established norms and conventions and routines; leaves me thinking there was some executive at Ford with a sweet, sarcastic sense of humor.

That La Moree house was in a rural part of town, out by a chicken ranch, and it wasn't unusual for my father to park a couple different vehicles out back or off to the side. He was always trading one ride for another—a car for a truck, a board for a bike.... We'd already used the camper a bunch of times for weekend trips to the beach, for longer road trips here and there. It was familiar, and filled with all our crap, just like any other room in our house. It's just that one day we looked up and there was no house.

We were gone.

Now, I'm sure there was a lot more to it, but this was how it registered for me. This is what I remember. And there's a great, buried truth in my take, even if my memory is off—namely, that it was no big deal, all of us moving into the camper and heading out. Really, it wasn't.

Plus, it was summer, and those days we were in the habit of heading down to the beach by the nuclear power plant in San Onofre, where there were great waves and a state-run campground; even when we had our house in San Marcos, we'd stay at San O for days and days at a stretch, so at the top this stretch was no different.

To hear my parents tell it now, it sounds like they had some sort of grand plan, to hit the road and follow our whims, but I don't believe that's how it went down. That's just the romantic, revisionist way to look at it. I believe it was more of a transitional thing, a temporary thing. It just kind of happened. We'd had to sell the house, for some reason or other, and we'd hang in the camper until the next move presented itself. Only there was no next move, except to roll on down the road to the next parking lot, the next campground, the next beach.

It helps to realize, too, that this was the early, early part of the 1970s—which was all tied into the laid-back, free spirit, California dreamin'–type lifestyle of the 1960s. I've always believed it was a sign of those times that my parents were even in a position to consider dropping off the grid. Don't think it would have ever occurred to them ten, twenty, thirty years earlier—or even ten, twenty, thirty years later. It fit with the times. With this one move, my parents seemed to embrace that whole counterculture movement, which was weird because in almost every other way they were supertraditional, superstraightlaced people. No, they didn't exactly care if we went to school every day, especially if the sun was out and the surf was up. But they didn't drink or smoke or fool around. They weren't hippies or dropouts. They had good, solid values—*do unto others* and all that. They were smart, caring, disciplined in their own ways. They believed in God, although they couldn't always agree on what He looked like or what we could ask Him to do for us, or even how to go about asking.

One day we looked up and we were in the middle of a freewheeling, counterculture lifestyle that had almost nothing to do with us, and underneath there was this emerging surf culture that had taken off in and around Malibu and all along the California coast. Back when my father started surfing down at Mission Beach as a teenager, there were maybe hundreds of surfers; now, thanks to the Beach Boys and *Gidget* and *Endless Summer* and a burst of activity on the California surf scene, there were millions. And it wasn't just the sport itself that had taken hold; it was the whole package, the easy mind-set. Surfers tended to be cool, bohemian, drifter types—at least, that's the picture that took shape, although most of my dad's hard-core surfer pals were also hard-charging drinkers and partiers. That wasn't my father's way, but it was the way of the beach. You surfed hard, you played hard … and you worked hardly at all. That was the ideal, to free up your days so that when the surf was up you could paddle out. And here we found ourselves living a surfer's wet dream. We could come and go and do as we pleased, and I think a lot of our surfer pals sparked to that, in their own ways. Can't say I blamed them. We lived without restraint, without constraint. We followed the sun, our moods, the tides. We would not be bound to any one place, to any one set of expectations.

Might not have started out like that, might not have been my parents' intention, but after a while folks started to notice. Our life wasn't meant to be a statement. But surfers would hear what we were up to and want to check us out; and even more than that, they wanted in. We'd tapped into something bigger than any of us could have ever imagined; soon, people were writing articles about us, and pointing us out on the beach, and reading more into our lives than we were. More than our lives could justify.

Turned out we could throw an awful lot of shit in and on that camper. We'd pile our boards and bikes up top; by this point, we all had our own boards; some of us had two, a longboard and a shortboard. This left a lot of room in the cab for us to cram our must-haves, but when it came time for all eleven of us to go to bed we were jammed in good and tight. We were already used to sleeping on the floor, on mats, on the beach … so this was no different. There was a big bed up top, in the cab-over portion of the rig, and that's where my parents slept. The youngest, Joshua and Navah and maybe Salvador, slept at the foot of their bed to start. And the rest of us fought for position in the back of the camper, staking out our own territory. The way it worked was the biggest kids got dibs on the best beds, only they weren't really beds; they were more like pads or mats; from time to time, maybe there'd be an actual mattress.

There was a breakfast table in the corner, and at night we'd turn that into a little sleeping area. There was also a side sofa that flipped out into a bed, and we could fit three or four of us on it when we were little. Basically, each of us claimed a tiny piece of camper real estate and called it our own, and at night, if you had to go outside to pee, you'd almost always step on a couple brothers on the way.

Us older kids tried to sleep as far from our parents' cab-over compartment as possible, because they went at it just about every night. Like wild animals, they went at it. They had a complete lack of inhibition when it came to sex, which meant we got an earful. If you weren't careful, you'd get an eyeful, too, although I suppose there were worse ways to see and hear your parents. Reporters would pick up on this, because we made a joke out of it, but when they asked him about it my father would put it back on them. He'd say, "Would you rather they heard their father beating their mother?" It was the *make love, not war* sentiment of the day, rubbed in our faces every single night. Soon as we were old enough to figure what our parents were up to, making all that noise, we thought it was gross and funny; they'd fuck, and we'd giggle, and the little kids would giggle right along; they had no idea why they were laughing, but they saw us big kids laughing and that was reason enough. Eventually, even the littlest ones picked up on what was going on; to this day, my sister, Navah, jokes that having to listen to my parents' loud fucking every night scarred her for life.

You know, in their own, weird way, my parents modeled an especially loving, intimate relationship for their children. They were completely devoted to each other, completely crazy about each other, completely supportive of each other. And they couldn't keep their hands off each other, which was kind of nice. Yeah, it weirded us out, as kids, to have to listen to all their groping and grunting... but it was kind of nice.

One of the first things my father did when he got the camper was remove the holding tank and receptacle part of the toilet. He thought the trapped methane would kill us, being closed up inside that camper all day, every day. Plus, he was still worried about his asthma, so he was determined to breathe clean air—which was tough to do in a recreational vehicle, with all those fumes coming in through the vents. But, mostly, it was disgusting. The toilet would fill with all our piss and shit, and the piss would slosh all over the place as we rode, there'd be muck all over the bathroom, so he pulled it out and had us shit in these tiny little blivet bags. That's what we called them. We'd do our business and tie them off and leave them off by the side, in neat, tiny rows.

Wish I had a picture of that now—a bunch of shitted-up, knotted-up blivet bags, up against one of the camper's walls. All neat and tidy and good to go.

My father fitted us out with a row of cubbies—little cubicles all our own, where we could stuff all our worldly possessions. In mine, I kept my clothes, a couple bathing suits, and a journal. That was one of my father's requirements, once we stopped going to school, to write every day in our journals—and for the first couple years we stuck to it. He made an effort to check in with us every once in a while, to see what we were writing. He was still in the habit of going around the horn and asking us to share something we'd learned each day, and writing was another way to keep us thinking and looking at the world in new ways.

After just a short time on the road, my cubby was overstuffed with my hobbies and interests. For a while, I was big into photography. I got an old Nikon camera, one of those underwater Jacques Cousteau models, and I started taking a lot of pictures out in the water, documenting all our trips and adventures. I did them all on slides, because they were cheaper to develop and easier to store. For another while, I kept jars of sand from all the beaches we visited, which I lovingly labeled. Shells, too. Actually, a couple of us had really nice shell collections going. But when things started to get a little crowded after so much time on the road my parents decided to put all our stuff in storage, and after a while my father got behind on the bill and our stuff was tossed. The owner of the storage place sold what he could and threw out the rest. The lesson there was to keep it simple. To pare down. We were already living pretty simply, down to the bare bones of what we needed, but after that we cut back even more. After that we learned not to get too, too attached to material things.

For laundry, we'd hit the nearest Laundromat, usually as a family. We'd put it off as long as we could, and when the funk finally got to my mother she'd drag us down for a couple loads. Sometimes, she'd just take the little ones while the rest of us were off at the beach, but my parents liked it when we were all together. I don't remember being any kind of help on these cluster trips to do our wash, but we hung out and goofed around and tried to keep out of trouble. Sometimes, while we were busy with the wash, my father would set off foraging for whatever it was we needed at the time—and we *always* needed something. Whatever money he managed to save when he was working, we went through it quick enough when he wasn't, so before we were too long in any one place my father would go out and see what he could see. He used to call it cockaroaching, and he'd go cockaroaching around, looking for deals on food, surfboards, places to park the camper, sideline work for us bigger kids. Wasn't exactly begging, but he definitely had his hand out—and folks were intrigued enough by our story and by the sight of us that a lot of them wanted to help out.

Even at ten, eleven years old, I hated to see my father out asking for stuff. I knew the deal. I knew we didn't have any money. And I also knew we didn't have any money by choice. In my little-kid head, this made a difference. After all, my father was a doctor. All of his friends had money in the bank. His friends from medical school, from the jobs he left behind ... they were all rich. Back then, doctors made a ton of money. They had nice houses, nice cars; their kids had nice clothes. If he'd just worked at it, and saved some of it, my parents would've been all set. But he was never any good with money—probably because he was never any good with work, either. It wasn't that he didn't see the need for money; he just didn't attach the same value or importance to it as everyone else. He was generous to a fault. If he saw someone in need, he emptied his pockets. But then he'd be in need—*we'd* be in need!—and I don't think he ever made the cause-and-effect connection.

Yeah, Doc. No shit. You give away your money, there's nothing left for your family. That's usually how it happens.

Once, after the roof of our camper collapsed in a killer rainstorm, my father was looking at a bunch of bills he couldn't pay, so he hit on one of his nutty schemes to make fast money. He'd heard on the radio that the price of silver was sky-high, so he scraped together whatever money he had and traded it in at the bank for dimes. Bags and bags of dimes. Then he had us kids sort through these bags of dimes to see if we could find any old silver dimes, which the government had stopped making a couple years earlier. A lot of these dimes were still in circulation, so my father thought he could unearth a couple fistfuls of them and we'd be all set. We sat around the small table in the camper, sorting through these bags and bags of dimes. For days and days, we did this. We worked in shifts, and after a couple days we'd turned up maybe two or three of the old dimes, which turned out to be worth only two or three times more than a regular dime.

All that work, for fifty fucking cents.

The idea was whenever my father started scraping at the bottom of his accounts he'd push himself to get a job. At one job, he used to get paid in crisp ten-dollar bills. He walked around with a wad of crisp bills, which he'd peel off one by one. Eventually, the wad grew thinner, and then it disappeared altogether, and we'd set off looking for something, someplace new. He'd take out this big book that listed different medical jobs all across the country, and he'd pick some out-of-the-way place he and my mother thought might be interesting and that's where he'd apply. He'd work in hospitals, clinics, wherever there was a need. He had this romantic notion that he was bringing twenty-first-century medicine to some of these backwater places, but it's not like he was on any kind of cutting edge. He wasn't really up on the latest advances or techniques, and he certainly didn't have any equipment or resources. He kept his medical license current; that was about it. He treated Native Americans on remote reservations, and migrant workers in New Mexico. Some of these places hadn't seen a doctor in years, so he always got the job, and for a while there'd be money coming in...until my father got restless or the waves turned out to be shit or the weather started to turn and it was time for us to break camp. There was always some new adventure, some new beach, some new part of the country... and my folks were open to all of it.

The idea, now that we kids weren't going to school, was to build our days around surfing. That was the key part of the whole transaction, only it didn't always work out that we could surf. Sometimes we'd be landlocked, like the time we lived in Portales, New Mexico. Or, for another stretch, in Martin, South Dakota, near the Nebraska border. They'd never seen people like us in South Dakota—and we'd never seen snow! Didn't know what to make of it at first, until one of us figured out we could ride it. We spilled out of that camper like caged monkeys, busted out our boards, and rode the hills just beyond where our camper was parked. The local muskrat hunter and Indian kids wanted nothing to do with us. Wouldn't go so far as to say we brought surfing to the region, but folks certainly scratched their heads and wondered what we were up to.

We crisscrossed the country a bunch of times, those first couple years, when I was eight and ten and twelve. All the way to Rhode Island, down to Florida, and back along the Gulf coast through Louisiana and Texas. Summers, we'd find our way back to California, usually through Mexico, where there was almost always great surfing along the Pacific Coast. At each stop, we'd set up camp and fall back on our routines. Remember, we were a full house by the time we hit the road—or, I should say, a full camper. There were nine of us kids, ranging from toddler to teenager. My father would get up early, usually with the sun. If we were on the coast, he'd grab a couple waves first thing; if we were feeling up to it, a few of us might join him. Then he'd come back and say his morning prayers. He'd put on the tefillin and start chanting, though sometimes he'd forget the prayers halfway through. Or he'd lose his focus and drift towards something else—some problem with the camper, some drama playing out on the beach, something.... I don't believe his morning ritual was about the prayers so much as it was about the ritual itself, the routine. He was a religious man, but only in a *going through the motions* sort of way. If he had to stop his prayers halfway through, he might never get back to them, because they were mostly meaningful in the setting out to do them.

He made the effort, paid his respects. And, to him, that was everything.

For a while, he kept up with our Chairman Mao march; each morning, he'd put us through our paces. It got to where we were so leaned out by our no-fat, no-frills, no-fun diets and by our morning calisthenics we started to look like skinny little sea urchins; we were all brown-skin-and-bones. When we'd stop for a visit with friends or family members every few months for a hot shower and a short breather, they'd ask after our health and well-being. We were ridiculously fit, but we looked so skinny and dirty and dusty. We'd always relied on each other for just about everything—love, support, friendship, partners in mischief—but now that we were living in the camper this was especially so. We'd created our own little world, moved to our own rhythms. We didn't really see ourselves in any kind of objective way. But folks would look at our skinny selves and how we lived and wonder what the hell my parents were up to.

Now, I sometimes wonder the same. My siblings, they probably do as well. I mean, it was a pretty messed-up childhood, even though it was messed up in mostly wonderful, exciting ways. We made our own rules, made our own adventures, so that part was great. We had our own little cultural immersion program going, and we were totally immersed in the water, totally at ease on our surfboards and in any number of whacky social situations, so that was great, too. I don't think I was ever bored—not even on the long drives we sometimes took, from one beach to the next. I don't think I ever felt scared or alone. Wouldn't trade any of it. Not a single day. But there's no denying we missed out on a lot of the fundamental elements of growing up. We didn't have any kind of formal schooling, other than a couple years, here and there, for the oldest. We didn't stay put in any one place long enough to develop any real or lasting friendships, other than with each other. And we certainly didn't have parents who modeled any kind of traditional work ethic, or showed us how we might make our ways in the world beyond the family camper, away from the beach.

But, like I said, I wouldn't trade the way I grew up for anything. Because, hey, when we were in the middle of it, hopping from one town to the next, one wave to the next, one adventure to the next... it's like we didn't have a care in the world.

That would come later, I guess.

5

San O

Once we lit out for the open road and started living in the camper, the beach at San Onofre was the closest thing we had to a home. It was the place we'd return to each summer; it became like our base of operations, our Northern Star. And if it wasn't for good old Richard Nixon, our lives might have spun in a whole other direction. We might never have taken up with our good, life-long pals the Tracys, or started our family surf camp, or ridden the hell out of Trestles, a collection of sweet surf spots up and down the beach where we learned to really rip.

Yep, say what you will about Tricky Dick, but surfers in Southern California hold a special place in their sun-splashed hearts for the man, and to us Paskowitzes in particular he was a kind of godsend. Or, at least, a slightly out-of-step old uncle who might have fucked up from time to time but still looked out for us. Don't know that my parents were all that thrilled with Nixon's politics, but as kids we didn't know the first thing about politics. We all knew who he was, of course. With or without San O, we knew who he was. And it's not just because he bought a Presidential retreat up the road in San Clemente. It's mostly because I don't think it was possible to grow up in that time and place without hearing his name, even if you didn't go to school or read the newspaper or live in a house, and if you grew up like we did you tended to hear it in a negative way. For us as little kids, his name was like a punch line to every anti-establishment or generation-bashing joke we could think to tell. We blamed Nixon for Vietnam, for the generation gap, for whatever else was dragging us down. And all of this was way, way before Watergate, before folks knew the guy was completely corrupt.

But Richard Nixon's one saving grace, far as we were concerned, came when he opened up the state beach at San Onofre, which for years had been run as a private surf club. You needed to be a member to surf there, or know somebody who was a member, or know how to sneak past the gatekeepers who ran the place, and that just wasn't my dad's thing. He'd grown up on the public beaches of San Diego, and it rubbed him a bunch of different wrong ways that folks wanted to privatize what he'd always thought should be public and open and free. It went against his nature, especially since he used to surf that break as a kid. The way it works is that the beach itself is public land, up to the high-water mark, but the access to the beach can be owned or controlled. At San O, the bluffs hugged so close to the shoreline for such a long, long stretch it was difficult to reach the water if you weren't a member without a really long trek from the nearest access point. There was no place to park, and you certainly couldn't camp, so most folks just took their surfing business elsewhere. But then Nixon came along and bought his famous Casa Pacifica, the Western White House, in San Clemente, which overlooked the Upper Trestles surf spot, just north of the San Onofre Surf Club beach, and he decided to turn the area into a state park.

To my dad and his surfer pals, it was like a great gift.

Guess we should have another special place in our hearts for Ronald Reagan, who was our governor at the time, because he was the one who upheld Nixon's Presidential decree and set the whole thing in motion. Almost overnight the California surf scene tilted to San Onofre. Just like that. Over the years, going back to when my dad was just a kid, a lot of the real diehards found a way to surf San O, to bypass the club, because the break was just too, too special to leave to a privileged few, but it was a real sea change when the government opened up the beach and set up campgrounds where we could park our rig and hang for the summer. Don't think the surf club guys were happy about having to share their private little sandbox, but to the rest of us it was huge. Even today, more than forty years later, you can still find grizzled surf bums at Trestles with nice things to say about Nixon and Reagan. It's an odd picture because for the most part these are left-leaning old hippies, but they don't give a plain shit about Nixon's politics or Reagan's policies; they just care that these guys made it possible for them to surf one of the best damn beaches on the Pacific Coast.

'Nuf said.

The good news/bad news was that the beach was directly alongside the San Onofre Nuclear Generating Station—or SONGS, but nobody called it that. The iconic features of the plant were these two giant containment structures, which always looked to me and my brothers like enormous breasts, rising up from the sea. I don't remember there being too much talk about what it meant for us to be spending all that time in what was basically the middle of a nuclear power plant. It wasn't really an issue. Also wasn't really an issue that the beach bumped right into Camp Pendleton, the primary West Coast base of the United States Marine Corps, which occupied an absolutely huge tract of land along the coastline. It was just part of the deal—if you wanted to surf San O, you had to deal with the military base and the nuclear power plant.

Back when he was young and single my father used to do a lot of surfing at Malibu Point, another legendary surf spot. To hear him tell it, the guys on the beach in Malibu were always up for a good time, which wasn't really my father's thing, but he got along well enough with these guys in the water, on the beach. He didn't drink, but he didn't mind that everybody else did, so when the sun dropped from the sky he'd spend his time checking out all the pretty girls. This was back in the 1950s, when surfers like Miki Dora and Terry "Tubesteak" Tracy ruled the beach. Miki was known as the King of Malibu, and Tube was like the mayor. He lived in a hut right on the beach, and all these Hollywood types would come down and hang and surf. It was like a never-ending party, with bonfires on the beach, music, cookouts... the whole deal.

The legend of Tubesteak was that he was the original Big Kahuna, the inspiration for the character made famous in all those *Gidget* movies. The way that came about was through a girl named Kathy Kohner, who used to hang with these guys. All day long, all summer long, she'd surf and play with the crowd around Tubesteak's hut. She fit herself right in. Each night, she'd go home and tell her father all these great beach stories. Turned out her father, Frederick Kohner, was a Hollywood screenwriter and a novelist and he grew his daughter's stories into a book called *Gidget, the Little Girl with Big Ideas,* which became a big success and led to a bunch of sequels, and a bunch of movies, and eventually a television series and a whole other bunch of movies.

Turned out, too, that Tube was the guy who gave Kathy Kohner the name Gidget. In those days, you didn't see too many girls out there surfing, so a lot of the guys didn't bother to learn Kathy Kohner's name. She was just known as the girl surfer. That was enough of a peg. Plus, she was short, so she was sometimes known as the midget surfer—or the girl midget. Tube mushed it all together and start calling her Gidget, and the name stuck. Frederick Kohner used it in his book, along with a lot of the other nicknames he'd pinched from his daughter's stories. Apparently, there really was a guy who went by Moondoggie, and there would have been a Tubesteak, too, except the name was a little blue for mainstream America, so he became Big Kahuna instead.

My father was a San Diego surfer and Tube was a Malibu guy, but they hung out from time to time. (Up in Malibu, the hard-core surfers knew Doc as one of the old-timers—because, hey, he was a veteran surfer even then. Anyway, he'd been at it awhile.) When the break was just right, Tube and Doc even snuck into San O together, which I guess would have been neutral territory for them. In the water they were both pretty hard-core, but on the beach Tube's Big Kahuna–type personality took over. Down at San O, they were like lone wolves, each out of his element but thrown together on the same break. And yet somehow the two of them developed a nice friendship, before they fell off of each other's radar for a stretch. Wasn't like it is now, with cell phones and e-mail and Facebook. It was easy to lose touch, and that's what happened with Doc and Tube. They started having families, and the tug and pull of work and kids meant they didn't see each other all that much anymore. Soon, the tug of the open road pulled Doc off the map altogether, and they drifted out of each other's lives, same way they'd drifted together.

But then San O opened up in 1971 or so, and there was a place to park our rig and a way to surf Trestles without the hassle. A lot of the old-timers were pumped about it, and for the first couple summers the place was packed. We pulled into the lot one day and it just so happened we'd parked right next to the Tracys' Ford Country Squire station wagon, with the fake wood on the door panels—a classic SoCal surfer ride. Don't know when the last time was that Doc and Tube had seen each other, but they fell right back into it. There was a lot of hugging, and clapping on the back, and wondering what the hell they'd been up to. Tube had had a bunch of kids, and Doc had had a bunch of kids, and we all started spilling out of our rides and checking each other out.

Took a while to introduce everybody. In fact, I don't think our dads even bothered with introductions, that first time. It was more like, "Hey, that one over there, that one's mine." And, "Those four over there, they're mine, too."

There were probably seven of us Paskowitz kids by that point, and seven Tracy kids, and we matched up close in age, so we just kind of paired off and hit the beach. No big thing—except, you know, it kind of *was*. I mean, for all of our adventures and road trips, we Paskowitzes had been pretty sheltered. We never really had any friends, other than each other, and here were these Tracy kids, a bunch of crazy little Irishmen. Looking at them was like looking in a mirror. They were a raggedy bunch of sea urchin kids, same as us, only they lived in a house and went to school. Their clothes were a little nicer. They lived in Lakewood and ran with a rough-and-tumble crowd from Huntington Beach we called the Hole-in-the-Wall Gang. Seemed to us like the Tracy boys knew just about everybody. First couple times we hung out it was all we could do to keep track of who was who and what was what, but we figured it out soon enough.

One of the great side benefits of hanging out with the Tracys was we got to ride their boards. We'd trade off—usually just for a couple hours, sometimes for a day. My brothers and I all had our own boards by this point, but our equipment ran towards the crappy side. Doc did a decent-enough job, touching up his old pals and recycling some of their used and tossed-off gear, but the oldest of us were becoming pretty strong surfers and we had our eyes on some of the newest and best equipment. This was still a couple years before we started competing in local tournaments and were able to pick up some local sponsors to help us out with our gear, so we scrambled for our rides.

We never complained about our equipment. We made do. We were happy with what we had. When you're a kid and you get your first board, you tend to fall in love with it. Doesn't matter if it's a piece of shit, it's yours. You fix every ding. It becomes like your pal. So we learned all the little quirks and nuances of these throwaway boards and came up with all these different ways to compensate and adjust, which I guess made us better surfers. We had to really work at it, you know.

But we saw what the other guys on the beach were riding, and we wanted in. And then along came these Tracy kids, with their sweet, sweet rides, so we were all over it. And it worked out great for the Tracys, too, because some of our ancient gear was throwback, so they got to ride old-school style. Never gave up on our own boards, but it was a chance to kick things up a notch, to grow our game.

After our first summer together, it's like we'd known the Tracy kids our whole lives. We found all kinds of ways to make all kinds of trouble. A lot of the time, we were out in the water, surfing, but for hours and hours we'd be on the beach, exploring. We'd sneak onto the base at Camp Pendleton and make our way to the commissary or the PX, where we'd scarf back cheap pizzas and chips and all this good stuff we would have never thought to eat if it weren't for our new friends. Remember, for years and years we couldn't eat anything refined or processed, but now that we were out in the world and the Tracy boys were giving us our first taste we were hooked. They were like our dealers. They turned us on to this whole other world, a world of fast food and soda. We used to spend a lot of time hanging at the visitor center at the power plant, where there were huge vending machines set up on a kind of deck area. People would drop loose change between the wooden slats of the deck and it'd pile up, so we'd crawl around underneath the boards, scrounging for money. There'd be spiderwebs and rats and all kinds of crap, but we didn't care. We just wanted to collect a couple fistfuls of change, which we'd then use to buy cheap, crappy food.

The best was when we'd find some old surfers getting ready to head into town on a beer run and we'd give them money to buy us donuts. The surfers would bring back three or four boxes of donuts, which we'd eat until we were sick; after so many years without sugar and sweets, it's like we were starved for this stuff. When we were just a little bit older, we'd grab these same guys on their beer runs and ask them to bring us back some beer instead. We just traded one kind of contraband for another.

On hot days, we'd sit in a small, air-conditioned theater in the visitor center, where plant officials would play a syrupy, ancient film about the benefits of nuclear power, over and over. We weren't really listening, just chilling, but the message must have seeped in, because we never thought to question the safety of the plant. Nobody did—not even our moms. It was just there, that's all, looking like a giant-breasted eyesore, and for a while the plant infrastructure created a killer break, thanks to a big, gnarly seawall that had been put up by the power plant engineers. During construction, they erected these piers that also made for some incredible waves, so we spent a lot of time surfing right in the shallows by the plant. Can't imagine it was any good for us, swimming in those waters, but we had a blast. There was one spot in particular, right by a return pipe that poured hot, steamy water directly onto the shore. The water had been pumped from the ocean into the core of the reactor, to keep it cool, and then it would get pumped right back out with such tremendous force it could knock you on your ass, but we'd splash around and bodysurf in these waters for hours and hours. On some days, when the current was just right, you could find that hot-water stream from the plant a full mile off the shoreline.

It was like a wonderland, that place, a playground. And the thing of it is, our parents never had any idea where we were. Life at San O was pretty much like it was on every other beach we called home in those days. We'd set off in the morning and wander back for dinner. That was the drill, same as always, only here there were miles and miles of beach to explore, and acres and acres of open land reaching way up into the hills overlooking the water. And tons and tons of kids, who descended on San O for the day, for the week, for the summer...

The Tracy kids knew their way around, but my brothers and I caught on quick. Soon, we were ducking in and out of the storm pipes that were cut into the hill every here and there. We were on a constant recon mission to figure where those pipes went. Some reached all the way beneath the dirt road on the other side of the campground and all the way out to the freeway—probably a mile or more. Some were so small you had to crawl through them on your belly, and some were big enough you could almost crouch, or maybe turn yourself completely around and double back to where you started. It got to where we knew the maze of pipes pretty well and we had our own special haunts. There was one series of pipes that led to a spot we called the Butt Cave—either because it reminded us of the secret hole in the hills on *Batman,* which led up to the Batcave, or because all you could do once you crawled inside was slither around on your butt.

You could walk along the beach and tell which kids were hanging in those storm pipes, because we'd all have these little scrapes and scars on our backs from crawling up against all that corrugated metal without our shirts. Welts, even. They were like badges of honor. Some of the little kids who were too chickenshit to crawl all the way up into the hills would even scrape their backs, just to brag that they'd been in on the same deal.

Eventually, we started taking girls up there, which was a whole other adventure. Wasn't much you could actually *do* with these girls, once you got them up into the pipes, because there was no room to maneuver (and, granted, it wasn't the most romantic setting), but it was still the thing to do. We'd grab a flashlight, because even during the day it would be pitch-black once you crawled your way in and most of the girls we knew weren't into the pitch-blackness.

Once, I caught a bunch of shit for taking this one girl up into those hills. We all knew her brother, who ended up becoming a big-time Hollywood producer, and she hung with us every now and then, and she was totally into the storm pipe scene. They lived in a big-ass mansion in Beverly Hills. The reason I caught shit was because we got stuck on the wrong side of the power plant gates after dark, when they closed the place up. We had to walk back up the cliff and then hike all the way around the road, and it was almost ten o'clock at night by the time we stumbled back to the campground and walked right into a bunch of high-beam headlights. Apparently, Doc and this girl's father had gotten all these campground dads together to go out looking for us and they were driving around using their cars as searchlights. Soon as they saw us, our dads started yelling and yelling, mostly at me—hey, I was the guy, so it had to have been my fault, right?

I don't think my dad would have been all that pissed if the girl's father hadn't been all that pissed—and, man, was that guy pissed! He actually came at me, like he wanted to take a swing, but Doc jumped in and held him off, and once that happened I don't think my father was all that mad anymore. Not at me, anyway. He'd flipped his anger onto this other guy, instead.

Very quickly, my dad became an authority on the ways of the beach. A lot of the places we stayed we were off by ourselves, but at San O we were part of a community, which I guess made him a kind of community leader. He came up with a bunch of rules you had to follow. The Tracy boys called them Dorian's Beachcomber Rules, and they were the unwritten laws of San O. Here's an example:

Doc was big into beachcombing, which was not a whole lot different from cockaroaching on dry land. Here on the beach, though, he wasn't looking for handouts so much as leavings. The first (and, really, *only*) rule of beachcombing was it only counted first thing in the morning. If you were out at dawn, looking for stuff people left out overnight—towels, T-shirts, bikes, shoes—it was there for the taking. But if you found any of this crap during the day, or even late at night, it wasn't really fair game, because someone might come back for it.

And he practiced what he preached, my old man. Every morning, he'd step from the camper before first light and start prowling around. He wasn't *just* looking for other people's crap. He'd surf, pray, exercise...but he'd keep his eyes open as he went about his business. If he saw something that looked like it had been abandoned, that was wet with morning dew and had clearly been out all night, he'd grab it, but only if it was something he thought we needed; that was another key rule of beachcombing—it had to be something you could actually use, or maybe trade for another something you could actually use.

One morning one of the Tracy boys found a boogie board that had been left by the side of the exit road to the park. It was Michael, who we all called MT.

(By the way, for whatever reason, most of the Tracy boys went by their initials. There was PT [Patrick], MT [Michael], JT [John], and Moe, whose real name was Stephen, so he should have probably gone by ST.)

MT was a couple years older than me, and he matched up with my oldest brother, David, only they had a real falling-out over this one boogie board. What happened was MT had been out early, first thing; he'd spent the night in one of the caves up in the hills, and as he was heading back he came across this board, and right away he was thinking of my dad's beachcomber rules. And then he went those rules one better. He went around the beach all that day, asking if anybody'd lost a boogie board. Nobody claimed it. Nobody recognized it. Nobody knew anything about it, so MT figured it was free and clear. He ended up swapping it out to some guy for some sandwiches and beer—which was in keeping with my dad's secondary rule, because MT was hungry and thirsty.

Well, cut to a couple hours later, or maybe even the next day, and David saw the new "owner" with the board and started claiming it was his. Started saying things like, "Hey, man, you stole my board." But then the story came out that the guy had traded for it with MT, so David went after MT, and there was a whole mess. It became this big, big deal, and for a while it looked like there'd be a real rumble over this one stupid boogie board. David got some of his buddies together, and MT got his buddies together, and it was a real standoff. Eventually Doc got wind of what was going on and came to smooth things over. He set up his own little beachcomber tribunal. He looked at MT and said, "Did you, Michael Tubesteak, find this board by the side of the road at first light?"

(By the way again, Doc addressed all of Tube's kids in this way, like their dad's nickname was their family name.)

The way it shook out was Doc took MT's side, which ended up pissing David off mightily, but one of my dad's big things was that rules were rules, and David had no choice but to accept his decision. That didn't mean David couldn't go around the beach talking shit about MT and stirring up trouble, and for a long time there was a whole lot of tension flowing from this one beachcomber/boogie board incident. But once Doc weighed in, the matter was meant to be closed.

◎

Even with a sheriff like Doc, we kids couldn't help but make our share of trouble at San O. For example, we were in the bad habit of skulking around the campground looking for booze. You see, once Nixon and Reagan turned the beach into a state park, the state put in these camping facilities as well, so my family usually parked our rig there for most of the summer, and over time we pretty much had the run of the place. That's where my dad got the idea to run the Paskowitz Family Surf Camp, which he did the very first summer they opened up San O. Nobody was doing anything like it. There were surf schools, of course. And you could walk up and down any beach and find someone to give you surf lessons. But Doc's idea was to get people to live and surf and play together for a couple days and really absorb the entire culture of the sport. So he recruited me and my older brothers to help out in the water and my mom to help with the cooking, and set up a bunch of tents for the campers. And do you know what? People came. Adults, kids, families...people heard what we were up to and wanted in, so the camps were successful, right away. All of a sudden, there was money coming in. Not a lot, but enough to keep us at it, summer after summer. Enough to cut short our vagabonding each spring and keep us coming back to San O on something of a real schedule.

Getting back to the trouble we couldn't help but make, most folks, they camped out at the beach for just a couple nights, maybe a week or so. That's how it worked with the Tracys. But we camped out like it was our own backyard, so we kids knew which campsites to target; we knew where the heavy drinkers parked their rigs.

Now, there's no defending our actions on this. (Stealing is wrong, kids! Don't try this at home!) But let me go ahead and try: we were underage, and we couldn't think of any other way to get beer; we didn't think of it as stealing so much as helping ourselves. We'd wait until the middle of the day, when everyone was down at the beach, or sometimes we'd hit early in the morning, when everyone was asleep. We'd scope out these big-ass coolers and make off with them. We were a happy band of little idiots, because we'd move about in groups of eight or ten or twelve. Not exactly stealth, a group of that size, but we must have thought there was safety in numbers.

Once, we recruited a kid named Joey Conroy from the beach to do our dirty work. Somehow, we'd convinced him it was his turn. We'd spotted a sweet cooler, figured there'd be a ton of beer in there, or maybe some wine, and it was just sitting out for the taking. Only trouble was, a couple of rough, surly guys were sleeping right next to the cooler. So all of us Paskowitz and Tracy kids kind of hung back in the bushes while poor Joey Conroy went out and did his thing. He was superquiet about it, ended up pinching a big jug of wine, but just as he was making his getaway one of the surly guys woke up and said, "Hey, what the hell you doing?"

Naturally, Joey started running like crazy, and the guy chased after him, and the rest of us just started laughing like crazy. Gave ourselves away, we were making so much noise, so as one guy was chasing down our buddy two other guys came chasing after us. Then Joey must have panicked, or tripped, or something, because he dropped the jug of wine, and it shattered on the asphalt they had all over the campground area. We ran in all different directions— but, idiots that we were, most of us ran straight back to our own campsite. So of course these guys started banging on the door of the camper, and Doc came out and had to apologize and make things right. He ended up replacing the wine and adding in another couple jugs as a kind of peace offering.

Doc wasn't too happy with us that time. He didn't like it that we were starting to drink, because he made it a special point to never touch any alcohol, but he was smart enough to know we were just a bunch of stupid kids, letting off steam. It's not like he thought we'd crossed over to the dark side or anything, but for the most part we managed to keep him out of the loop. The place was so big, stretching all the way to the power plant on one side, and all the way to

Nixon's Casa Pacifica on the other, we eventually got smart enough to spread out and make our mischief where he couldn't find us out.

One of our favorite activities was throwing shit off the cliffs overlooking the beach. This, to us, was big, big fun. Patrick Tracy and John Tracy, PT and JT, were really good at making life-size dummies. They'd find some thrift-store clothes, and stuff them with newspaper, and get them looking real lifelike. Then we'd drag these dummies up to the cliff, to a spot that jutted out over the beach or the campsite or parking lot area. Each time out, we'd have the whole thing choreographed. We'd have a group of us down on the ground as plants and another group up top with the dummy. At some point, one of the guys up top would just start beating the crap out of the dummy, and yelling all kinds of shit, while the group of us down below would point and start screaming things like, "Oh my God, look! He's gonna kill him!"

What's amazing to me is that people always fell for it. Not just once or twice, but a bunch of times. We moved around, of course, and we picked our spots, so we didn't do our thing in front of the same group of people, but we'd get everyone's attention and people would gather around and there'd be this great, horrifying scene. It was all rehearsed, and we played it up, really sold the drama. Oh, man, we were such a bunch of little shits. Once, we were so convincing a lifeguard actually left his station and started sprinting up the hill to try to save the dummy, and as he got halfway up we threw the dummy down and some poor woman on the beach actually collapsed. Really and truly. At the time, we all thought she'd had a heart attack, but I think she just fainted. (At least, I *hope* she just fainted.)

For a while, the cooler pinching overlapped with the dummy tossing, and we thought it was funny to toss the coolers off the cliff after we'd picked them clean. Looking back, this was insanely stupid of us, because someone could have gotten hurt, and because we ruined a bunch of perfectly good coolers.

We'd hang back in the bushes, eyeballing these great big Coleman coolers, the metal ones with the heavy-duty handles, and we'd try to keep superquiet, waiting for just the right moment. Usually, the superquiet would be broken by one of the Tracy boys, making like Yogi Bear and saying, "I have a hunch, here comes my lunch," which was a phrase, frankly, us Paskowitz kids had never heard. We'd never heard of Yogi Bear. A *talking bear* who hangs out at national parks, *stealing picnic baskets*? What the hell was *that*?

That's how it was with us and our pop culture references. Once we hit the road, we didn't watch much television. We knew some shows—like *Batman* and *The Brady Bunch* and *Sigmund and the Sea Monsters*—and then there were others, like *Yogi Bear,* that completely passed us by.

Once or twice each summer, we'd head to the Tracy house in Lakewood, check out their television, root around in their fridge, maybe stay the night. They always had the not-so-good-for-you kinds of cereal, and we cleaned out their cupboards soon as we burst through the front door. One of the first times we went over there, I sat in front of the television the whole time, fisting so much cereal into my face I got diarrhea—whether from all that television or all that cereal I'll never know.

For these reasons, and I guess a whole bunch of others, my mom wasn't too crazy about the Tracy family, not at first. She didn't think they were the best influences. I mean, Tube wore his hair in a ponytail. The boys all had long hair. She blamed them for introducing us to beer, and she knew they smoked weed and would probably turn us on to that before long. For their part, I'm not sure what the hell the Tracy family made of us. Tube told us that when we drove to Lakewood to visit he could hear our camper rattling down the street for miles, like we were some beach blanket version of the Beverly

Hillbillies—a pop culture reference I somehow managed to get at the time.

But in the end my mom got along pretty well with Tube's wife, Phyllis, and my father got along great with Tube, and after a couple years my folks just gave up complaining about the other stuff because we'd become like family. But at first my mother definitely felt they'd been a disruptive, negative influence. And do you know what? She was probably right. They *were* a disruptive, negative influence, but without their disruptive, negative influence we wouldn't have had half as much fun. And it's not like *all* we did with the Tracy kids was make trouble. Hell, no. In fact, mostly what we did was surf. All day long. All this other stuff took place when the waves were crap, when the weather was lousy, when we needed a break—because, really, it was all about the surfing. It was at San O that we learned to surf a world-class break, and it was at San O that we developed enough confidence as surfers to start teaching other folks how to get up on a board and have at it.

And it was at San O, really, that we got our first taste of competition. My dad started entering us into all these different contests they'd run out on the beach, most of them organized by the displaced San Onofre Surf Club guys, who I guess got over the invasion of their private beach pretty quick. Tube had his kids entered as well. It was like the San O version of Little League. Usually, there'd be a couple different events every weekend, and soon there was a Paskowitz at or near the top of almost every leaderboard, which was way cool.

Doc told us that surfing wasn't any kind of competition, that it was a very personal experience that didn't need to be judged or quantified or measured against anyone else's very personal experience. But at the same time he was pretty damn stoked that we were winning a lot of the events.

And once we got our first taste of competition, we wanted more.

Back then, even in the middle of summer, there weren't a whole lot of events scheduled in the middle of the week, so we started staging our own. We divided ourselves into teams and ran our own contests. I was on the Oinky Surf Club, which we named after my brother Moses, who was kind of big. (Sorry, Moses. . . .) Wasn't the best name for a surf club, but it made us laugh; I think it even made Moses laugh. We made membership cards and everything. And then, on the other side, there was the Sigmund Surf Club, which they named after Salvador. They didn't bother with membership cards—because, hey, they weren't as cool as us.

I even went out and recruited some of those gnarly Hole-in-the-Wall guys from Huntington Beach—serious, kick-ass surfers like Randy Lewis, who went on to have a big-time career as a shaper when he was done competing. He was eventually elected to the Surfers' Hall of Fame in 2010, but to me and my brothers and the Tracy boys, trying to outduel each other in our own do-it-yourself events, he was just a world-class ringer—the best surfer on the beach, come to help us claim our crown. As soon as Randy and his buddies showed up on the beach and flashed their Oinky Surf Club cards, Abraham and MT and the other Sigmund surfers knew they were screwed.

6

The Other Last Dime

A lot of folks, they hear how we grew up and they get
to thinking we were on some long and winding and never-
ending road to nowhere.

Well, we were and we weren't. . . .

It's not like my parents threw darts at a map on the wall of
our camper and left it to fate or chance to figure where we'd go
next. We followed the seasons. We followed whatever job leads
or opportunities my father was able to line up. We followed the
tossed-off recommendations of road warrior surfers, who might have
mentioned a sweet spot for us to park our rig and catch a few
waves for the next while. There was at least some rhyme and reason to our comings and goings. And there was a rhythm to them
as well. Wherever we were, however we happened to land there,
we fell into a nice, simple routine. We were vagabonding nomads,
yeah, but there was a structure to our lives—at least, a little bit.
Didn't much matter to us kids if we woke up on a beach in Florida

or Texas or Rhode Island or all the way down at the tip of the Baja Peninsula, or even in some motel parking lot, tucked way in the back where the streetlights didn't quite reach, long as we could surf and hang and make our little pieces of trouble. We were like sea turtles, I guess. Our home was on our backs, and once San O opened up for us it meant we would always circle back to Southern California. It gave us a place to come home to; it meant we could have our friends and be a part of a community, without the hassle of going to school and staying in one place all the time; it meant we could be at home all year long, in our sea turtle sort of way, and then when summer came around we could be really and truly at home.

The thing of it is, the high-concept hook of how we lived—nine kids growing up in a twenty-four-foot camper! surfing all day, every day! the call of the open road!—really only lasted seven or eight years, stretching from the time Navah and Joshua were born in the early 1970s to round out our clan, to when Jonathan and Abraham and I started lighting out on our own, 1978 or so—basically, from when I was eight or nine until I was fifteen or sixteen. For those years, the one constant was the camper. The backdrop kept changing, the view outside our window, but the camper was our steady frame of reference. We ran through two or three rigs over the course of those years, but on the inside they were much the same. When I close my eyes and think back to when I was a kid, to those seven or eight years when we were all together, I see us in some version of camper, coming back from the beach after a day in the sun, or bunched together at our tiny table, sucking back whatever gruel my mother would set out and call breakfast, or heading off on some new adventure, watching the world unfurl outside our window. That is what I see of my childhood.

Sometimes, the routine was in the getting there. Oh, man, we crisscrossed the country so many times, it's like I spent half my childhood looking out the grimy windows of our ratty-ass campers, taking in the sights. We had a bunch of different ways to pass the time. My mother used to sit in the back with us, while two or three kids would sit up front with Doc. It was always considered a great treat to sit in the cab with my dad and help navigate, but personally I preferred the freedom we had in the back. We didn't have to sit still. We could lie down and stretch out. Mom would play her favorite operas for us on the tape player, or maybe another classical recording. In her one attempt at homeschooling, she taught us to recognize the works of all these great composers—and to this day most of us can hear a piece of music and get close to identifying it. With her music in the background, we'd pair off into groups of two or three or four and play a road game or board game. Some of us would read, or write in our journals. Or maybe we'd just let the *rickety-rack* of the road lull us off to sleep.

Probably our favorite thing to do on road trips was play a game we called Pilot to Bombardier. Don't know who gets the credit for inventing this one—or the blame. Wasn't exactly good, clean fun, but it was fun. And endlessly amusing. Here's how it worked: One of us would take the lookout post by one of the rear windows. That person would be the pilot. Another one of us would take his position over the toilet. That person would be the bombardier. Remember, my father had removed the holding tank and receptacle, so the toilet was really just a hole in the floor of the camper, which came in pretty handy for this particular game—the object of which I'm guessing must be coming clear.

The key to the game was in the timing, and in choosing our targets. Also, it helped if the bombardier hadn't taken a dump in a good long while and was raring to go, on command. The pilot would check out the traffic behind us. The ideal target, we all believed, was a convertible, but it was just as good to find a conservative-seeming couple dressed in their Sunday best. The more prim and proper the target, the better. The cleaner the car, the better. Frankly, any target would do, as long as we hit it, although direct hits were pretty rare. Everything had to go just right. The bombardier had to have just the right consistency in his "load" so it would splash against the pavement in such a way that it would bounce and explode at the same time, and if that same time happened to catch a windshield about a car length behind us we counted it as a great victory.

It was a real team effort, and what's amazing to me now, looking back, is that none of our victims ever hightailed up to us after they'd been strafed by one of our Paskowitz bombs. I mean, they had to have known that the steaming pile of shit that had just exploded onto their windshields had come from the camper directly in front of them, right? That stuff doesn't just fall from the sky. But in all those years, over all those miles, no one ever chased us down or pulled up alongside our driver side window and motioned for my father to pull over.

My father had to know what was going on. He had a mischievous sense of humor, so I'm guessing he found all of this pretty damn funny, but he'd never show it. My mother was a whole other story, though. She absolutely did not approve—which was probably one of the reasons she rode in the back with us so often, to keep us from playing. Whenever she was up in front with my dad and she'd hear us howling in the back of the cab, she'd holler back to us. She'd say, "Are you boys playing that disgusting game of yours?"

We'd bite our lips to keep from laughing, and hang back for a bit until one of us had to go again.

◎

One winter, mid-seventies, we lit out for New England. My father had been hired on as a kind of town doctor on Block Island, just off the coast of Rhode Island. It was like the land that time forgot, that place, with grand old buildings and a rich seafaring history and good old-fashioned Yankee charm. There was even a decent surf scene, except it was a little too cold to surf when we hit town.

First thing I remember about that Block Island trip was that we almost didn't make it there. The folks who ran the ferry from the mainland didn't want to take our camper on the vessel, which put us in a jam. Everything we owned was in and on that camper. And it wasn't just our home; it was also our ride; we needed it to get around. And so, after a whole lot of back-and-forth, my father somehow managed to persuade the dockmaster to let us drive our rig onto the ferry.

For some reason, the hands on board called the ship *Corky*. I'd read enough to know that most ships had names, but I never knew people actually called them by those names. Our arrival had caused a big stir, so everyone kind of abandoned their posts to check us out. They kept telling us that *Corky* was a sure, strong ship. "*Corky*'s sailed the world's oceans," one member of the crew said.

But then, once we pulled away from the dock, the ferry started to list and moan, and all of a sudden the crew started freaking out—like they weren't sure how *Corky* would handle our weight. They thought we were going down!

By some miracle, we made it across to Block Island without sinking. Once on the island, we Paskowitzes drove to a gigantic white Victorian house, which came with the job. The house was huge! We were all completely excited to spill out of the camper and race inside to claim our own rooms. Just the idea of being able to sleep through the night without getting your hair stepped on every time someone had to go to the bathroom…it was such a luxury, such a thrill. Adam ran upstairs and claimed two rooms for himself—one to sleep in and one to study in. He was our little scholar, with all his chemistry and biology books, so he spread his stuff all around and let it be known this was his space. There were three or four floors of bed-rooms, so we each grabbed our own. I don't think the bedrooms were furnished, so we'd have to make do with our sleeping bags to start, but nobody minded, and as the sun went down that first night we all settled into our separate rooms and went to sleep.

We tried to, anyway. There was a storm that night, with big booms of thunder, big cracks of lightning, and it just about scared the piss out of me. After a couple hours of tossing and turning, I started to panic—a little bit. Finally, I made my way to my parents' room. I was maybe twelve years old, maybe thirteen, but I wasn't too old to sleep with my parents on a dark and stormy night, in a big, strange house. Apparently, the rest of my sibs all felt the same way, because when I opened the door they were already there. Every last one of them! Curled on the floor in their sleeping bags. And they were all sound asleep, which meant they'd given up on their own rooms *way* before I'd given up on mine.

And that's how we slept, the whole rest of our time on the island. All of us in that great big house, with all those rooms, packed tight into our parents' bedroom just like we were back in the camper.

I have very specific memories of our trip to Florida, which came a couple years later, when I was about fourteen. The trip marked a kind of turning point for our family. For the first time, I caught a glimpse of my father carrying himself in a less-than-heroic way, and I didn't like how it made him look. Shook me up pretty good, but I don't want to get ahead of the story. I remember crossing through Texas and hugging the Gulf coastline as we snaked our way past Louisiana and Mississippi. Once we left Texas, the air seemed sud-denly different—the people like from some other time and place. We ended up camping in some sketchy-looking places on the Gulf and on into the Panhandle, but this didn't seem to bother my father too terribly much. We had that whole safety-in-numbers thing going on. Plus, we were such a rolling novelty, most folks could only look at us and scratch their heads.

We were really scraping, on this trip. Money was especially tight. We never had a ton of money, even back when my father was peeling off ten-dollar bills from that great wad of cash he used to carry. But the trip to Florida felt like the beginning of a jam. I remember money being a constant topic of conversation between my parents, although they made an effort to keep the talk from us kids. Still, it's tough to keep secrets when you're living in a camper, so some of the tension filtered through. There were a lot of whispered conversations, as I recall. A lot of comments about money being tight, although it's not like my father was ever too terribly worried about not having any money. Wasn't really any kind of big deal to him, but being broke did change our circumstances. It meant we had to stretch in order to eat and gas up the rig and pay for our other supplies. It meant we had to think about things we'd never given a thought to.

In fact, another one of those "last dime" stories I hinted at earlier might have taken place as we passed through Louisiana, because (as I learned later) our prospects then were pretty damn bleak. (And because once we got to Florida they went from pretty damn bleak to really fucking grim.) In the *Surfwise* documentary about my family that was released in 2008, my brothers remember that we were at a roadside rest stop on the coast of Louisiana when this story happened. I remember that it happened on one of our drives back from Mexico to California. And my father... well, he doesn't remember the story at all. I'll tell it from my Mexico-based perspective, but I'll leave room for the fact that it might have happened on this pass through Louisiana. I suppose it's even possible that something like this happened more than once—because, as you'll see, the story is mostly about being down-and-out and up against it, and we were certainly down-and-out and up against it a time or two.

In my version, we were driving back from Mexico in the camper. We'd just crossed the border and were headed back up the 5 freeway, really excited to be back in California. We'd just come from a long stay in Mexico down at the tip of Baja, at a funky shack on the beach we rented from an old-time photographer named Ken Kay. That was a particularly cool trip, because Ken let me use a lot of his gear. He was only there for a couple days when we arrived and then he bolted, but before he left he taught me a lot about underwater photography and how to take pictures out in the break, adjusting the aperture and the speed in order to shoot my brothers surfing. He also showed me how to pinch the grease off your nose and rub it around the perimeter of the lens to give the picture a kind of blur.

The waves were unbelievable, some of the best we'd ever surfed, and I should mention here that as we got older this last was becoming a bigger and bigger deal. I must have been about thirteen or fourteen, and I was getting pretty good. Already I'd won a bunch of San O competitions, and a couple other contests here and there, but more than that, I was beginning to appreciate what it meant to ride some serious surf, what it meant to exert my will on a board—to ride the wave instead of letting the wave ride me. In fact, all my brothers were kicking things up a notch, which I guess is inevitable, unavoidable, if you lived to surf the way we did. I can remember one contest around this time, in Padre Island, the biggest of the Texas barrier islands, with some nice Gulf swells. There were separate age divisions for each one of us, right down to Adam, and we ran the table; there was a Paskowitz on top in every category, and Doc was jazzed about that. The local papers picked up on it, too, which was happening more and more whenever we breezed into some new town; there'd be an article about this nutty Stanford doctor with a camperful of champion surfer kids, and folks would head down to the beach to check us out.

So now here we were down in Mexico, each of us a kind of amateur champion, each of us really learning to rip, all day long. And here's the thing: When we were younger, we all had started out on my father's hand-me-down Hobie board—a big, heavy monster none of us could carry. We had to help each other haul it down to the beach. But slowly we graduated to smaller, newer boards, and we each developed our own style. There was always a huge competition among us brothers. Even when we were just out by ourselves, doing our own thing, we competed with each other. Early on, it was just the oldest four of us. We went at it hard, always looking over our shoulders to see what the other brothers were doing. We didn't want to miss a trick. Even when I took off on my own wave, I'd check them out, just to make sure I wasn't missing out on some new maneuver, some twist or turn I could add to my repertoire, some way to get better. We'd all inherited my dad's approach, catching every wave and riding it all the way in, so a lot of times we'd take off all at once, especially when we were at this beach in Mexico, where we pretty much had the break all to ourselves.

One thing about this photographer's house: it was covered with dogs. Don't know if they were Ken Kay's dogs or just a pack of wild dogs that had the run of the place, but there were a whole bunch of them. I remember one dog in particular, a skinny short-haired retriever we all called Crab Dog. You could point to a hole in the sand and he'd dig out a crab; then he'd play with it and chase it all over the beach.

Poor Crab Dog was hit by a car one day, right in front of the house where we were staying. The house was on a remote road, wasn't a whole lot of traffic, but we heard a yelp and a tire screech and we raced outside to find Crab Dog half-dead, half-alive, just lying in the road. It was so incredibly sad. There were just a few of us kids around, big and little, and none of us knew what to do, so I raced inside for my dad's .22, which was almost always along for the ride. He'd taught us older kids how to use it, so I came back out and pointed it at Crab Dog, thinking I'd do the humane thing and put him out of his misery, only when I went to shoot him I ended up missing completely. (Guess my dad had been so busy showing me how to use his damn rifle he'd forgotten to teach me how to aim.)

It was so lame! So sad! I was at point-blank range. Crab Dog had his mouth open, and he was panting furiously, his tongue hanging down to the pavement, so I figured the thing to do was go for his mouth, but I didn't hit anything. Not even his tongue, which was hanging way, way out. So I reloaded and this time put the barrel right at his forehead, and this time I didn't miss.

We were all crying. Some of us were too old to be crying, but we were bawling like babies. Don't know where my parents were, but we were all a little older at this point, a little more independent, even though we were crying. Anyway, it was just us kids, and after that we picked up the dog and gave him a good and proper burial. For a long time, nobody spoke.

The drive back to California that year was spectacular. The weather was perfect, the wide-open spaces breathtaking. Doc usually took his time when the camper was fully loaded, but on this trip things seemed to be moving especially slow. We drove along some really radical ridges and cliffs and past these gorgeous bays on the Gulf side of Baja. We'd stop every now and then for a swim, because the water looked so clear and warm and inviting. I remember one stop, on the Pacific side, in a lagoon-type spot where we could see the whales cresting offshore. It was a magical thing to see and I raced inside the camper for my camera, but by the time I came back out the whales had moved on.

Turned out the real reason Doc was taking his time on this return trip was because he was especially low on cash. He thought if he nursed our last few drops of gas he could squeeze an extra couple miles out of the tank. I remember gassing up at one of the last gas stations in Mexico and we didn't have enough to fill the tank. We still had a couple hundred miles to go, and we started to think we might not make it. For the rest of the ride to the border, it was like a race against the fuel gauge.

Somehow, we made it all the way back to San Marcos, our old stomping grounds. The tank was almost bone dry and we were completely out of food and water, so we pulled over by the Hollandia Dairy, an old-school market where we used to shop. At this point, us kids didn't really have a clear idea about our money situation, so we were thinking this was just business as usual. This was just us, stopping to load up on supplies, same as always. But before heading inside the dairy my father sat us down around the table in the back of the camper, said he something to tell us. Then he reached into his pocket and took out a dime and slapped it down.

"You see that?" he said, pointing to the dime. "Who can tell me what this is?"

We all looked at each other, thinking this was some kind of trick question. The older kids knew enough not to answer, but finally one of the younger kids piped in with the obvious: "It's a dime."

"Ah, but it's not just any dime," my father said. "It's our very last dime."

He was dead serious, but he was also excited. I thought, *Hmmm, something's a little off about this.* And then, underneath that thought, there was another, more unsettling thought—that maybe this was something my dad couldn't fix. Up until this time, there was no trouble he couldn't steer us through. No wave bigger than we could handle. Nothing he couldn't fix or troubleshoot or negotiate away. When you're a kid, and you're old enough to understand about money, and you hear that your family is completely broke, it kind of scares the crap out of you, but my old man was pumped about it. His attitude, his whole demeanor, didn't fit with the way I saw it. To him, it was a thrilling, romantic moment, to be completely out of money. He didn't have a job. We had no place to go, nothing to eat, nothing lined up. But he wanted us to see this low moment as the start of a great adventure.

Then he said, "I'm just going inside to pick up a couple things we need." Left us all right there in the camper, to scratch our heads and wonder what the hell was going on. I followed him in after a few minutes, saw him throw some milk in his shopping cart, some eggs, some bread, some chicken. The usual...only what was *unusual* about this trip to the market was he didn't have any money to pay for it. But that didn't stop him. He made his way to the register, took out a checkbook, and paid with one of his "Dorian Paskowitz, MD" checks. He knew no one would question a doctor's check, and in his head he must have done whatever calculations he had to to justify the transaction, but I didn't see that there was any justification in it at all. I was too scared to say anything, too embarrassed, but I thought about it long and hard. I thought about what it meant, about how we were living, about what people would think if they knew we were stealing like this—because, hey, that's what it was, stealing.

I was up all night, thinking about it. Best I could tell, I was the only one who'd seen Doc pass the bad check, and I didn't know if I should tell anybody about it, if I should tell my mom. Frankly, I didn't know what to do—so I did what us Paskowitz kids did best: nothing.

Don't know what Doc was thinking. Probably, he put a little spin on it. Probably, it wasn't the first time he'd passed a bad check—just the first time I'd seen it for myself. Probably, he just figured it was his turn to have his hand out, and the Hollandia

Dairy folks, it was their turn to help. And that he'd pay them back, if and when he could.

There was no justifying it, really, but this was who we were. This was how we lived.

⊚

So there we were, headed across the Gulf states to Florida. Because we were up against it all over again, and because my father was a bit of a showman when it came to this kind of thing, I suppose it's possible some version of this same scene played itself out in Louisiana, the way my brothers remember. The year before, the year after... somewhere in there. Doc liked to serve up these little life lessons for us, even if the lesson didn't fit with the way the rest of the world seemed to operate. Even if it scared the plain crap out of his kids.

The setup to Florida was that my father had landed a job at the *National Enquirer*—probably the strangest gig on his résumé. They didn't hire him to be a doctor but to serve as a kind of medical authority and to stand behind some of the more ridiculous stories they published. You know, if the headline said someone had found a six-headed alien that breathed through its elbows, it helped if there was a medical professional to support the claim. My father grabbed at it because, after all, a job was a job. And it was an excuse to head out to a part of the country we'd never seen before.

We were all psyched for Florida. We'd heard there was supposed to be some really good fishing down there, and at that stage in our lives we were big into fishing. It started in San Diego, when we used to surf Tourmaline. We'd park somewhere at the end of the day, and I'd splinter off with Abraham and Moses and head out to the jetties. We had no fishing gear of our own, not even a line. We had to scavenge among the rocks at low tide and scrape together other people's discards. Half the time, we'd be untangling all these lines or knotting all these short pieces together. We could always find hooks, too. For weights, we'd use rocks or spark plugs or whatever washed up onshore that seemed like it would do the trick.

Bait was never a problem. We'd dig for sand crabs, or collect the flat crabs on the rocks, and then we'd cast our homemade lines into the water and wait. It was hillbilly fishing, but it worked. We'd always catch a mess of small fish and end up throwing most of them back, but there was always enough to take home. Sometimes, when we were a little older, we'd get a fire going right on the beach and cook 'em up right there.

So when the idea of Florida came up, we were all over it. The *Enquirer* building was in a town called Lantana, not far from Palm Beach. There was a pier there, down where we used to surf, so once we got a feel for the Atlantic our days were pretty much the same as they'd been back in California. We'd surf and fish and goof around. The surfing was good—nothing like we were used to out in California or Mexico, but this gave us a bit of an edge in some local contests. A lot of the locals had never seen kids our age with so much confidence on their boards, but that just came from spending so much time in the water, on much bigger breaks.

We rented a small house with a big backyard leading down to the Intracoastal Waterway, which had a whole bunch of little canals feeding off of it. Wasn't exactly the Everglades, but it had that look, that feel, and at night we'd grab one of our new friends and hop into his small boat and head out fishing. It was real swamp country, real spooky, but there was something thrilling about it, too. The landscape was like nothing we'd ever seen.

I loved how these local kids all had their own little putt-putt boats to get around. They'd zip in and out of the canals like the kids in California would cruise the strip in their hot rods. We fell in with a crowd of kids who liked to sleep out on the banks of all these weird back waterways. We'd make a fire and set up our tents and it was like a scene out of Mark Twain. There were feral cats running around everywhere. No gators, though. Don't think we were deep enough into Everglade country for that, but we saw our share of giant cane spiders.

One night, we even saw the great Skunk Ape.

What's that you say? You've never heard of the Skunk Ape? Well, best we could tell, it was South Florida's version of Sasquatch, a local legend that had somehow managed to scare the crap out of local kids for generations. And, on this one night, it scared the crap out of us. The legend of Skunk Ape is that you start to smell a hideous odor before he appears. He's half man, half ape, and he stinks to high heaven, so we were sitting around the fire one night, smelling this god-awful smell, hearing these thundering footsteps. And then—we could swear it!—it sounded like a tree was falling, off in the distance. Not just the snap of a sapling, or the crack of a branch, but a real, serious tree. We heard it land with a giant thud, and at this point we were all freaking out. Even the local kids who'd dragged us on the adventure were terrified. One of them got so spooked he fired off a couple rounds from his .22 into the swamp, and after nightfall the footsteps seemed to fade and the smell disappeared.

For some reason, we stayed the night. Don't think we slept at all, but we toughed it out. We were too cool to let any Skunk Ape chase us from our adventures.

Meanwhile, the fishing was incredible. We'd catch these giant sheepshead, some ballyhoos, some goggle-eye…fish I'd never even heard of would just come tugging on our lines, all day long. It was crazy. Giant jellyfish, cobia, snook…more species of fish than we could even count, and we'd bring home whatever we didn't eat there and then and my mother would find a way to feed them to us.

It was in Florida that my father first put us big kids to work. David and Jonathan were probably old enough to work legitimately at this point, while Abraham and I, at fifteen and fourteen or so, were close enough. My father gathered us around one afternoon and told us we were old enough to go out and find jobs. I think David and Jonathan might have gone out and worked before, but it was a first for me, and probably for Abraham. And so in many ways this was a turning point for our family, the first time the older kids were sent out into the world to earn our keep. My father even lined up a job for Moses, even though he was only twelve or thirteen—too young for working papers, certainly, but that kind of detail never got in the way of a Paskowitz family plan. I mean, it's not like we were being paid on the books or anything.

It was like the end of our innocence—although we were hardly innocent. It's like my parents had been stiff-arming the real world since we moved into the camper—and here, finally, the real world pushed back. In some ways my older brothers and I were excited to be let loose and start earning our own money, but in other ways we were scared shitless, because we knew how little we'd be making at these minimum wage gigs. We knew that if our thin paychecks were supposed to make a dent in the family finances, we were fucked.

All five of us started out working at a concrete water park that was being built along the highway. Can't imagine how my father managed to get five of us hired on, but he was good at that sort of thing. Touching people up ... that was one of his specialties. My job was to sand the imperfections out of the concrete slabs, so the customers wouldn't get cut sliding down after the slabs had been painted. It was a miserable job, and it didn't help that there was 100 percent humidity, on top of one hundred–degree temperatures. The job was so terrible we all stepped away from it, one by one. My father didn't mind, long as we had something else lined up. Abraham was the first to go, I think. He got a job as a bag boy at Winn-Dixie, a big supermarket chain. I followed soon as I could, with a gig at the Piggly Wiggly, a much smaller, much lower-end market.

The guy who hired me insisted that I needed working papers, but he was a kind man and he let me work on an interim basis, and every week he'd check in with me and ask if I'd submitted all the forms through my school. Each time, I'd just nod and tell him everything was cool, and buy myself another week.

I never saw any money—my paycheck went directly to my dad—but I remember feeling a sense of autonomy, like I was finally making my own way. I used to get this big rush of independence every time I broke for lunch, because I'd fix myself these great meals and eat like a prince. I'd have to pay for it, of course, but I'd get an employee discount and the money was deducted from my paycheck, so Doc never really knew the deal. But it was the one chance I had to break from the healthy gruel my mother was still feeding us, so I'd load up on fried chicken, coleslaw, chocolate milk ... all the good stuff I could never get at home. I'd serve myself these big, heaping portions and walk with my tray to this employee picnic area that had been set up behind some hedges in the parking lot. I'd sit there all alone by the junction box that powered the place and eat my fill, kind of loving it, digging the independence of it, thinking I'd finally arrived.

The job didn't last long. My boss kept after me. He spoke in a thick Austrian accent. He kept saying things like, "Izzy, *ve* need your *vork* permits. I shall have to call at your school."

I put him off as long as I could, which just about coincided with the day a bunch of repo guys came to claim our camper. Turned out we really had been up against it. Turned out Doc really did need our tiny paychecks from Piggly Wiggly and Winn-Dixie and wherever else my brothers had managed to line up work. He'd always leased our campers, and we learned later on he was forever ditching his payments. For some reason cutting out on the camper payments struck me differently than the time I saw him passing that bad check at the dairy in San Marcos. This time it didn't feel like stealing so much as trying to stay one step ahead of the man. It had a *catch me if you can* feel to it, and here they'd finally caught up to him.

I came home one day and saw all our shit spread out in the yard. The camper was gone. Nobody seemed too upset about it, though. The little kids were freaked, but us older kids just shrugged it off. It was something to deal with, that's all. Mostly, there was just a bunch of sleeping bags and some loose clothing, plus whatever crap we'd been keeping in our little half cubbies. Nothing we couldn't find room for in our tiny house, until my father could scrape together enough of a stake to lease another rig. And that's just what happened. We hung on in Lantana for another couple weeks, and my father did his thing at the *Enquirer,* and I think I probably worked another odd job or two, and at some point we got our shit back together and piled into a new rig—which, of course, wasn't really a new rig at all, just another run-down cab-over, with just as many miles on it as the one we'd lost.

But it was new to us, and this added to the excitement, so we filled up all the spaces where the previous owners had been and set out for home—wherever the hell that happened to be.

◎

Long as I'm on the East Coast, I'll slot in a New York story. Didn't happen on this same trip—probably, it was the year before—but somewhere around my thirteenth birthday, 1976, we lit out from California for a meaningful journey. We pointed the camper to the Big Apple for my bar mitzvah. My older brothers had all been down this road, but David had done his *rite-of-passaging* in Israel and Jonathan and Abraham did theirs on the West Coast, wherever my father's free spirit–type Judaism happened to place him at that moment. When my turn came, it was decided we'd head out to my grandparents' synagogue on the Upper West Side of Manhattan—a place called Congregation Rodeph Shalom, one of the oldest temples in the city, going back about 150 years.

The place pretty much echoed with the New York Jewish experience, and it pretty much intimidated the crap out of me, but my grandfather set it up and I had no choice but to just go for it.

To be clear, my father was a proud and selectively observant Jew. He raised us kids to be the same way, but at his core I don't believe he thought of himself as *only* Jewish. He was Jewish and then some, Jewish and a little bit more besides. We were taught by his example to be children of the whole wide world. We were children of faith, yeah, but it was a deep, all over, no-labels kind of faith that also included a faith in each other, in ourselves. We cared deeply about Israel, and the many friends we'd made there over the years. We said the Shema—even if we said it in a Pledge of Allegiance, going-through-the-motions sort of way. We sometimes joined my dad in his daily prayers, although he was quick to point out that we didn't truly "count" in this until we had become bar mitzvah. We didn't keep kosher or observe the rituals of the Sabbath, but we were aware of what these things meant, the sacrifices they carried. This was our Paskowitz brand of religion. Didn't always mesh with how we passed bad checks or had our rigs repossessed, but it was an elastic system of beliefs that Doc could stretch to cover our sometimes funky circumstances.

And so we grew up knowing it was this great big deal, to chant from the Torah and to be welcomed into the Jewish community as an adult. It meant a lot to my grandparents as well. Remember, my father's parents, Lewis and Rose, were Texas Jews, so I imagine they went at this whole religion thing in their own, frontier-type way, but somehow they wound up in New York at this heavy-duty synagogue. Somehow they arranged it so I could be counted there. They arranged it with the rabbi who sent me a tape with all the blessings

I was supposed to chant and the section of Torah I was supposed to read. I couldn't actually read Hebrew, of course. I'd had those few weeks of training at that Israeli *ulpan*, back when I was little, but that hadn't exactly stuck. Looking at the letters of the Hebrew alphabet for me was like looking at hieroglyphics, so the only way I could keep up was to do it phonetically, to try to piece the sounds to the melody and memorize the whole deal.

Wasn't a whole lot to memorize, looking back, but when I was in the middle of it, obsessing, it felt like the lines stretched on for just about forever. I spent the entire trip to New York huddled in the back of the camper, learning my prayers, going at it over and over until I thought I had it down, only I never quite got to where I had it down. The closest I could get was close enough, but my dad kept grilling me, pushing me. He also kept telling me not to worry about it, and my older brothers kept telling me not to worry about it, but that didn't keep me from worrying about it.

So there we were, a mostly happy band of wandering hillbilly Jews, careening across the country for a rendezvous with some ancient scrolls at a landmark Manhattan synagogue. We must have made an unlikely picture as we rolled towards town in our weighted-down camper. We had our boards piled high up top, same as always, only this was probably the first time we'd driven through such a densely populated metropolitan area. Don't think my father had it in his head to account for the clearance of our rig, he was so used to driving in wide-open spaces. But in New York, of course, there's no such thing. The approach to the city is booby-trapped with bridges and tunnels and overpasses, so truckers know to proceed with caution.

Unfortunately, we Paskowitzes knew no such thing.

We must have had twenty boards loaded onto the roof, tied down in our improvised, homemade way, and as my dad pulled into the city he drove under an overpass and sent them flying. He miscalculated, was all. Or he wasn't paying attention. I was sitting in the back, minding my own, learning my prayers, when I heard this sick, horrible, banging-clanging noise: the whole fucking roof rack was clipped off the top of the camper. Fell right back down onto the highway behind us. We all turned in the direction of the noise, and you could see sparks kicking up off the road where it hit.

Oh, man, we were freaked! By some weird rush hour miracle, my dad managed to cross a couple lanes of traffic and pull the camper to a stop on the right shoulder, just a football field or so up the road from what was left of our surfboards. There was just enough room for us to park, and soon as we did the big kids all spilled out of the rig and scrambled to collect our gear, which had been scattered all over the road. The real miracle was that no one was hurt. All those boards flying every which way, bouncing and flipping and skipping across the pavement and the hoods of the oncoming cars... and yet there wasn't even a fender bender or a cracked windshield.

Kind of amazing, really.

The boards didn't fare too well, though. About half of them had been split in two, but as we dragged them in bits and pieces back to the camper my father announced that we would fix them up or turn them into belly boards. This was the Paskowitz way: nothing was ever wasted; everything was recycled, refurbished, and put to second and subsequent use.

This time, we didn't bother tying everything up top. We just threw all those battered and broken boards into the back of the camper and rumbled into the city. We didn't have far to drive, anyway. I think we drove directly to the shul. We pulled right up front and parked alongside this magnificent old building, and I went straight inside with my father to meet the rabbi. Don't remember if my grandfather was there to meet us or make introductions. And I don't think I was really dressed for the occasion—probably, I was wearing my usual Shabbat outfit, a weird combo of a buttoned-down shirt and a blue blazer with a full-Windsor tie over a pair of board shorts—but I had other things on my mind.

The rabbi spoke with a deep, daunting voice. He was nice enough, and welcoming enough, but I think I kind of cowered in his presence. It's like the weight of the entire history of the Jewish people was suddenly pressing down on me, and I choked. I'd thought I knew all the prayers, all the blessings, but they flew right out of my head. The rabbi took me aside and helped me through the material.

When Saturday morning came around and it was my turn to read from the Torah, I choked again, but then I finally figured out to treat it like a piece of music. I'd listened to the tape of the rabbi chanting my portion so many times, over and over, it had been burned into my memory. Music I knew. Hebrew I didn't know. So I went with the music, and soon as I did the stuff came pouring out of me. I stumbled a couple times, but the rabbi stood behind me and fed me my lines—not *all* of my lines, but a word or phrase to help jump-start my muscle memory until the tune kicked back in for the next while.

I sang my little sun-splashed heart out.

At some point during all the sweep and big emotion of the moment, I stepped outside myself for a beat and tried to take it all in. I tried to embrace what it all meant. My grandparents were there. My aunt Sonia was there, with all my cousins. My brothers and sister were there, of course. It was kind of mystical, kind of wonderful—and, yeah, kind of weird, too. I mean, here we were, going through these ancient motions in a storied, moneyed Manhattan synagogue—a solid, certain place that had almost nothing to do with our uncertain life on the road—and at the end of the day we'd climb back into our camper.

But not before I collected some great gifts. Best of all, I got my first high-end surfboard—a Gerry Lopez Lightning Bolt, a stinger-swallowtail model that had been made for me by a legendary surfboard maker named Danny Brawner, who in another ten years or so would become my father-in-law.

(More on *that* in another few chapters.)

I flipped for that board. Struck me as just about the most beautiful board I'd ever seen, and I was thinking I was just about the luckiest bar mitzvah boy in recorded Jewish history. My brothers were probably crazy, stinking, drooling jealous that I got such a sweet ride out of the deal, and we all took turns riding the crap out of it—until it was stolen from our campsite at Campland, an RV park in San Diego where we stayed for a couple weeks the following summer. I was crushed. We all were, I think, because it was the nicest board in the family.

Luckily, I got another, more lasting gift—a beautiful Nikonos II camera, which I managed to keep for a while longer. But it wasn't about the gifts, really. Even at thirteen, I appreciated the significance of the moment, the connecting fabric that now wrapped around me and my older brothers, as well as our father and grandfather, and every card-carrying Jewish male who'd ever walked or surfed or chanted Torah. But it was a neat bonus that I now had a professional-type camera to record it all with—and, briefly, a professional-type surfboard to keep me pushing, reaching, striving in the water.

Turned out I was the last of my brothers to have a bar mitzvah. By the time I was thirteen, our camper was full up with rambunctious teenage boys. Our lives, which had always been a little bit crazy, were now a whole lot bigger and busier. And crazier. We began to develop our separate interests, our own friends, so there wasn't really room for any kind of formal ritual. Wasn't really room for any kind of formal *anything*. We were being pulled in so many different directions, all over the country, we seemed to lose this one, all-important connection to who we were and where we'd been.

◎

Sometimes, our Mexican border–crossing stories seemed to bump into our broken-surfboard stories, or our on-the-road shit stories overlap with one of our rite-of-passage stories. That's about what you'd expect from a fucked-up American surfing family, right? Everything all bundled up neat and tidy and knotted into one of my dad's special blivet bags we used to leave by the side of the road.

For this one, we were goofing around on a beach in Mexico, back when we were kids. I was eleven or twelve. Moses, who figures in this story, was ten or eleven. We weren't very far from the California border, probably at the K-181 surf break, about 120 miles down the Baja Highway. These days it's a serious surf spot, but in the middle 1970s it was quiet, desolate. Basically, we filled up the beach all by ourselves.

The day started out like any other. The brothers would break off into groups of two or three and hit the water. My father would go off to surf on his own, maybe catch up with some friends on the beach. And my mom would hang back with the little kids. At this spot we were even more spread out than usual. There's a popular rock reef at K-181, with a heavy kelp bed that makes for a lot of fun lefts, but on this day we'd found this perfect little cove area, and to get to it you had to kind of hand-board or shimmy down a small cliff. The place was remote, but once we got down there we didn't want to leave. We were going at it hard, and there were some decent waves, and at one point one of us big kids snapped a board right in half. This happened sometimes, with some of our old, ratty-ass equipment. No big thing. And what also happened sometimes was that the little kids would splash around in the white water on the broken pieces of surfboard. That's what happened here—and again, it might have been no big thing. But Moses was laying on his belly on one of these half boards, along the shorebreak, just as a powerful wave came along and flipped him over in a violent, sudden way.

As Moses rolled over, the board rolled with him in such a way that it pierced the sand and he was thrown on top of it in a straddling position . . . *right on the fin.* The fin on this particular board was ridiculously sharp, and thin, and tapered almost like a scythe. Lodged itself right up his ass. It was such a fluke, freaky thing, but dangerous as hell, because the blade of this board tore about a foot into Moses' rectum and into his colon. I don't think he even screamed—anyway, I don't remember a scream, just the kind of commotion that made us turn our heads and check it out. By the time Jonathan and I got to him, Moses was completely still, almost in a standing position, with this broken board hanging from his butt. He was in shock. And right away we could tell it was bad. His bathing suit was cut. There was blood—not a lot, but some. Oh, man, it was bad, bad, bad.

One of us raced to fetch our father. He got to Moses double-quick and did what he could to remove the board and inspect the wound. He could see there was a substantial amount of tissue damage, figured there'd been a lot of internal bleeding. Moses's ass was basically cut in half, so we went into fire drill mode. We grabbed all our stuff from the beach, clambered up that cliff, threw everything into the camper, and got our boards tied on up top . . . all in the time it took Doc and a couple of the brothers to get Moses back to the vehicle. Everyone was crying, and completely panicked.

Dad got in the back with Moses and wrapped him in a blanket. Don't remember who drove, to start, but we knew we had to really hustle. Doc didn't think there was any good place in Mexico we could go to get help, so the idea was to book it to the border and hit the first hospital in California. He didn't think Moses was in a desperate spot just yet, but then as we started driving Moses' temperature began to spike. We were stuck in some heavy traffic. I think it was a weekend, and there were a lot of day-trippers down from California, making their way back north. As we got closer to Tijuana, things started to back up. My dad remembers that there was a bull-fight letting out just as we were crawling into town, so that backed things up even worse.

At this point, my father was up front doing the driving and my mom was in the back, tending to Moses. He was comfortable, but as his temperature climbed he seemed more and more out of it. It had been about four hours, and my father knew that if we didn't get Moses to a hospital soon he'd be in real trouble. Getting across the boarder was always a bitch, but this one time, when we were desperate for some smooth sailing, it was a bitch on top of a bitch. We went from a crawl to a standstill.

Finally, my dad found a cop and called him over. Doc's Spanish was lousy, and so was the cop's English—not a good combination, as far as getting our situation across, so my father figured he'd *show* him what was what. He led the cop back into the camper and the guy took one look at Moses and kicked it into gear. He ended up ditching his own vehicle and getting into ours and driving us across the border himself. Took us along all these back roads and emergency lanes—and, even, into oncoming traffic for a stretch. It was probably the hairiest ride I've ever been on.

By the time we crossed into California, Moses' temperature was up to 105 or so. Doc didn't quite know what to do, so he headed for the house of a colleague he thought might be able to help in an emergency. He thought maybe Moses was developing sepsis. This was back before cell phones, of course, so we couldn't call ahead to see if my father's doctor buddy was home. We just pulled up to this guy's house, and Doc frantically explained the situation, and the guy dropped whatever he was doing and drove with us to the closest hospital, where I think he had admitting privileges.

Thank God he was home.

Meanwhile, the rest of us were all in the camper, watching this whole drama unfold, worrying like crazy about our brother, doing what we could to keep it together. A few of us hopped out at the doctor's house and waited out the emergency there, but my parents continued on with Moses and the doctor right in the camper. They didn't even bother to call an ambulance. They just peeled off.

On the way to the hospital, with the doctor driving, Moses looked up at my father and said, "Hey, Dad, you're not gonna be mad at me if I don't surf anymore, are you?"

I heard that later and thought it was just about the saddest, sweetest thing.

Moses made it to the hospital. They rushed him into surgery and fixed him up. After, he had to wear a colostomy bag for the longest while—don't think he took a proper shit for about a year. He had to shit out of his stomach, essentially, but he was okay. And, soon enough, the rest of us were all okay, too. It got to where we could joke about it, and we had no choice but to joke about it, really, because when you're a kid and you're living in close quarters like that and one of your brothers has to shit through his stomach into a bag . . . well, you have to tease him mercilessly about it.

Basically, it's your job.

I've got to hand it to Moses, though. He was tough. And he gave as good as he got. He'd get back at us at night, when everyone was asleep. There was a simple, paper clip–type apparatus that held his colostomy bag shut; he'd have to roll up the bag and clip it shut to keep it from leaking. Once Moses got comfortable with the routine and how everything worked he'd open up that bag late at night, releasing what amounted to a couple thousand farts into our tiny, unventilated space. I'd never smelled anything so deadly, so toxic in my life. One by one, we'd be startled awake by the smell, and there'd be Moses off in the corner, giggling into his sleeping bag. The little shit.

About a year later, we were back at San O for the summer, and Moses was finally ready to shit on his own. We made a whole ceremony out of it, a whole party. For the ceremonial shit, Moses went to the old kook shacks, which was what we called the plywood shitters they used to have at the park campsite. The whole family gathered around for the blessed event. The Tracys were there. All the friends we'd made over the years. There were like thirty, forty people, all bunched up outside the latrine, waiting for Moses to take his first legit shit in just about forever—and when he was done, he put it in a little bag and held it out for all to see, like it was a stinking trophy.

Everybody cheered.

That night, we had a big party. Lots of food. Lots of music. A real celebration. We all remember it for the big deal that it was. Even the Tracy boys remember it, all these years later, although they remember it as Moses' bar mitzvah—which I find pretty hilarious. I guess this means they have no clear idea about our traditions and rituals. To them, it makes sense that Jews shit into little bags and call it a rite of passage.

But it *was* a rite of passage, in a sick little way. It was a coming of age for Moses, a symbolic shift from being sick to being well, but it was also a transition for our whole family. At least, that's how it seemed to me. To almost lose Moses like that, and to now have him back, whole . . . well, it combined with us losing the camper in Florida a couple years later, with us older kids having to take on jobs, with Doc letting us know we'd run out of money, to leave me feeling like the ground beneath our feet was a bit unsteady. To have to watch my dad pinch those few items from that dairy, it kind of rocked my worldview. I went from thinking that nothing could ever go wrong, that nothing could touch us, to knowing full well that our time together was precious, and that we were precious to each other, and that if we didn't take time to nourish and nurture what we had it'd all turn to shit.

7

Break

One by one, we lit out on our own.

Jonathan was the first to leave. David was the oldest, but he stayed on in the camper into his twenties. Jonathan was the rebel child, the one who made the biggest trouble, the most noise; he wore his hair long, back when we were all still sporting the clean-cut, leaned-out look that had become a part of the Paskowitz family mystique. David was more about toeing the family line; he was my father's deputy, there to uphold authority. Jonathan was there to cross that line, to go against authority.

He was also the best surfer of the bunch, by far. I used to watch him all the time, trying to pick up on this or that. He had all these sick moves, used to surprise the crap out of me, watching. Always looked like he was surprising the crap out of himself, too, with some of the tricks he pulled, the confidence he showed. My other brothers, they were all strong surfers, but there was a kind of grace about Jonathan on a board. Like he was dancing, almost. Like he was answering every question the wave threw at him. When we started surfing in all those competitions, Jonathan was always the one to beat. He was the one the locals came out to see, the one they'd heard about, and most times he didn't disappoint. If the waves were with him, he'd rip, and the rest of us would do our thing and sometimes catch a trophy or two, but Jonathan was definitely the star.

Guess it was inevitable he and my father would clash. Mostly, it was over a bunch of small arguments, a growing rebellious streak, which I guess is how it happens in most families. Only here, we weren't like most families. We were nine kids, of various stripes and sizes, living like surf rats in the back of a crappy camper, following the urges of our loopy, freethinking parents. At sixteen or so, Jonathan got it in his head that he was ready to live on his own, so he went off to find what work he could, wherever he could, and to find a way to compete in more of a full-time, full-on way. He lined up a couple low-end sponsors, who kept him in decent equipment and made it possible for him to find a place to live and move about on his own. Wasn't about money or glory for Jonathan, I don't think, so much as it was about independence, making his own mark. I looked on, at fourteen or fifteen, and picked up on *that*, too.

Soon, Abraham followed Jonathan, only not by his own choice. My dad actually tossed him from the camper, for some youthful fuckup I'll leave for Abraham to tell. He might have left on his own, soon enough, but the upshot for me was that my buddy was gone. Abraham and I had done everything together, since we were super-little, and I couldn't see hanging back without him. Really, that's what it came down to. Hadn't been thinking of leaving, but it felt to me like I was about to be left behind. Already our little family dynamic had been upended, with Jonathan gone, and I didn't like how my days were looking without Abraham, so I told my parents I was going off to live with him for a while.

Wasn't a lot they could say: it's not like my prospects were any bigger or better staying on with them; it's not like I had school or a job or any other pressing worry. So I bolted. I was fifteen years old, and I was gone. No real plan. No real thought, other than it seemed like a good idea at the time. In the moment, it didn't strike me as any kind of big-deal decision. And it's not like my parents set out any kind of point-of-no-return ultimatum; I knew if things didn't work out, or if I had any kind of change of heart, I could always find my way back to the camper. There wasn't any kind of blowup or tension; it just felt to me like it was time to go, so I went.

First thing I did was move in with my friend Bob Bueno, at his place in San Clemente. Abraham and I moved in with Bob together, but I don't think we contributed to Bob's expenses in any kind of meaningful way. Not at first, anyway. It's more like we just crashed there, as long as it was okay with Bob—and, lucky for us, it was okay with Bob for a good, long while.

Every young, upstart surfer with no education and no plans should have a friend like Bob Bueno. He was a sweet, funny, giving Mexican dude we'd met a couple summers before, and he was like our savior. He'd moved to San Clemente from La Puente, up in the San Gabriel Valley, and for him the contrast was startling. He used to say it was like he'd died and gone to heaven, to be able to live and work in such a beautiful setting, surrounded by beautiful things. But he wasn't the type to take his good turn for granted. He was a hard worker who made good money in construction and who really enjoyed spending that good money. His fridge was always stocked with good food and good beer. He worked up near L.A., so there was a long haul back and forth. It meant he was always putting in serious hours, but he never complained; he was always happy to come home and kick back and enjoy the hell out of what was left of the day. He surfed a little, too, which I think was part of his motivation for moving to the area. That's how we met, surfing. I had my lifelong, hard-core San O pals, but through Bob I met a bunch of kinder, gentler, more laid-back surfer dudes—guys who hit the beach when they could. Guys who'd give you the shirts off their backs before they'd ever drop in and pinch one of your waves. And Bob was the most generous soul on dry land, happy to have me and Abraham underfoot, along with anyone else who needed a place to crash.

My deal was to focus on my surfing, to get as good as Jonathan, to line up some sponsors and see if I could make a living at it. Wasn't much of a living to be made, but I was young and stupid and determined, so I went after it. Bob's place was right by Trestles, so I knew the beach, knew the break, knew the locals. Wasn't the worst place to ride out the next bunch of waves and crank things up a couple notches until something good had a chance to happen. I was riding piece-of-shit, hand-me-down boards, whatever I could scrounge or borrow, just trying to focus on eating right and surfing hard.

Abraham got a job right away, as a box boy at a local supermarket called Alpha Beta, but I continued to just go to the beach and surf. Didn't have the head for anything more than that. Didn't have the background, either. I mean, when you don't go to school, when your parents leave you to fend for yourself on the beach, you don't exactly have much of a foundation, and for the first time I realized what I might have lost, all those years outside the classroom. It's not just that I might have needed a high school diploma, if I ever hoped to get a decent job, but I needed the discipline, the focus, the follow-through that would have found me in school.

All of which meant my best bet was to find my way on a surfboard. There were plenty of contests in the area, although occasionally I'd hitch a ride to a competition down in Mexico. Wasn't really any prize money back then, just bragging rights and gear and maybe a couple sponsors looking to get you to wear their shorts or use their wax. Early on, my best showing was at the San Miguel Pro, down in Baja, where I finished fifth out of a field of over one hundred. It was a huge validation, to make it to the finals, against all those guys. I went up against all these big names—so it felt absolutely great. It also earned me a hundred bucks or so, but more than that, it meant I could compete; it meant I had a shot.

I should probably mention here that the idea of competing on a surfboard is antithetical to a true, hard-core surfer. Yep, that's a big word for a true, hard-core surfer. For me. "Antithetical." Doesn't come up in my everyday conversation, but it popped into my head and I looked it up and it fits pretty well here. It means it goes against my nature—*our* nature as watermen. And yet, at the same time, it doesn't—because, let's face it, we compete for waves all the time. We compete for position. We fight the hassle of work and family and all the pressures of the world around, just to get into the water. That's a kind of competition, don't you think? In a way, that's what was behind Doc's decision to step away from the workaday world and raise us kids off the conventional grid, just so we could surf and surf and surf. It's because he didn't want to have to compete for those small pockets of freedom and wonder he found on a board, didn't want us kids to have to compete for our own version of the same, but at the same time it's because he'd faced down whatever he thought the world expected of him and come up with his own approach instead. In his own way, he'd already competed . . . and *won*. And now all there was left to do was surf.

But competing in a contest is a whole other deal. It's not like a race, where there can be a clear winner. There is no clock, no fast and finite set of rules, no way to defend yourself or protect your lead. It's all about style and approach and degrees of difficulty. On our own, we don't measure or judge. We don't rank ourselves against our buddies, or spend our days worrying about a bunch of subjective scores that may or may not have anything to do with our rides. We just rip. We look at each other and think, *Yeah, that guy's got it going on.* Or, *Nice try, fella.* We know where we stand and what we can do and none of it much matters. It's not like any other sport, where in order for you to *win* someone else has to *lose.* It's not a battle. It's more like a state of mind.

Okay, so if that's the way I feel—if that's the way *most* surfers feel—then why do we bother competing? Why do we fly all over the world, to the biggest, baddest, most remote breaks known to man, just to line up against each other and have at it and hope like crazy we make it to the final heat? It cuts against who we are, but at the same time it *is* who we are. Or here's a better way to put it: it *allows* us to be who we were. It keeps us going. After all, if we didn't compete, we couldn't afford to ride all of this gorgeous, state-of-the-art gear, we couldn't afford to skip out on work, we'd have to hold a real job, and we'd be expected to put in time at that real job, time that would take us away from surfing.

And so, yeah, it was a big boost to post such a strong showing down in San Miguel, against such a deep field, at such a young age. I had made a giant splash, only it didn't come out of nowhere. Folks in and around surfing already knew who I was, because of my dad and the way we lived. We were like mini-celebrities in the surfing community. Wherever we went in those days, there'd be a reporter looking to do a story on us, or a news crew hoping to get some footage of all us Paskowitzes, riding eleven across. My dad had a bunch of friends who'd found a way to make a living out of the sport—shaping boards, making or marketing gear, writing for surfing magazines . . . not to mention all the guys who'd gone on to become true champions. So the Paskowitz name alone might have opened doors for me eventually, and I would have been completely fine with that, but making it to the finals in this one contest early on meant it wouldn't *just* be the Paskowitz name doing the opening. It'd be *my* name, too.

I still had to work, though. Still had to put in my hours, somewhere. Ended up working at a Carl's Jr. burger joint, about a hundred yards down the road from Bob's house. Seemed like a reasonable commute. Plus, we ate there all the time, so it made sense to punch their clock and get a deal on their food. Hadn't counted on how miserable I'd be, in this ridiculous outfit I had to wear, seeing all my buddies running in and out of there all day. It was a big hangout for our crowd, and it was embarrassing to be seen in this campy hat, this cheesy triple-knit polyester uniform they made us wear. I felt like that character in *Fast Times at Ridgemont High* who had to wear a pirate costume to work. Plus, just to add to the indignity, we had to pay for our own uniforms. They took the money out of our paychecks. I only lasted a couple weeks, which wasn't exactly long enough to pay down my uniform advance, so for weeks afterwards I'd get these calls from Carl's Jr. management, telling me I owed them seven dollars and forty cents. That's what it ended up costing me to work there.

Not too long after that I got a job working with my friend John Meade, cleaning boats at Newport Beach. John was an ex–coast guard guy I'd met on the beach who had a thriving sideline business maintaining boats for high-end yachtsmen. The money was good, and I got to be outside on the water all day. The drag was I had to ride the bus from San Clemente to Dana Point, so John and I could drive to Newport Beach together. I looked up one day and realized I'd gone from not working at all, to working at a burger joint down the street, to commuting an hour back and forth and putting in the same long haul Bob Bueno logged. But I didn't really have any other options. I was too young for a driver's license; even if I could drive, there's no way I could have afforded my own car. I couldn't afford to just surf all day, so I sucked it up and cleaned boats.

Turned out to be a great job. It was good, honest work. The money was decent, the hours flexible. I ended up working with John for years and years, even after I started having some big success on the circuit. I'd come home from my world travels, after blowing through whatever prize money I'd managed to collect, show up at the marina, and get right back to work.

※

I didn't stay at Bob Bueno's for long. Didn't want to overstay my welcome—although I don't think Bob would have ever kicked me out. For a while I stayed with a mutual buddy of ours named Lyle Fuller. He lived in a beautiful house in San Clemente with his mom, Patricia; they were kind enough to take me in for a stretch, and I was smart enough to take them up on it.

Lyle and I made our share of trouble together. The absolute biggest of trouble came about on a whim. We were hanging around one day, thinking it'd be nice to head down to Cabo for an adventure. Neither one of us had a whole lot going on at that point, and John Meade never minded if I grabbed a couple days every here and there, so Cabo sounded like a good idea. Lyle drove a Subaru Brat, a mini-truck with the two useless seats in the cab facing back. I thought it was such a cool ride, but it wasn't very practical—soon another friend of ours was fixing to join, a guy named Gilbert Roybal, so the Brat was out. It only sat two people up front, and nobody was too keen on riding all the way down to Cabo in the open cab, facing back. Plus, we needed all that room for our gear.

For a while it looked like we'd have to scratch our plans, which was basically what happened to most of our grand schemes and big ideas, but then I hit on what I thought was a perfect solution: the family camper. In the big-ideas department, this was huge. My folks were off on some remote, landlocked adventure. By now, Moses and Adam had gone off on their own, so it was just David and the three youngest, Salvador, Navah, and Joshua, at home with them. The camper was less and less necessary as our little family unit got smaller and smaller, and that winter Doc was storing the vehicle with my aunt Josephina and uncle Emilie, at their place in Paris, California, right off the Ortega Highway. Aunt Josephine was my mother's oldest sister. We all called her Auntie Grandma, and she and my uncle had a big spread, ten acres or so, which made a convenient way station for the camper when it wasn't being used.

I still remember the way my dad always complained, driving our campers down the Ortega Highway, that it was a treacherous stretch of road. Our campers always had shitty brakes, and you had to press down on them as hard as you could as you came down that pass to the main road. It was a bitch and a bear.

This rig was another in our long line of Class C campers, with the big cab-over built on top of a standard, one-ton Ford body. The only "custom" piece to the ride was the surfboard rack Doc had fitted to the roof, which was big enough to hold up to forty boards, or a whole bunch of other crap if we were traveling light.

I called ahead to Auntie Grandma, told her I was coming. Told her my father said it was okay to grab the camper and head down to Mexico for a surf competition. This last part was just a white lie on top of a big-ass lie. There was no contest, of course; I just figured it would throw my aunt off the scent if I made it sound like it was a road trip with a purpose, instead of just a road trip for no apparent reason. I needed to dress up my lie every which way, because my father would have never given me permission to take the camper, for a whole bunch of reasons—mainly, I didn't have a driver's license.

I hated that I was lying to my aunt, because she'd always been good to me, good to my family. But when you're sixteen or seventeen and you've spent your entire life watching your father stretch the truth to get what he wanted or needed or thought he deserved, lying comes easy. No, I'd never seen him lie to family. He was honest with my mother; he was honest with us kids. But a lie is a lie, and I always felt like I came to it naturally, like there was some default mode in our hard-wiring…and Auntie Grandma didn't suspect a thing. She might have, though. She might have known I was too young to drive, but I guess she just didn't put two and two together. She was too busy trusting me.

I suppose we could have squeezed into Lyle's Brat, but we had a nice momentum going with the camper. We liked that we wouldn't have to worry about a place to crash. We liked having all that room.

I took the wheel to start. Before heading out, we stopped at a Triple A office in town. One of our guys had a membership card, so we loaded up on maps, figured out a route, an itinerary. I'd made the drive a bunch of times, but never without my dad. All I knew was to head south and keep going.

First leg of the drive went great. Made it past Tijuana, no problem. Started thinking we would make it to Ensenada and hang for a bit—because, back then, Ensenada was a happening spot. There were tons of kids our age, California kids down for the day or the weekend, so we pulled into town, got something to eat, had a few beers. Probably, I had a few too many, because our pal Gilbert didn't think I was in any shape to drive. He was right, I'm sure. Gilbert didn't drink—or, at least, he didn't drink that day. Made sense to let him drive for a while; the idea, all along, was to share the driving. Before I gave him the keys, though, I explained to Gilbert about the brakes. I told him they were a bitch and a bear. Told him the rig was a little top-heavy, and reminded him that it was a scary road, with a lot of twists and turns to it.

Now, Gilbert was a tiny guy, maybe five feet in socks. He looked like a little kid trying to drive a school bus, but he was a decent driver. I sat with him up front for a bit, until we pulled out of town. The steering wheel was one of those lap-height, oversized, counter-steering types, with a whole lot of play in it, but Gilbert seemed to get the hang of it. After a while, I told him I was going back into the camper to lie down. Lyle switched places with me and got in front, and I climbed into the cab-over and tried to sleep. If there's one thing I was good at, after logging all those years, all those miles, it was falling asleep on the move. The rhythm of the road was like nature's Ambien, and, mixed with the beers, I was gone within a couple kilometers. I wasn't in a deep sleep, though. It was more like a half sleep. I could feel the camper lurching this way and that way, my body being rolled to one side or the other with each shift.

And then, I was shaken from my half sleep by a sudden lurch to the right side of the camper. I popped right up off the pillow, and as I did I could feel the rig kind of dip into a rut on the shoulder of the road. At that point, I could just imagine Gilbert up front, trying to spin that oversized, counter-steering wheel the other way, to adjust, and it turned out that's just what he was doing, only he threw the rig into such a sudden hard left we flipped over on our side. It was a massive camper and we'd been moving at a decent clip, so once we flipped we kept going and going, just sliding along with our own weight and momentum. Behind me I could hear the sick, scary sounds of the appliances coming off one wall and crushing into the other.

There was a tiny window in the cab-over, and I'd had it open, but now that we'd flipped I was in danger of slipping right through it, so I straddled the frame of the window to keep myself from flying out. I put myself in this weird, spread-eagle position, and I tried to brace myself against the side walls like Spiderman. I knew we would crash eventually, but while we were sliding I had all this time to frantically figure how to position myself to keep myself in one piece and inside the cab. Of course, I had no idea how we would hit, or what we would hit, but I was scrambling just the same.

Well, just as I was bracing myself, and straddling that cab-over window, I noticed we had crossed to the other side of the road, into oncoming traffic, and I could see a truck coming our way. I could hear it, too. The driver was leaning or pulling on his horn, so there was this long, loud peal. We were in the middle of a big straight-away. The truck driver had been going at his own decent clip, headed down a small incline; he'd seen us spinning up ahead and slammed on his brakes, but he couldn't bring his rig to a full stop before smashing head-on into our side, spinning us around and around and right off the road.

Once everything stopped, I shook myself alert and realized I was covered with fuel. Also, I saw that the back wall of the cab-over compartment had been crushed and pressed all the way to the front, locking me in. The only way out, really, was the narrow, viewfinder window in the front, but I did a quick survey and saw there was nothing within reach that I could grab to bust out the window. There was just me and my bare feet, reeking of fuel.

Lyle and Gilbert were screaming at me from outside the vehicle. Somehow, they'd made it out. They asked me if I was okay. I hollered back that I wasn't hurt, but I was stuck. Suddenly, I was overcome with a sense of urgency. I panicked, thinking the rig would burst into flames at any moment, so I started kicking violently against the window, trying to bust through. Ended up cutting right through the bottom of my foot. (I still have the scar!) Pushed away the glass and managed to fit my way through.

There were big hugs all around. Gilbert and Lyle had thought I'd been crushed to death, and after that they thought I'd been seriously hurt, so we were all happy to be alive and in one piece. A little cut up and bruised, but okay. Poor Gilbert was falling all over himself with how sorry he was. Really, the guy was pretty broken up about it. I told him it wasn't his fault, that it could have happened to any one of us.

Soon as we stopped celebrating/commiserating, I checked the damage. The rig was completely destroyed, flattened. Our boards up top were like pancakes. Everything inside the camper was demolished. It was a giant miracle we hadn't been killed.

Incredibly, there wasn't a lot of damage to the truck. The driver took in the scene and bolted, quick as he could. I imagined he was driving his rig on even less authority than we were driving Doc's. We were on a fairly remote stretch of road, but a couple cars stopped and people offered to help. I remember hearing a bunch of voices, in English and Spanish, and not really understanding what anyone was saying. I was pretty rattled, pretty freaked.

Finally, one of the English voices pierced through whatever fog I was in. The voice came from a guy with blond hair. He spoke perfect English, perfect Spanish. He was Mexican, but he didn't look Mexican. He could see I was shaken, confused.

He said, "Dude, you're gonna get charged for all this damage. They're probably gonna toss your asses in jail."

Turned out this guy's family ran one of the oldest, most famous cantinas in all of Mexico—Hussong's, back up the road in Ensenada. We'd been there a bunch of times. It's where the margarita was invented, so the place was a big, big deal, a real landmark.

Our Good Samaritan offered us a ride back to Ensenada, so we grabbed what was left of our crap—clothes, mostly—and jumped in the back of his car. Lyle had some nice tools with him, so he was able to salvage those. I had my bar mitzvah camera, so I was able to snap a few pictures of the rig. Those pictures turned out to be very helpful to my father, when he was dealing with the insurance mess, which basically meant that instead of him being hugely fucking pissed at me he was only somewhat fucking pissed at me.

Don't think any of us talked all that much on the way to Ensenada. When we finally hit town, the guy dropped us off at Hussong's and set us up with drinks, a place to wash up and stow our gear...

whatever we needed. Really, he couldn't have been nicer about it. It was a lucky thing he'd come by when he did, which takes me to another idea: to all of you no-good kids out there, planning on jacking your family camper and rolling it on a big straightaway on your way to Cabo, you should only do so when you know you'll be picked up by a guy who'll take you back to his family's cantina, where there'll be pretty girls and free drinks and good music and where you and your friends can all pretend that whatever the fuck has just happened to you has just happened to some other group of no-good kids, from some place other than where you happen to be from.

We were so completely fucked, but at the same time it was easy to ignore that we were so completely fucked, because right away we started running into a bunch of people we knew from San Clemente. It was almost surreal, the way we'd slipped from this giant disaster scene into this giant party. I disappeared into the bathroom for a couple minutes, to clean my wound and bandage up my foot, and by the time I got back Gilbert and Lyle had scored a ride for us back home. Trouble was, I started talking to a pretty girl, and drinking my fill, and when our ride was ready to go I just waved Gilbert and Lyle off, figured I'd get back home somehow or other. I was having a good time talking to this girl, who'd just pulled into port on a cruise ship and was out partying with her friends.

So here's where things went from a little bit out of control to all the way out of control, because the girl invited me back to her ship. She said, "Hey, I'll sneak you on."

Sounded good to me. I didn't know the first thing about cruise ships or protocol. I just figured it was another good time, a change of venue, so we did just that. Snuck our way past the ship's guards who'd been assigned to watch our comings and goings, and by the time my drunk started to fade I realized we were out at sea. We'd pulled out of Ensenada, and I was officially a stowaway. Of course,

I'd been a stowaway all along, but now that we'd left port it seemed worse, so I did the only thing I could think to do. I started drinking again. At some point during our too-long, too-wild evening, the girl and I parted ways, but I met up with a group of guys who seemed up for a whole other good time, and they got a charge out of my story. At the end of the night, they let me crash with them on a roll-away. Woke up the next morning, head pounding, and saw that my leg had bled all the way through the sheets. All the other guys in the room had gone; we had arrived in some new port and everyone had disembarked.

I tied a towel around my still-bleeding leg and hobbled to the deck like some wounded warrior, not knowing quite what to do. As I walked, I realized we were back in the United States, and I realized I didn't have a passport, I didn't have any identification, I didn't have any money. I was totally screwed. I started shaking.

There was no way out other than to go through the customs area, so I stood in line and came up with a plan. When my turn came, I told the customs agent that my luggage had been stolen, along with my passport and my wallet. I said it in my most convincing, most distraught voice, like I was a weary world traveler and not some deadbeat stowaway who'd just totaled a vehicle in Mexico and stepped away from the accident scene before a report could be filed.

The customs agent was nice enough. He pointed me to a room across the way, where I would have to fill out a bunch of forms, so I thanked him for his help and walked in the direction he'd pointed—only I just kept walking. I told myself to look straight ahead, to look like I knew exactly where I was going, like I belonged. And as I walked, I picked up my pace a bit, until I was finally through the main gates and stepping from the ship onto the dock. Even then, I just kept my head down and kept moving, until I finally looked up and saw that we'd arrived at San Pedro Harbor. I found the nearest pay phone and called Lyle, who came by and picked me up in the Brat and took me home.

I caught a whole bunch of shit from Doc, but not for a couple days. Not until he was back in town. Looking back, I think he must have known, Auntie Grandma must have told him I'd borrowed the rig, but he was waiting for me to come to him, and when I did he lit into me something fierce.

You know, I think my brothers and I had always been a little terrified of my father when we were kids, although maybe "terrified" is not quite the right word. Because Doc was such a mighty, larger-than-life figure in our lives, because we were all in such awe of him, we didn't want to do anything to disappoint him. We were afraid of letting him down, as much as we were afraid of any beating or dressing-down that might come our way as a result. In other words, we didn't piss him off lightly. Oh, we pissed him off. Many, many times—in many, many ways. We were rambunctious, devilish boys, after all. But we felt bad about it, each time. Like we were doubly guilty. And here, after stealing-turned-destroying his camper, I felt extra-doubly guilty. I was out on my own—not quite an adult, but close—and yet I quaked like a little kid at the thought of having to tell him what happened.

Those pictures I'd taken? They ended up saving my ass . . . and Doc's. He didn't own the vehicle outright, it was financed, but he was able to say that the car had been stolen, and to send in documentation of the damage. The insurance company paid off the loan and my father was in the clear.

Wouldn't go so far as to say it all ended up to the good, because things weren't right between me and my father for a long time after that . . . but at least it didn't end up costing us anything more than a couple of sweet surfboards, some misplaced trust, and a near-death experience.

Oh, and there's just one more thing. A couple years later, I was driving along that same stretch of road and right there at our crash site a taco stand had gone up. I pulled over to check it out and saw that the folks who'd built the stand had salvaged one of the sides of the camper and used it for one of their side walls.

Thought that was way cool... and fitting. For me and my buddies to destroy our family camper like that and to have it retrofitted as a taco stand... well, it was nothing more than the circle of life, Paskowitz-style.

8

Danielle

I'm afraid I didn't make a good first impression on my wife, Danielle. In fact, it's a wonder she ever wanted to see me again. First time we met, I saw her across the room at a party, and she struck me straight off as just about the most beautiful thing I'd ever seen: animal, vegetable, mineral...whatever, she had 'em all beat. She was absolutely breathtaking. Tall, blond, with great tits and a sweet, sweet smile.

I didn't think I had a chance with her, but I knew I had to find a way to talk to her, to at least give it a shot. Don't think I would have ever forgiven myself if I didn't make some sort of move, but the "breathtaking" part was turning out to be a problem. Why? Because I ended up taking her breath away, too—only not in a good way. In my stupid defense, I'd been working on my car all day—a '65 Impala—so there was grease in my hair, on my clothes, under my fingernails. I looked like shit, felt like shit. Wasn't really in the mood to go to this party in the first place, but it was a party for this girl who used to go out with my brother Jonathan, who happened to be pregnant with his baby, although she hadn't really acknowledged that it was his at the time. Everybody knew, in a *kind of, sort of* way, but it was one of those things that weren't really discussed.

Anyway, when I got there, I was greasy and tired and wanting to be someplace else. I went to the party basically to support Jonathan, even though it wasn't clear to any of us at that point what his involvement would be with this baby, or if it was even his. Don't mean to go all soap opera on you or lay on too much information, but I want to set the scene. Plus, I'd had a few beers, and eaten a bunch of junk food, and my stomach started acting up in a big-time way. It got so bad I had to take a major, major dump—in a tiny little apartment, with no ventilation—but I was so *not* into being there I just didn't care. I didn't really know anybody at the party, wasn't looking to meet anybody, so I dropped a big-time load and stunk up the place like you wouldn't believe, and then to make matters worse as I was coming out of the bathroom there was Danielle, waiting with her knockout friend Terri, next in line.

I was so thoroughly and totally embarrassed I could have shit, all over again. It was bad enough just seeing Danielle as I came out the door, but then to have these two gorgeous creatures slip inside together to inhale my shame... well, it was like someone had taken my thorough and total embarrassment and put it on a billboard.

It was probably one of the ten lowest moments of my life, to that point—the ultimate party foul in every sense of the word—and to hear Danielle tell it later it was just as bad as I thought. Apparently, she and Terri closed the door behind them and Terri turned to Danielle and said, "Hey, that guy was cute." Or something similarly flattering and positive and hopeful. To which Danielle could only scrunch up her face in disgust and say, "What a pig! Are you serious? How could anybody do this? This place smells awful!" Or something similarly mortifying and negative and doubtful.

Mom with all her little beach rats.
That's me in the center with Adam
rubbing my head.

Caravanning through Israel in our
pop-top camper.

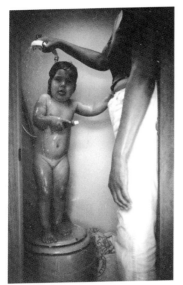

Mom giving my baby sister a
cold shower in the camper (sorry,
Navah).

Mom whipping up a little something for
Joshua to eat.

About to set off on a hike with Dad. Love my red shirt.

The little rascals—except for Joshua.

Mom lining us up for inspection outside the camper (again, without Joshua, but you can see his playpen on the right).

With Doc at Tourmaline Beach around the time I started surfing.

Prepping my board for competition.

Hanging Ten—Salt Creek, California.

Mugging for the camera off the coast of Florida.

Here we are in our standard size-ordered poses: Navah, Joshua, Salvador, Adam, Moses, yours truly, Abraham, Jonathan, and David.

How smokin' hot were we? Danielle and I used this picture for our wedding invitation.

With Isaiah and Elah.

Mom and Dad in Baja, Mexico—early 1970s.

The Paskowitz men—with Isaiah and Elijah in Makaha, Hawaii.

Teaching Isaiah how to surf.

Surfers Healing—
Folly Beach, South
Carolina.

Surfers Healing.

Life among the savages—all prettied up for the filming of the *Surfwise*
documentary.

I knew who she was, of course. By reputation. She was Danielle Brawner, and in addition to being gorgeous, she was California surfing royalty. Her father, Danny Brawner, had been a drummer for the Sandals, a surf rock band that had made a big splash in the 1960s with the sound track to *Endless Summer*. Even today, you can hear the Sandals' distinctive instrumental surf tunes on classic rock radio stations. And Danny had since gone on to become a legendary glosser, making boards with Dale Velzy and managing production at Hobie since we were kids. It was Danny Brawner who'd designed the Gerry Lopez Lightning Bolt board I got for my bar mitzvah. He'd known my father, for years and years. They used to surf together at Tourmaline, at San O, at Malibu. They ran with the same crowd—so I'm guessing Danny gave Doc a deal on my board.

I knew Danielle's brother Damian, too. Damian was the drummer in a popular club band that always played around San Clemente, and everyone thought it was cool that his father had been the drummer in this famous surf rock band. I knew Damian had a sister, but I had no idea she looked like … *this*.

I left the party soon as I could, making my apologies to Jonathan's ex, but I couldn't shake thinking about Danielle. I got home and wished like hell things had gone differently, so I drank a couple more beers and started feeling sorry for myself. I had a girlfriend at the time, a pretty little Irish-Mexican girl I'd been seeing for a while, so it's not like I was out looking to meet anyone. I suppose I could have called my girlfriend and invited her over to take my mind off what I'd missed, but instead I asked my pal Scott Ruedy to call Danielle for me. Scott and I were living together in a tiny little apartment in San Clemente. Apart from friends whose couches I'd crashed on and my buddy Bob Bueno, whose kindness I'd abused, Scott was the first guy I'd lived with who wasn't a brother. We've been friends for over thirty years; we would be best man at each other's weddings; that night I recruited him to call a girl for me, because I was too chickenshit to call her myself. That way, I fig-ured if Danielle shot me down, she wouldn't be shooting me down directly.

It was lame, I know, but I'd dug myself such a deep, deep hole I didn't see any other way out.

Scott didn't mind being my wingman. And guess what? Dani-elle was happy to hear from me, even in this lame-ass, once-removed way, so I got on the phone and we ended up having a nice long conversation. Really, it was such a great conversation, I hung up and called the Irish-Mexican girl and broke it off with her. I didn't want to string her along or to have Danielle thinking I was some sort of two-timing asshole, so I cleared the decks and made myself available.

Whatever happened now, I was all in.

And what happened was this: Danielle and I set off on a whirl-wind two-week romance. It was incredible. She was smart and funny and sarcastic, just like me. (The *sarcastic* part, I mean—never really thought of myself as smart or funny.) More than that, she had a big, generous heart and she was smoking hot, which basically made her the girl of my wildest dreams. The reason it was only a two-week romance was because she was leaving for Europe on a long-planned trip with one of her girlfriends. It sounded like an amazing adven-ture, and a part of me was excited for her, but another part thought it sucked that just as we were getting going she was going away. We'd been thrown together in this chaotic way and now there was a clock on our relationship—or whatever the hell we wanted to call it. Plus, she was planning to see an old boyfriend in France, so that was kind of weighing on me, too.

I was still surfing on the professional circuit, but in a half-assed way. It had been a couple years since I'd made the finals in that San Miguel competition, and I'd had other small successes, here and there. Nothing major. Nothing sustained. Enough to land some low-end sponsorship deals with a local apparel company and a local surfboard company, enough to maybe even call myself a professional surfer and not be laughed off the beach, but hardly enough to keep me in beer and utilities. I was still working with John at the marina, making good money. By outward appearances it might have seemed like I had it going on, but it felt like I was treading water. Wouldn't say I was washed up, but I was certainly stuck, languishing, and before Danielle showed up I'd been wondering if I really wanted to give myself over to surfing. It can be a tough slog, a real grind, traveling to all these out-of-town tournaments, not making any real money, having to keep fit and focused. Before meeting Danielle, I was leaning in the direction of packing it in and finding some other way to fill my days. I didn't think I had it in me to live like my father, to eat healthy, to live, sleep, and breathe surfing, to do whatever it took to make it on the professional circuit. But then, after hanging with Danielle those two weeks, I started leaning in a whole other way. I'd never been with a woman like her. She was incredible, really—and it wasn't just that she was drop-dead gorgeous. She was decent and wonderful. She was twice the woman I deserved, at least, and I found myself wanting to double down and step up my game, just so I could measure up. She made me want to be better.

Also, she made me want to be in a serious relationship. With her. Only with her.

When our two weeks were up, I drove Danielle to LAX from San Clemente. We didn't leave ourselves a ton of time, although in those days you could breeze into the gate just a couple minutes early and still make your flight. That's about how it shook out that day. I had to ride the emergency lane the whole way there, but nobody pulled us over, and there was no time for a long, emotional good-bye, which I guess was just as well. I had my too-cool-for-the-room pro surfer exterior to maintain, but deep down I was a wreck. Deep down I was quivering. It felt like the love of my life was slipping away. Danielle had burst into my world like a comet, and taken me on this wild, wonderful ride, and now she was off to blaze some other path, on some other continent... maybe even take up with that old boyfriend.

I wanted to cry.

◎

I moped around for a couple days after Danielle left, not quite sure how to jump-start my life. But then an opportunity came for me to leave town, too, in the form of a one-way ticket to Israel. My dad's old pal Topsi Kanzapolski had a couple kids in the surfboard business, Amor and Nir. They sent the airline ticket for Abraham, actually, but he wasn't up for the trip, so we switched it up. Their idea was I'd help them with their designs. My idea was to just get away, maybe wait out Danielle's European tour with a change of scenery.

I stopped for a day or two in New York on the way over. In recent years, the city had become a kind of hang for the Paskowitz clan. My grandparents had been there awhile, and now my brother Adam was living there, working in a motorcycle shop; also, my sister, Navah, had just left the camper and decided to give New York a try. This meant it was just down to Joshua living under my parents' roof, and their roof at this point was down to a Chevy Nova—so the times they were certainly a-changing in our family. (Just to be clear, the Nova was like a base of operations, a place to keep their stuff; they also had a couple tents, so it's not like poor Joshua had to sleep in the glove compartment.)

I had thirty bucks in my pocket and a backpack with a pair of board shorts and a couple days' worth of clothes. I was still bumming about Danielle, missing her like crazy. I borrowed twenty bucks from my sister, which she didn't really have, to get myself a killer leather jacket at Adam's bike shop, using his employee discount—

basically because I thought it'd cheer me up to have a killer leather jacket.

It did and it didn't.

When I boarded the plane for Tel Aviv, I was down to some loose change, but somehow I made it from the airport to Amor's flat. Amazingly, I found that I still knew my way around. It'd been about ten years since I was last in Tel Aviv, but I had a sense of where I was, where I was going. Amor had a really nice setup across from a marina. You could see the beach from his window, and it was filled with surfers. I remembered the stories my father used to tell, about bringing those first boards through customs in the 1950s and teaching guys like Topsi to ride. I thought about our two trips to Israel as a family, and the growing popularity of the sport, especially on weekends when the surf was up and the crowds were out. And now here I was, about to start work with Topsi's kids at a surfboard factory, across from a break where hundreds of kids lay on their bellies waiting to drop in and ride. Surfing had become a big, big part of Israeli culture. In some areas, among young soldiers especially, it was such an all-consuming passion you could look on and think you were back in California.

The only thing missing, really, was a world-class break. The surfing wasn't bad, but it was a lot like surfing in Florida, where the shores are buffeted by islands and you're unable to get a clean swell. The Mediterranean can behave like a giant lake, with low pressures and an occasional wind that will drive the swells into little waves. Sometimes, when it's especially windy, it can whip around and blow up the face of these small waves and make them taller, instead of blowing on their backs and crushing them.

On a good day, the surfing was fine. Better than good enough, really. The water was crystal clear and warm and completely different from what I was used to back home, so there was something exotic about it, too. I really dug it, the whole scene. I dug the language, the culture, the vibe. Wound up working there for a couple months, although "working" is probably too strong a word to describe what I was actually doing at first. Basically, I was hanging out and letting these guys bounce their ideas off of me about their boards, their designs; sometimes, I'd bounce my ideas right back. We commuted to the factory on Amor's Harley, which had a bitchin' sidecar, so we tooled around the streets of Tel Aviv like an Israeli Batman and Robin, making the beaches safe for Middle Eastern surfers.

On Friday nights, we'd have Shabbat dinner with Amor's parents, Topsi and Naomi; they cooked these amazing meals, and we talked deep into the night about what was going on in Israel, among the young people especially. The Kanzapolskis' English was perfect, but they sprinkled in a little Hebrew if they thought they needed just the right word to get a point across. Soon, whatever Hebrew I'd retained in my fog of little-kid memory started to come back to me and I could hold up my end pretty well.

I didn't make any money, but I got a place to stay. And food and beer. At the time, early 1980s, beer wasn't a big thing in Tel Aviv, so I was a bit of a trendsetter on this one. Most of the folks I was hanging with seemed to think beer was filling, that it would make them fat. They'd rather smoke hash—that was their way of unwinding after a day on the beach or a day at the surfboard factory. Personally, I'd never been into weed back home. It always made me feel drowsy, dopey, paranoid. Beer was much more my thing. But hash was a whole other high, and I came to really enjoy it, so that became a part of our days, too. Surfing, food, beer, hash ... the ideal recipe to chase me from my funk about missing Danielle.

It's not like we weren't in touch. Over the next three or four months, she wrote me letters. (Remember letters?) Told me what was going on with her adventures. She got pickpocketed in France, had all her money stolen, so that set her back. The much-dreaded reunion with the old boyfriend—much dreaded by *me*!—came and went without incident, so that gave me a lift.

After a while, my friend Dovoleh found a way to rig one of his neighbor's lines so Danielle and I could talk on the phone and we'd have these long, loopy conversations that stretched on for hours. Each one was like that first conversation we had back home, the night of that shitty party. Just the sound of her voice was enough to get me thinking I should drop everything I was doing in Israel and find my way back to wherever she was. She returned home to California ahead of me, but we kept up with our late night phone sessions, and after a while I couldn't take being away from her. Trouble was, I had no money for a flight home. So Amor's girlfriend hooked me up with a couple modeling gigs, and I started doing some coloring work down at the surfboard factory, which earned me a few shekels. I'd apply watercolors to the blank boards after they'd been shaped; then we'd wait for them to dry and laminate over the fiberglass, giving the boards a hip, distinctive look. Nobody was doing that over there at the time, and it threw a little money my way and soon I'd managed to scrape together enough for a return ticket.

Danielle came to meet me at the airport in a limo, which I thought was way cool. It belonged to a buddy of hers who lived up the street, and the guy wasn't doing anything that afternoon, so she convinced him to go for a ride. (First time I ever had sex in a limo! Historians, take note!)

Seeing her again was like coming up for air.

I'd given up the apartment I was sharing with Scott, so I needed a place to stay, and Danielle convinced her folks to let me crash in her brother Damian's room. They weren't too keen about it, I don't think, but Danielle could be very persuasive, I was learning. Don't think Damian minded one way or another; we got along well enough, and it's not like I was actually bunking with him the whole night; I'd sneak into Danielle's room when her parents went to sleep, and sneak back in the morning.

I'd loaned out my car, too—to my brother Abraham, which ended up being a big mistake. Oh, man, I loved that '65 Impala. It was my first car. Bought it for $650 off this old dude, who made me drive around with him in it for a half day before agreeing to sell it to me, like he wanted to check me out and see if I'd be a worthy owner. It had sixty thousand miles on it. The chrome was in perfect shape. Hadn't really wanted to lend it to Abraham, but he had no other way to get around and promised he'd take good care of it, and I couldn't see letting it sit for a couple months when I was in Israel.

It took Abraham a couple days to get the car back to me after I got back to town, but once I got my car back I was able to feel a measure of independence. Kind of tough to feel like you're on your own and moving in the right direction when you're living with your girl-friend's brother in his boyhood bedroom. So the car helped, definitely. I could come and go as I pleased, and do as I pleased...until we were all woken up one morning a couple days later by the bleat of the telephone and a loud knock on the door. It was way early, still dark, and all of a sudden the house was filled with all this noise and activity. I'd already ducked back into Damian's room, and he and I were both startled awake by two cops, who came busting into his room with their guns drawn, barking out questions.

One of the cops turned to me and said, "Are you Israel Paskowitz?"

I nodded.

Then he slapped a pair of handcuffs on me and started pushing me out the door of Damian's room. It was a crazy, chaotic scene. Danielle's parents were half-asleep, standing in the hallway outside Damian's room, but her mom, Sharon, was alert enough and pissed enough to go off on me. Sharon turned to Danielle and screamed, "See, I fuckin' told you he was no good. Goddamn surfer!"

Danielle's dad was laughing. Danny was a cool guy. Took a lot to set him off. Plus, we got along pretty well. I think he knew one of the cops, because Danny was a volunteer fire captain and he worked with all these law enforcement types. He thought the whole thing was pretty funny. He even asked the cops to hang back for a beat so he could go get his camera. Said he wanted to take pictures, because this was something we'd all want to remember—Doc Paskowitz's kid, being led from Danny's house in handcuffs.

Damian was freaking out—mostly because of the drawn gun, I think, but also because he'd nodded off with a jarful of coins on his bed. He'd come back from a gig, was counting out his tips, and was a little bit hammered, so I'd taken the time to stick a bunch of pennies on his skin while he was passed out—you know, just to goof on him. Danielle had said I should make myself at home, and this was the kind of thing my brothers and I would do to each other all the time. An hour or so later, as Damian stumbled out of bed, with all these coins stuck to his body, I didn't think I'd done such a good or thorough job, because they started dropping to the floor—one by one, at first, and then in clumps. Poor Damian couldn't figure what the hell was going on. He was half-asleep, half-baked, fully confused.

The whole scene was a little too confusing to process. Sharon was yelling at Danielle, and Danielle was yelling back at Sharon, telling her to shut up and leave me the fuck alone, and Danny was off to the side, trying not to laugh.

Wasn't exactly the picture of domestic bliss, I'll say that.

I managed to grab my passport and jump into a T-shirt and a pair of shorts, before the cops threw me barefoot into the back of their car and drove me to the station. The whole time thinking, *Great, Izzy. Welcome the fuck home.*

At this point, I still had no idea why these guys were arresting me, but it came clear that Abraham had run up all these parking tickets and moving violations while I was in Israel. The car was registered to me, but whenever Abraham got pulled over they'd run the plates and he'd say he was me and that he'd misplaced his license, so now there were all these outstanding warrants for my arrest. After a while, they came looking for me.

Ended up spending the rest of the morning in a jail cell, before I was dragged in front of a judge. There were a bunch of other cases ahead of me, all similar traffic violation stories, and it seemed this judge was giving about a week of jail time for each warrant. I did the math and figured he could put me away for a month or more, because there were four or five outstanding warrants—but luckily I was able to produce my passport, to show that I was out of the country at the time of each violation. I said I'd left my car behind and that a lot of people had access to it, but when the judge pressed me to give up some names I pretended like I couldn't really say for sure, like the list of people who might have had a key was just too long for me to be any more specific.

I didn't want to give up Abraham on this, even though he'd been so quick to give me up every time he was pulled over.

Danielle was hugely pissed, though, because the whole scene created a mess of tension between her and her parents—between *us* and her parents. She was pissed at me for not turning Abraham in, and at Abraham for putting me in this spot, and at her mother for being so quick to write me off, and at her father for not taking it all that seriously.

I couldn't be mad at my brother just for being stupid and selfish and irresponsible. It wasn't Abraham's fault that his stupidity and selfishness and irresponsibility ended up getting me arrested; it's just how it shook out—and it all shook out to the good, because my passport put me in the clear.

And because it forced Danielle and me to push our relationship to the next level and move in together. We couldn't stay on in her parents' house after something like this. I'd overstayed my welcome, and we rode that swell into our first apartment, knowing that whatever happened next, whatever adventures lay in wait, we would face them together.

9

Going Long

Okay, so now I had one part of my life figured out, the part that said I would be with Danielle, but that still left me to figure the earning-a-living part, the surfing part.

Turned out some of the answers found me on the beach on a day when we weren't looking for anything more than a good time. Danielle and I were just surfing, laying in the sun, groping each other to make up for all that time we were apart... when we met an old friend of Danielle's father, a former world champion surfer named Gary Propper. I knew Gary, but only by reputation; he was like a guru to a lot of the young surfers on the circuit at that time. He was also a bit of an entrepreneur in the entertainment world— what they used to call an impresario. He was a record producer, a movie producer, a talent manager, a publisher, an artist... basically, he was into everything. A couple years after that day on the beach, he'd help discover an obscure comic book series called *Teenage Mutant Ninja Turtles,* which he'd develop into a series of blockbuster movies and television shows, and he was especially plugged into the surfing world.

Gary used to ride for Danny Brawner, who sponsored him back in the 1960s, so we built on the connection and got to talking. Gary had seen me surf. He knew I could compete, and I think he also knew I had drifted away from it in the past couple years. Eventually our talk turned to longboarding. He kept telling me longboarding was making a comeback. I hadn't realized it had ever left, but I knew as well as anyone it had always been a kind of poor cousin to the shortboard circuit. It's not that longboarders were disregarded; it's just that they'd never been as highly regarded as shortboarders, at least not in recent years. Traditionally, all of the big-time, marquee champions had been shortboarders. That was the money play. Shortboarders were the ones who got the big sponsorship deals, the girls, the glory; they were the guys who could really rip. But I was always a big fan of longboarders. I'd only been riding shortboards in competition, but longboards were a big part of my experience. As kids, we each had our own longboard and shortboard atop the camper and we would switch back and forth. Doc's thing was to get us comfortable on all types of rides, on any type of surf. I always felt I could express myself better on a longboard, like I was more in control, more myself. There was something more elegant about a longboard ride, compared to the more choppy, more in-your-face approach of a shortboard. It was like choosing between a classy limousine and a sleek sports car: each made a statement; you just had to figure out what you wanted to say.

This powwow with Gary Propper took place around the time Corky Carroll was coming back out of "retirement" and riding in longboard contests, making a big-time name for himself all over again. For years Corky had been known as one of the founders of professional surfing, and then he stopped competing. Now he was back at it and in some ways more famous, more successful than ever.

He was even doing commercials for Miller Lite, talking about "not getting filled up and groovin' on Lite's great taste." That commercial made a big splash on the surfing scene, because it put it out there that we were real athletes, deserving of at least a sliver of spotlight, all of which fit neatly into Corky's place in surfing history. A lot of folks credit him with being the first surfer to win any kind of national endorsement deal—in his case, with Jantzen sportswear and Hobie Alter, the largest surfboard manufacturer in the world back in the early 1960s—so, clearly, he was an icon of the sport.

By the time I was done shooting the shit with Gary he had me thinking I'd enter my first longboard contest. And I did. There was a contest right in my own backyard, at San O, over the coming Fourth of July weekend, part of a Budweiser pro surf tour that would take shape over the next couple years. Some of the best surfers in the world were scheduled to attend, so I didn't think I had a shot, but I wanted to get wet and get going, see if I could maybe measure up. I didn't even have a decent longboard, so I had to beg and borrow. Started out on Herbie Fletcher's nine-foot board, which was essentially the minimum length for a longboard. Technically, you could ride any board that was at least three feet over your head and still be eligible, but nine feet was the minimum standard.

Now, the way it works in a typical pro event is that you have twenty, thirty, or forty minutes in your heat to catch as many waves as you can and then you're judged on your top three rides. There are usually five judges, and they rank you on a scale of 1 to 10; in those days, they didn't use decimal points, so the best you could hope for on one ride was a total score of 30, after tossing out the high and low marks. Most guys, they caught maybe seven or eight waves in the allotted time, up to a maximum of ten, but I tended to be selective, especially when we were at a break I knew well. And that was certainly the case here. I'd been surfing San O since I was a kid, so

I had a serious home-field advantage. There were maybe a hundred surfers in the field to start, maybe more, and they'd all surfed this wave a bunch of times, but I kept telling myself I'd surfed it longer, harder... *smarter.* Kept telling myself I knew that break better than I knew myself, so I was at a big psychological advantage—enough, hopefully, to make up for the fact that some of these guys were way out of my league.

I could afford to be selective because I could pretty much predict what was coming, so I'd wait for the right wave, let the other guys in my heat battle for position while I hung on the outside, picking my spots. Yeah, I'd grown up with my father's credo to ride every damn wave, to believe no wave was as good as the one you were on, so this approach cut against everything I'd learned as a kid—but this was a competition, which also cut against everything I'd learned as a kid. We were taught to prevail over the wave, not over the guy surfing next to us, but to succeed on the circuit you had to mix in elements of both.

I knew enough to be selective, to wait. I knew I only needed to post three good scores. Only needed to impress five judges, three times, in thirty minutes. That's how I broke it down in my head; that's how I made it manageable.

For the moment, I counted myself lucky to be riding Herbie's board. It felt to me like there was some good karma in it. Herbie was a bit of an innovator on the longboarding circuit; he helped to move the sport away from the slow, heavy boards they used to ride when my father was younger to a lighter, more modern design. And it wasn't just the weight of the board; it was what he did with it. Herbie's board even had a square nose; that was like his trademark; he could control his board and spin it around in a helicopter-type move, like what you'd expect to see on a shortboard. In this way, and in a bunch of other ways, Herbie was really revolutionary in his approach. He was one of those Huntington Beach guys we used to hear so much about as kids, and growing up, we all looked up to him, tried to copy him.

First couple heats, I tore it up on Herbie's nine-footer. I was really feeling it. My thing was to ride without a leash, which I thought was a great way to psyche out the competition. Wasn't just me, a lot of guys didn't like to use a leash, but I liked how it put it out there that you know you're not falling. You ride without a leash, it's another way to get an edge. It's not about showing off so much as showing confidence.

I started off so strong the event organizers actually pulled me over in one of the first heats to measure my board. They'd seen some of the moves I was pulling, some of the turns I was making, they figured it had to be less than nine feet, so the other surfers picked up on this and it gave me a whole other kind of edge. It set me apart. Already these guys knew who I was, but not because of my surfing; they knew who I was because of Doc, because of how we lived. I'd had some decent showings as a shortboarder, but I don't think that was relevant here. I guess I had a certain credibility, but not the sort that would have earned me any respect in a longboard event. It was more like, *Oh, you're a Paskowitz? Well, then, I won't kick your ass for spilling that drink on me.* Or, *Your dad's got class. He's a cool dude. He's surfed with legends, so maybe I won't drop in on you.*

Anyway, I was in my element, and I surfed my way into the final heat against big names like Corky Carroll, David Nuuhiwa (a Hawaiian surfer who'd won the 1971 U.S. Surfing Championship on a tri-fin shortboard), Dale Dobson (a virtuoso on the longboard, from Oceanside)... and Herbie Fletcher. Herbie took one look at the field and probably decided there was no way he'd let me beat him on his own board, so he came over and told me I'd have to find another ride. Struck me just then (and still!) like a dick move—and a perfect example of an anti-surfing move. It's not like *he* wanted to ride the nine-footer; he just wanted it to sit on the beach, so I couldn't use it against him in the finals.

Can't say I was surprised. Disappointed, maybe, but not really surprised. Herbie had taken a bunch of us younger surfers under his wing. We all used this product of his called Astrodeck, a rubberized traction system he'd developed that had yet to catch on, meant to replace the wax we were all used to. Also, he'd put us in these famous surf movies he used to make, but we'd always be in the background, while he was front and center. He was a selfish, self-centered guy—nice enough, but only when it suited him, and here I guess it didn't suit him.

And so I had to scramble. Wound up borrowing an eleven-foot board from my friend Vaughan Moran—a nothing-special, banana piece of shit that was much harder to maneuver than Herbie's board, than anything else these other guys in the final heat were riding. Still, I wasn't complaining. I was happy to have *something* to ride, happy to just be in the finals, and it turned out I maneuvered the crap out of Vaughan's board, despite the long odds against me. Ripped my way through the finals like you wouldn't believe.

You have to realize, back then I was a lot tinier than I am now. I think I weighed about 160, 165, compared to the 220 or so pounds I carry today. Since I was so light, I could ride the nose of my board and hold a Hang Ten for a lot longer than anyone else. I could turn my big board in a modern-type cut—a much more abrupt, almost violent turn, more like you'd see from a shortboarder, as opposed to the more graceful, more subtle turns you expect from a longboarder. I could hit the lip of the wave with that clunky eleven-footer, and instead of just cruising along in a traditional way I could make all these surprising, aggressive, radical turns. I could even do my own helicopter-type, 360-degree turn, and steal a page from Herbie's playbook, but I'd do it cleaner, tighter, faster, and I'd do it at a critical point in the competition.

And that's just what happened. I ended up winning the whole thing. Earned myself a whopping six hundred bucks—big, big money for me at the time. But even more than the money, I'd earned myself a reputation. Some cred all my own. I'd chased down all these giants like Corky Carroll, Dale Dobson, and David Nuuhiwa, and at the other end I was a longboarder... a *champion* longboarder.

Ended up changing just about everything.

In competitive surfing, as much as you think you're an original and trying to bring something new, we're all doing essentially the same thing: you have some idea what you want to do out there, but you also have to let the waves decide. You have to know where you are in the competition, what kind of scores you're looking to pull, whether you should play it safe or go all out. You have to know what the judges are looking for and how to catch the biggest ride or make the most difficult maneuver at the most critical point of the wave. It also helps if you know who's riding in the heat with you, if you have some sense of their scores to that point, if you know what they're trying to accomplish, so you can set it alongside what you're trying to accomplish and do what you can to come out ahead.

The traditional Hang Ten move? That almost always landed you a big score, because there weren't a whole lot of guys who could pull it off. Whenever you were able to get out onto the nose of the board and wrap your toes over the end, you were greatly rewarded. The degree of difficulty is way up there, but it's also an absolutely gorgeous move. And pulling it off, it's like you're flying. It's like you're perched on the roof of a car, surfing down the freeway.

The guys who can Hang Ten tend to be soulful surfers. It's in them—hey, it has to be, because it's not really something you can teach.

One of my favorite things to do in competition was to catch a wave early on and get up on the nose right away, way outside. Some waves are so steep, so strong, it's just about impossible, but whenever the wave gave me the move I'd take it. I'd actually be looking for it, waiting for it. If I could take off and get out in front and throw a nice little Hang Ten and then get back before the wave crashed... it was like jumping out to an early lead. I'd be ahead of the game and start to feel like I'd accomplished something, and I'd have the scores to show for it.

Another move I always looked for was a 360, also a big crowd pleaser. A lot of guys, they have their own ways of pulling off a 360, but my thing was to catch that early Hang Ten and then step back into a Hang Five, where I'd just have five toes hanging over the nose. From there, I'd get my fin to come up, in such a way that the whole board began to sideslip down off the wave and whip around double-quick.

Weren't a whole lot of longboarders doing 360s when I started out, but that was another great lesson: push the edge one day and the edge pushes back the next. In surfing, as in anything else, you have to keep stretching yourself and challenging the notion of what's possible, what's expected.

◎

That first tournament earned me my first serious sponsor—Gary Propper, who was looking to introduce his own line of surfboards. Gary invited me and Danielle to his beautiful penthouse apartment overlooking the Pacific Coast Highway and Sunset Boulevard, to talk about it over dinner. I'd never been wined and dined before, so it was way cool to be on the receiving end of this kind of attention. One of Gary's ideas was to sign a bunch of up-and-coming longboarders to ride for him, and I guess now that I'd won this Budweiser event I was as up-and-coming as anyone.

He offered to pay me a modest monthly salary, about one

thousand dollars, and to provide me with gear and travel expenses for out-of-town tournaments. Danielle and I went home that night to talk about it—but, really, there wasn't a whole lot to talk about. I called Gary the next day and accepted his offer. The one wrinkle to the deal was he wanted me to go to acting school. He said he saw me as a kind of Latin heartthrob who also happened to surf. Remember, he was also a movie producer and a talent manager, so he believed it made good sense to connect the world of surfing with the world of entertainment. He knew I'd done some modeling, off and on, and said that if I was going to represent his brand, he wanted me to be poised and polished, maybe start doing some commercials, going out on auditions. Any gigs or shoots I'd book as an actor or model, he said, would benefit his surfboard line. With Gary, it was all about marketing and synergy—two concepts that were pretty much lost on me.

Another thing I liked about Gary was he wanted to go out surfing with me. I thought that was cool. A guy like that, he didn't have to prove anything to a kid like me, but I appreciated that he wanted me to know he still had some chops, that he understood what it meant to live for this type of thing. So we spent a day on the beach up at Malibu and I came away inclined to follow his lead. If the guy wanted to pay me to go to acting school, I'd go to acting school.

And so it was agreed. Gary set the whole thing up, arranged for me to attend classes with Stella Adler, the famous Hollywood acting coach. She had a studio on Hollywood Boulevard, and I started making the drive up there a couple times a week. Danielle was working at the time at *Surfer* magazine, so I'd drop her off on the mornings I had class and drive up to Los Angeles. My surf buddies would have given me a ton of shit—*acting classes?*—but I didn't tell anybody. Don't know why, exactly . . . I just didn't. I'd simply disappear for the day, and do my thing in class, and then head back home, hopefully in time to pick up Danielle at the end of her day.

It was a nightmare. For one thing, the traffic just about killed me. I wasn't wired to sit still like that, for so long. Plus, the city freaked me out. I'd get all weird and anxious and tense. I felt like a fish out of water. Literally. I'd get to the studio and race to the bathroom, just to splash some water on my face, to wet my gills. And then, all day long, I'd drink buckets and buckets of water, which meant that by the drive home I'd have to really, really pee. Like all the time. So I ended up keeping all these piss bottles in the car, just so I wouldn't have to get out and go. It was an old habit. Back when we were kids, my father would *never* pull over when one of us had to go. We always had to make good time, and so I felt the same way here; the drive was so draining and wearying, I couldn't see stretching it out any longer, even for the couple minutes it would have taken for me to stretch my legs and pee.

Then I'd pull up to collect Danielle in our Ford Escort, and she'd take one look at the back of the car, filled with all these golden piss-filled bottles, and scrunch up her face in disgust.

I kept up this routine for a couple months, but only in a random way, because Gary also had me entering a bunch of surf contests. The one kept pulling me from the other. After a couple months, I learned not to mind the commute or the hassle of the city, but it took a while to get used to some of the silliness of acting class. A lot of what they had us doing was just bullshit, and it used to bug me big-time that nobody else in that whole place would admit that it was just bullshit. Like I'd have to crawl around onstage and pretend I was a dog. The idea was to teach us not to just *act* like a dog but to actually *be* a dog, so I'd bark and crawl around and roll over on my back. I tried, but I don't think I ever *got* it, not in the way the great Stella Adler intended. I mean, I could bark like a dog, and crawl around on all fours like a dog, but I couldn't lose myself in barking and crawling like a dog and start to think it was real.

During class, Stella Adler would stop by to monitor our progress, but I don't think she ever had anything positive to say about my performances. She was pretty old by this point—in her late eighties—so she wasn't there every day, but when she was she made her presence known. Once, she interrupted me in the middle of a reading and said, "What are you trying to say, young man?"

I thought about this long and hard before responding. This was one of the most respected acting coaches in Hollywood. She'd taught Marlon Brando, Robert De Niro... all these greats. What was I trying to say? Well, whatever it told me to say in the script, for starters. I thought about telling the great Stella Adler just that, but I didn't want to embarrass myself any more than I already had, so instead I just shrugged and said nothing.

The other students in the class, they seemed to get it. Or, at least, they knew to *pretend* to get it. The room was filled with a lot of Midwest farm boys and fresh-off-the-bus wannabe starlets; they knew how the game was played, and there was a whole lot of sucking up and acting like what we were doing really, really mattered, when we all knew it really, really didn't.

At some point, I started going out on auditions. Gary's wife, Ruth Anne, would set them up for me. Somehow, I landed a jeans commercial, where I got to pose with this superhot model, but mostly I'd go out on these big cattle calls that never went anywhere but around and around. Usually, it came down to whether or not I could dance and the answer was always the same: no.

However, I did get one callback—for the movie *Say Anything*, directed by Cameron Crowe. Don't know how I slipped past the casting people to make it to the next round on this one, but they must have liked something about my look and figured they could work around the fact that I couldn't act.

I had a second callback, too, and this time I was supposed to read for Cameron Crowe, which everybody kept telling me was a great accomplishment, just to get that far in the process. Personally,

I couldn't think of it as an accomplishment unless I got something done, but pursuing an acting or modeling career was all about stages, I was learning. It wasn't about getting it done; it was about getting to the next stage, and here the next stage was just a second callback. No big thing—no matter how many people told me otherwise. I was reading for one of the off-leads in the movie, one of John Cusack's friends, but then when this second callback came around on the calendar it conflicted with a contest I was planning to attend in Australia called the Coke Classic. It was the biggest event on the tour that year, so I couldn't really justify missing it, just for the shot at a nothing-special role in a small movie that may or may not have amounted to anything. The casting people couldn't believe I'd pass up such an opportunity—although, like I said, it wasn't much of an opportunity. I mean, it's not like they were asking me to crawl around on all fours and bark like a dog, which at this point I could have done pretty well.

That first win at San Onofre kicked off a heady time for me on the longboarding circuit. Back then, there was no formal tour the way there is today, just a series of events that tended not to bump into each other. I'd go over my calendar with Gary, and we'd pick out the contests that made sense, and he'd make the arrangements. After a while, I started riding Hobie boards for Danielle's father, too, so I had access to the best equipment, the best gear. Any surfer just starting out, his biggest concern is to cover his expenses, so here I was good to go. The high-end surfboards were so ridiculously expensive, I could have never afforded them on my own, but if I meant to compete at the highest level I needed to have a quiver of surfboards at the ready, at all times. I needed to have the right board for the right break, just like all these big-time guys.

It was during this time, riding for Hobie, that I received the best compliment of my career—from no less an icon than Dale Velzy, probably the most influential, most creative shaper in surfing. I'd looked up to him from the time I realized who he was and what he did; he came up to me after an event and said, "Man, you've got great hands."

Just about blew me away. What Dale meant by that was that there was a kind of grace to the way I rode. It's what you strive for on a longboard, to be like Baryshnikov, like an artist. You want what you're doing to come across more like water ballet than break dancing, which is more of a shortboard ideal, and it starts with your hands. A lot of times, a guy might be technically proficient and do everything right, but there'll be nothing artful about the way he rides. There'll be no poetry it. So hearing a comment like that from a guy like Dale Velzy really had me flying.

Jonathan, too, started having some decent success riding longboards. We traveled to a lot of the same events. For a while, he was riding for Herbie Fletcher, who was a very entrepreneurial guy. He could be a selfish dick, but from everything I heard he was good to Jonathan; he took care of his team, and Jonathan did well with him; we even went head-to-head with each other in the finals of another Budweiser event in California, one of the first national events on a tour that was just getting off the ground.

I didn't mind losing to Jonathan.

Meanwhile, things were hot and heavy between me and Danielle. We were together all the time. We found a way for her to travel with me to most of my out-of-town events, so that was a great perk. She even came with me to that Coke Classic event in Manly, Australia—a suburb of Sydney. We worked it out so we took the per diem money that was meant to cover my hotel and crashed with friends instead; then we used the cash to take some of the bite out of Danielle's airline ticket.

We stayed with my good buddy Ian Reeder, a free-spirited New

Zealander I met on the beach a couple years earlier. (We've been mates ever since.)

One thing you need to know about surfing in Australia: it's big. Like Super Bowl big. For the Coke Classic, the beach was packed with spectators—over one hundred thousand, by some estimates. There were helicopters hovering above the break, for aerial coverage of the event, and it was broadcast live, all across the country. Front-page news, and all that. Even high school surfing makes the news over there; it's a completely different vibe, and you feel it the moment you step off the plane. Everywhere you turn for a world-class competition like the Coke Classic you're bombarded with billboards and promotions and headlines announcing the event, and it's easy to get caught up in the fuss. It's easy to feel like a celebrity. It was great, actually, unlike anything I'd ever experienced.

And then to find myself surfing in the final heat with the great Skip Frye and a local surfer named Andrew McKinnon, and Chris Slickenmayer, another famous shaper... well, it didn't get any better than that.

Now, to be on the outside in a final heat with Skip Frye is to be in the presence of a true champion, a true gentleman. And a true craftsman. Skip and Doc were great pals from the San Diego area; I'd known Skip my whole life, just about, and I always loved watching him surf. Talk about grace: the man fairly floated out there, like a pelican gliding over the waves. He made it look effortless, with his arms spread beautifully at his sides, like he was getting ready to take flight, but at the same time he'd carve these elegantly aggressive turns and really push the limits of what you thought was possible on a longboard. He was something to see, really—and here I was, up as close as could be.

The way it worked for this contest, best I remember, was that there were only the four of us in the finals. The heat ran forty-five minutes, longer than I was used to, and there were subtle gradations in the scoring—meaning you could go out to five-tenths of a point and score a 7.5 or an 8.5 on a ride, instead of just a straight 7 or 8. This tended to make for a tighter leaderboard, which I guess was the idea, to build up the excitement for the fans.

Oh, and about that leaderboard...it was much more obvious who was winning and losing in such a big-time event. Back home, there'd usually be a scorer's table, and the results would be tabulated by hand, and then some serious-seeming people would pass a score sheet around and eventually someone would announce the results. (It could take a while!) Here in Australia, it was almost instantaneous, which it had to be when you had one hundred thousand people waiting to find out what was what. Doesn't seem like such a big deal now, because these days everything's done by computer and the scores appear immediately on a jumbo scoreboard, but at the time it was all new to me. Australia was the first time I ever competed that I knew where I stood before the event was finished, because they kept announcing the scores over a public-address system, and posting them for all to see.

Okay, so here's an *anti-*, anti-surfing move—and I share it here as a kind of antidote to the way Herbie Fletcher pulled his nine-foot board out from under me.

I'll set the scene: I was out there with Skip Frye, just the two of us, waiting for a wave. I was in probably the best shape of my life, wearing tight pink shorts, riding a pink board. (Don't know why, but pink was my color that year. That's what Hobie had me pushing, only we called it punk rock coral, which made all the difference.) Time was running out. Up until this point, it had been a very small day, with mostly waist-high waves. All four finalists were tallying similar scores in the 4.5–5.5 range.

Nothing major. Nothing to set any one of us apart.

And yet even though the waves were kind of ho-hum, it was a

spectacular day. Not a cloud in the sky, which I guess was part of the problem, far as the waves were considered. There was no real breeze, nothing to kick up the current and give us something to ride. But the crowds were great, the energy off the charts, and now here we were, hoping we'd get to catch at least one more wave before the final horn.

Just then, Skip and I spotted the wave of the day rolling towards us. We both knew this wave could make or break our tournament. Wasn't one of those waist-high jobs, looked like it might even break over our heads, so I whipped my board around and started to go for it. As I did, I locked eyes with Skip. We were only a couple feet apart.

He just looked at me and said, "Take it easy, Iz. You got this."

I couldn't believe it—and yet, at the same time, I could. Skip Frye didn't try to take the wave from me. He just gave it to me. He didn't have to, but he did. It was a beautiful, beautiful thing. He didn't even try to go the other way, alongside. It would have been nothing for the two of us to split the wave; it was big enough for both of us. But he just waved me on, told me to go for it, like a true gentleman surfer.

And it ended up costing him. There were only a few minutes left in the competition, and there wasn't another wave like it the rest of the heat, so I ended up destroying this one wave and putting up a sick score—a 10, double what we'd all been posting. (My one and only perfect score!) And even as I rode that wave to the championship, I thought what it meant for a guy like Skip Frye to just hand me the title. Also, what it meant a couple years earlier, when Herbie Fletcher took back his board. Skip had had his day in the sun, and he wanted me to have mine; that's all. He was just that cool. It made him happier than if he'd won the thing himself, just to see me happy, and I've made it a special point to give that wave back to other surfers over the years. A bunch of times. Not to balance things out, but because I want to be more like Skip Frye than Herbie Fletcher.

Once, I was head-to-head at a world championship event in Haleiwa with Rusty Keaulana, the son of Doc's old pal Buffalo Keaulana, a classic big-wave surfer. I was on the inside when the wave of *that* day came in, and all I needed to do was stand up and ride it in. I was in position. But I went the other way so Rusty could take it, because I'd learned to be just as happy to see my friends win as to win myself. (Rusty wound up winning that tournament, pretty much on the back of that one wave.) That's how I felt whenever my brother Jonathan beat me, head-to-head. Really and truly. That's how Skip felt, seeing me win. Really and truly. And that's how I felt here, really and truly, because I wasn't about to jeopardize a lifelong friendship, hanging on the beach at Makaha together since we were toddlers, just to win a fucking contest.

Skip Frye taught me that—but, I suppose, I knew it all along.

◎

The footnote to that Coke Classic title was that I won a bunch of money—about three thousand dollars, more than I'd ever won in a single contest. There was an awards ceremony on the beach, after which I grabbed Danielle by the hand and made for the nearest bank, so I could cash the check and blow all the money.

The great thing about Australia and surfing was all the bank tellers knew who I was. I didn't need any ID. I just burst through the doors to cheers and shouts of, "Good on ya, mate!" and cashed my check like it was nothing at all. Spent about fifteen hundred dollars on a sexy cocktail dress for Danielle. She wasn't too happy with me for making her buy it, but there was a fancy ball that night for the winners and I wanted us to be stylin'. I found a slick little something to go with my short, Elvis 'do and the rockabilly look I was wearing back then. Then I rented us a limo, to take us to the hotel where they were holding the fancy ball that night.

We turned some heads when we hit that party. Better believe it. It was killer. We drank and danced and drank some more. Got back to Ian's place around two o'clock in the morning, and had another couple nightcaps with him, but after all that drinking and dancing and merrymaking I couldn't sleep. Plus, I think I drank myself sick, because I ended up in Ian's bathroom, hugging the toilet. I might have even nodded off, my head at the base of the bowl. I was in sorry shape, but at one point I opened my eyes and saw a conga line of roly-poly pill bugs, marching to a hole in the baseboard behind the toilet. It was like a scene out of a cartoon. Struck me just then as the most absurd thing.

Don't know what those bugs were really called, but the folks Down Under called them slaters. You know the bugs I'm talking about? You touch them, ever so slightly, they scrunch up into a little tiny ball. Back home, we called them roly-poly whatevers. Down Under, they were slaters. I'd seen them around, but never this many, marching in formation.

Somehow, in the middle of a full-on drunk, completely fucking blotto, I found a marking pen and crawled all the way to the back of the bowl, to the tiny mouse hole–type opening in the wall where the line seemed to form. Then I drew a proper door around the opening, and a sign above the hole that said: "Welcome all slaters!"

Then I passed out and forgot all about it.

It wasn't until some months later that Ian found my drawing. By that point, Danielle and I were back home in California. Ian had dropped something behind the bowl and got down on all fours to fetch it, and there in front of him was this cartoon mouse hole with my welcome message on it, and he could only smile to himself and wonder what the fuck I was doing down there in the first place.

10

Hitched

It was inevitable we'd get married. Not "inevitable" as in "unavoidable" or "predictable," but it was clear early on there was a course we were meant to chart. We were like a force of nature. From the moment Danielle picked me up at the airport in her friend's limo, really, I knew we'd be together always, always, always.

Took her parents a while to come around. Her father and I were cool, but Danielle's mom wasn't too happy with me after I was taken from her house in handcuffs; don't think she was too happy with me *before* that, actually, but the handcuffs didn't help. She was cool with me eventually, though. I suppose she would have liked it if I had a better job, or better prospects, or a better education—hell, even just a piece of a shred of a tiny little fragment of an education would have helped. My future mother-in-law, Sharon, was a strong woman, but she could tell Danielle and I were a team, so she gave us her blessing. She even agreed to pay for our wedding.

My father was a little disappointed that Danielle wasn't Jewish.

Oh, my parents loved Danielle, and they loved the Brawners, but Doc would have liked it if I had kept the faith on this one score at least. After all, he'd done his part to repopulate the tribe, with eight Mexican-Jewish sons, but it was probably his secret wish that each of us would have eight Jewish sons as well, and here I was, first to the altar, with a shiksa bride—just like him! He came around, though. Guess he figured he had eight more kids to marry off and that one of them would fall for a card-carrying Jew and produce a proper Jewish grandchild. (He's still waiting!)

Danielle wanted a traditional Catholic wedding, which was okay by me, but I did go to the trouble of seeking out a rabbi to perform at least a part of the ceremony—just to balance the scales. I thought we could do it up like one of those cartoon shorts they used to show at the movie theaters, before the main feature. We could say a couple prayers, maybe stomp on a glass, and then move on to the big show. Danielle was totally up for it, so we made some phone calls, started asking around. There were a bunch of rent-a-rabbis in Southern California, natch, but you'd be surprised how few of them wanted to share the stage at a Catholic wedding, especially in this *off-to-the-side* way; they all wanted to run the show.

Also, money was an issue. Danielle's mom, Sharon, was footing the bill, but I'd already been in and out of her doghouse too many times to ask her to pay for a rabbi, so Danielle and I were on our own for this part. And so we looked long and hard for a rabbi who'd take the gig on our terms. Finally found a guy in San Diego who agreed to meet with us for lunch at a deli, to discuss our plans. It was understood that Danielle and I would be paying for lunch— anyway, it was understood by the rabbi, who showed up and ate like a pig. He ordered a ton of food, plus a container of chopped liver to go. This last is what's known as chutzpah, a term Danielle would forever after associate with this gluttonous rabbi, who finally told us his fee for the ceremony was twenty-five hundred dollars. It seemed a little high, especially since the priest who was actually marrying us was only charging a couple hundred bucks, so we thanked the rabbi for his time and for doing his part to give Jews a bad name and sent him and his chopped liver on their way.

That was it for me on the rabbi front. Figured I'd given it my best shot.

Danielle and her mom found a beautiful church for the ceremony—St. Edward's, overlooking the ocean in Dana Point—and then I realized our wedding date conflicted with a contest I meant to enter off the San Clemente Pier. I was back and forth on whether or not I should compete. Wouldn't go so far as to say I was torn, but I was starting to fray. Why? Well, I was in the middle of a great run and I needed the points for my standing on the national circuit. Also, I always looked to compete in events around town, to make the most of my home field advantage, so I checked in with the tournament organizers to see if I could pinpoint the exact time of my heat and maybe find a way to towel off and still make it to the church on time.

Danielle wasn't too happy about this, and she said as much. I'm paraphrasing here, but I believe what she said was, "If you're even a minute late, I will fucking kill you." Or words to that effect. In truth, she only gave me a little bit of hell, probably because a part of her thought it was way cool, to be marrying this rad surfer dude who had to catch a couple meaningful waves before tying the knot. Probably, I should have had the sense to let them go and let the day just be about my beautiful bride and our beautiful wedding and our beautiful future together, but nobody ever accused me of having a whole lot of sense.

I had it all worked out—in my head, at least—and the night before the wedding we gathered at St. Edward's for a rehearsal, and while Danielle and her bridesmaids were figuring where to stand I was huddled with my groomsmen, going over last-minute plans for getting from the beach to the church the next morning. We ran through all these different scenarios, to make sure we had everything covered. The wedding was called for ten o'clock; my heat was set to go off at six thirty; wasn't a whole lot that could go wrong, really. A couple of the guys were also planning to surf, including my brothers Jonathan and Adam, but there were enough non-surfers in the group to cheer us on, help ferry us back and forth, and make sure we had everything we needed.

At one point during the rehearsal, I caught sight of my dad, standing around in a pair of worn-out shoes I recognized from when I still lived in the camper; the soles were coming apart from the tops, and he'd put caulking around the seams to hold the whole mess together. I took him aside and told him he couldn't wear those shoes to my wedding rehearsal, and then I slipped out of my own shoes and handed them to him.

I said, "Wear these."

It seemed way more appropriate for the rad surfer dude groom to be barefoot than for the father of the rad surfer dude groom to be walking around in a pair of shabby kicks that wouldn't have even made the cut at the Salvation Army.

Oh, and speaking of shoes, I'd gone out and bought all my groomsmen a pair of creepers to wear at the wedding. Remember creepers? They were a big punk-rockabilly craze in the late 1980s, so I bought a bunch from a British company called Nana for the wedding party. Mine were black with a leopard print—totally smokin'. My idea was we'd all line up for our groomsmen photo and look so spectacularly handsome in our custom creepers we'd have to hire extra security just to keep the ladies out of the shot.

◎

The wedding was shaping up to be a big, big deal. It was certainly a big deal in the Paskowitz family; we could fill a room and call it a party all on our own. Plus, we'd invited all these legends of surfing—friends of ours, friends of Doc, friends of my father-in-law. Tubesteak and the rest of the Tracys would be there, of course. Gary Propper, Hobie Alter, J Riddle, David Nuuhiwa, the Patterson brothers, Raymond and Ronald... just a sick, sick lineup of all-time great surfers. I was the first among my siblings to get hitched, so most of my aunts and uncles and cousins were there, on both sides, plus Danielle's large family... in all, over two hundred people, which made it like a highlight of the San Clemente–area social calendar. Folks were coming in from as far away as New York and Hawaii, so we were all pretty psyched.

Scott Ruedy was my best man, and my brothers were groomsmen, along with Danielle's brother, Damian. Don't think all the Paskowitz boys came to the pier on the morning of the wedding, but Abraham was definitely there, and Jonathan and Adam were competing, so they were there, too. The guys who weren't surfing were all dressed for the wedding in their monkey suits, looking snappy and out of place for six o'clock in the morning on the beach. My buddy Matt Archbold, one of the greatest shortboarders in the world, was there and for some reason he was dressed out in an embroidered Mexican poncho. Other guys were wearing smoking jackets, or fancy Hawaiian shirts, or whatever their wives or girlfriends had told them was appropriate. We must have made an odd picture, in our various styles of formal dress, still in our various stages of early morning sleep, descending on this scene for my preliminary heat, but to our thinking it was all part of the celebration. It all tied in.

Understand, I wasn't just surfing to go through the motions, or selfishly avoiding my husbandly responsibilities; this wasn't some last act of rebellion or a swan song to my misspent youth. No way. The competition was important. It was a big-time, Hobie-sponsored event—a sanctioned leg on the national tour, which was just getting started. But at the same time it wasn't *just* about needing the points to add to my yearlong total and securing my spot in the standings; I was also in it to win it. There was serious prize money involved—twelve hundred dollars as I recall, which I'd recently learned would have almost bought me half a rabbi. And I'd be going up against a strong, competitive field. I'd been in a zone for a good long while, and my goal was to keep a good thing going.

The waves were on the small side, but this was more of a problem for the other surfers than it was for me. I knew this sweet spot on the north side of the pier, where you're almost hugging the barnacles, that would put me in a prime position to catch the best of the swell as it came in. I was on my pink board, on the inside, ready to ride my way into the finals. And that's just how it happened. I caught my few waves and when the horn blew the guys came down to the shorebreak to meet me. A couple of them—already drunk, probably; or, possibly, still drunk from the night before—threw me on their shoulders and walked me out of the water, while I was still wearing my wet suit. Someone brought champagne, so we started passing the bottle around. I didn't even stop at the scorer's table to see if I'd made it through, because I knew I'd nailed it. Wasn't that I was cocky or superconfident, just that I knew no one was catching the same waves as me.

At this point, it was a little after eight o'clock; the wedding was in less than two hours. We were only a couple miles from the church, but we had to swing by Abraham's place so I could shower and change into my tuxedo. The other guys all disappeared into their own rides, while I hopped into Abraham's run-down BMW. It was such a crap set of wheels, we couldn't help but laugh. When we were younger, fresh out of the camper and scraping to buy our first used cars, we took a kind of youthful pride in what we were driving—throwaway American muscle cars, mostly, but we took such good and loving care of these vehicles. (My '65 Impala is a perfect example.)

But at some point, with Abraham, he flipped a switch, to where it was more about the brand than the ride itself. He'd always wanted a BMW, and this piece-of-shit was what he could afford; part of me worried if the thing could even get us to the church.

Happily, the car did its job. It was me who nearly didn't make it there. First we had to have a couple beers. After all, this was my wedding day, right? There was a lot to toast…and, it turned out, Abraham had laid in a cooler's worth of Pacifico. I showered between beers, jumped into my tuxedo, got started on my tie. My hair was still wet as I dressed, so my collar was soaked through, but I was making good time—that is, until I drained one Pacifico and popped another cold one. And another. Somehow, the time got away from us. Don't know what it was or how it happened, but all of a sudden it was almost ten o'clock—"go" time. Guess I was so distracted by all this different crap I had to wear, all these component parts to my tuxedo, making sure I didn't forget anything…I just messed up. Spent a bunch of minutes in there looking for Danielle's ring.

Ah, the ring…a head-turning, no-karat, no-grade, no-clarity stunner I picked up at Target for $180. The setting had four micro-tiny stones that had a beautiful dark color to them, which was about what I could afford, but Danielle didn't care. She only cared that I could haul ass to the church in time to put the damn thing on her finger.

Meanwhile, over at the church, people were starting to freak, wondering where we were. Scott Ruedy had gone back directly from the beach, along with Danielle's brother, Damian, and the rest of my brothers, and they reported that I'd finished with my preliminary heat and was on my way, so the woman who was coordinating everything decided we were on schedule. The rest of the bridal party was all there, so they started up the music, the procession… everything. Folks were walking down the aisle, and soon it was the bride's turn to walk down the aisle, and they just kept on going. It was like a runaway train. The wedding was underway, with or without the groom.

This all came to me later; all I knew at the time was we were running late. Not too, too late, but late enough. Apparently, Danielle was starting her walk down the aisle, looking mighty pissed. Mad as she was, though, she didn't have a single doubt about my intentions. She knew I didn't have cold feet; she knew I wasn't bailing. She just knew I'd fucked up, was all.

As I raced into the church, I glanced down and saw my father's shabby, caulked-together shoes, same pair from the night before. They were kind of tucked beneath the bushes by the entrance— tucked neatly, the way you'd rest a pair of slippers at the edge of your bed—and I had to laugh. Also, I had to wonder: Did he wear them back to the church this morning and suddenly remember they were all wrong? Was he barefoot? Did he leave them here last night? It looked like that scene in *The Wizard of Oz* where Dorothy's house has fallen on the Wicked Witch of the East and all you can see are her ruby-red slippers, only here it was like St. Edward's had fallen on poor Doc as he arrived to watch the first of his Jewish sons get married . . . in a Catholic ceremony.

Don't know why, but it struck me as just about the funniest thing.

Soon as I walked in the front door of the church, I was hurried down the aisle. Danielle was halfway down by that point, figuring out that I was not yet in position. I watched the video afterwards, and she looked so stunning, so pissed, so bewildered; her beautiful doe eyes were frantically scanning the room, trying to figure out what was happening, and in the moment I remember trying to avoid eye contact with her, because I knew she'd rip into me. I shot right past her on my way down the aisle and I tried to flash a look of apology, but she gave me the cold shoulder as I passed.

Other than the mess I made by running late, the wedding went off without a hitch. Before it was over, Danielle was all smiles and it was all good between us. And the reception, up the bluff at the Chart House, was kick-ass. Lots of good food, good music, good beer. One of the highlights of the reception was doing whiskey shots with Doc, pulled from a hundred-year-old bottle he'd been saving for a special occasion. He never drank, other than a cup of wine on the Sabbath, but some patient had given him the bottle years ago as payment for a visit or a consult back in Hawaii, and this seemed like a good time to pop it open.

I was a little hungover for the finals the next morning. Danielle, the new Mrs. Paskowitz, came down to the beach, and by this point she was fine with my wedding day screwup; by this time it had already become a story we'd tell over and over...someday, to our grandchildren. Guess she realized this was about what she could expect, marrying a professional surf bum, and that I'd just been holding up my end of the deal.

Jonathan ended up out-surfing me in the finals. I took second. And, as always, I was happy for him; I'd kicked butt in the preliminaries and he'd kicked butt in the finals, and that's how it shook out. I left the beach thinking, *Good for him.* And, *Good for me.* And, *Good for all of us.*

And it was.

◎

It's not like Danielle and I sat down and planned our lives together. Wasn't our style. We both wanted kids—sooner rather than later, I guess—but Israelah snuck up on us. I'll never forget the look of stunned joy on Danielle's face when she told me she was pregnant, but I imagine it was a lot like the look of stunned joy on my face as it sunk in.

Most people, seeing how we were living and with a kid on the way, would think we might have been stressed about money, but that never entered into my thinking. Might have kept Danielle awake a time or two, but not me. The way I grew up left me thinking kids didn't change a thing, in terms of your bottom line. What did it cost to have a kid, really? Just a package of diapers, every couple days. That's it. Ten bucks a day. To me, that was within our means, so I took a *no worries* approach.

Besides, I was at the height of my career, surfing out of my mind. I knew it wouldn't last forever, success at that level, so we couldn't count on it going forward, but I also knew I'd be crazy not to make the most of it. There was one stretch in there when I won eleven major championships in less than two years, including three in a row—at Trestles, at the Rabbit Kekai in Boca Barranca, Costa Rica, and at the Coke event in Australia I wrote about earlier. Wasn't a lot of prize money to be had on the circuit, but the endorsement money was rich enough to fool me into thinking I was making a living. For a couple years, I pulled in thirty thousand dollars or so, between winnings and sponsorship fees. One year, I even topped fifty thousand. That was the year I did a series of ads for Nike, with Bo Jackson, Andre Agassi, and Michael Jordan, so I was getting a ton of attention. When I threw it all together with the decent money I was still making up in Newport Beach cleaning boats, it was enough to keep us in surfboards and diapers.

Danielle had her gig at *Surfer* magazine, too, and it came with benefits, so we had the pregnancy and pediatrician covered. In most respects, we were better off than my folks had been when they started spitting out kids—even with my father's medical degree.

We had a funky setup on a ranch owned by Danielle's parents, high up in the hills of San Juan Capistrano. Wasn't much of a ranch, really. Back then, it was more like a big open field, pretty damn far from civilization. It was way, way up off the main road, and you had to take a twisty, unpaved access road to get to it. It was so rustic we didn't even have electricity when we started living there, had to operate everything off a hand-crank generator. We had the idea that we'd be like pioneers, which worked out great because Danielle was becoming more and more interested in horses, so there was plenty of room for her to ride and roam.

Turned out to be too much of a hassle, though. We'd come back to the property a bit later on, but at that stage of our lives it was too much, or not enough. It was one thing, getting up and down that hill under normal circumstances, but with a baby the twenty minutes it took each way left us feeling pretty isolated, like we needed to be a little closer to civilization, and a steady supply of hot water.

This was never more obvious than the moment Danielle's water broke. Racing down that hill to Mission Hospital took forever; on those hairpin turns it felt like I was about to drive us straight off the bluffs. Probably, that was the first we talked about having to find another place to live. But first things first, we had a baby to deliver, and by the time we got to the hospital there were a whole bunch of Paskowitzes and Brawners who'd arrived ahead of us. This was the first legit grandchild on both sides, so everyone dropped what they were doing to get in on it. ("Legit" because, technically, Jonathan's son was the first of his generation on the Paskowitz side, but Jonathan never really copped to being the boy's father.) At one point, there were about fifty friends and family members gathered at the hospital, waiting on this kid's arrival, so it was a grand welcome... until the nurse had to chase everyone out.

Don't remember too much about the actual delivery except that Danielle was pushing and pushing. For six hours, she pushed. I wasn't much use to Danielle, I don't think, but she hung in there. We didn't want to know the sex of the baby beforehand, but I knew it'd be a boy. Deep down, I knew. We were Paskowitzes, after all.

And it wasn't just me. Danielle seemed resigned to it, too, which explains the absolute bombshell rush of surprise that washed over each of us when the baby finally came. I'd thought about this moment about a million times, and it never occurred to me we'd have a girl.

Not once.

I was so happy for Danielle. She really, really wanted a little girl, and I think she'd been terrified to say as much during the pregnancy; mostly, I just don't think it occurred to her it would work out that way. But it did. Thrillingly, amazingly, wonderfully ... it did. I was blown away with how pumped I was for Danielle. It's like I'd given her this miraculous gift, only I'd get to share in that gift, too. Every day, I'd get to share in it.

I was totally stoked myself. I'd never really given much thought to having a girl or a boy. In my family, growing up, there was all this great weight and significance attached to the idea of having a son, but I never bought into any of that. Really, it was a lot of crap. To me, the weight and significance came with having a beautiful, healthy child. That's all. A girl or a boy, it didn't matter—and I think it only mattered to Danielle in an icing-on-the-cake sort of way. But to me, little Israelah was the whole damn bakery.

I must say, I was a great dad. And a full partner in parenting. Don't mean to blow smoke up my own butt, but I was very involved, very present. It helped that Israelah arrived in November, as the pro circuit slowed for the winter, so I was around a whole lot, but I was really into taking care of her and taking part. Danielle was breast-feeding, so there was a lot I *couldn't* do, but she pumped enough for a nighttime bottle and I always took the middle-of-the-night shift. All night long, I'd just stare and stare at this beautiful little girl—*my* beautiful little girl. The bottle would be long gone, and Israelah would be fast asleep, but I'd just sit with her in my lap, for hours and hours.

After six weeks, Danielle went back to work. We needed the money, but even more than that, Danielle had it in her head she'd be a working mom. That was the idea, the ideal, so we moved into a small, two-bedroom apartment right above Danielle's folks and I started spending most of my time running around with the baby. Danielle and I drove a Ford Escort in those days, and I'd be back and forth to all these different surf shops and warehouses around town, and it was always a trick to try to puzzle a bunch of surf-boards into that tiny car. The only way to do it, really, was to slide them directly over Israelah's infant seat, so I'd pull up someplace and a buddy would help me unload my boards and all of a sudden I'd hear, "Hey, there's a baby under here!"

First couple times, I pretended to be surprised.

Most days, we'd swing by the magazine for lunch, so Danielle could breast-feed Israeleh, and I remember stepping outside myself during these moments and wondering what I'd done to deserve such as this. I couldn't remember when I'd ever been happier.

Soon, we started calling the baby Elah, and the name seemed to fit. She was such a perfect, perfect baby. Never made a peep, other than to let us know she wouldn't have minded a little something to eat, or maybe a diaper change. We even hauled her to Australia, for another tournament the year after my Coke Classic win, and I re-member sitting down on the plane next to a couple of big old burly Aussies who didn't look too happy at the prospect of spending the next fourteen, fifteen hours next to a crying baby, but she was amaz-ing. Didn't cry once, the whole way.

By the time we got back home to California, we realized Danielle was pregnant again, so the loose plan was to keep doing what we were doing. By our math, Elah would be a big sister at about sixteen months, and she hadn't given us any trouble, so we thought things would continue to be fine and easy and wonderful. We thought all our babies would pretty much take care of themselves.

(Yeah, right.)

Danielle worked straight through her second pregnancy, while I did most of the hands-on heavy lifting with Elah during the day, whenever I was in town; when I wasn't, Danielle's folks would pitch in, so they were a big help. For a while, we lived in the apartment at the back of their house; for another while, we lived just down the street; always, they were nearby and happy to pitch in.

I made sure to be home for the weeks surrounding our due date, of course, and when Danielle finally went into labor I talked her into a little detour. I remembered that she'd been at it for hours with Elah, so I assumed we were in for another long haul and suggested we stop at the beach. We'd already parked Elah with her grand-parents, so I pointed the car towards San O and figured I'd catch a couple waves before Danielle's contractions got bigger and closer together.

Full disclosure: I only half-expected Danielle to join me in think-ing this was a good idea, but I thought it was worth a shot. And do you know what? She was completely down with it. We both thought the sound of the surf and the smell of the sea would clear her mind for the ordeal ahead, so while she walked I grabbed my board and paddled out. I left Danielle by the shack on the beach, pacing back and forth, told her I'd keep checking in with her. It helped that she had a killer whistle—one of those loud, piercing trills that come in handy when you're calling farm animals or expectant surf bum fa-thers who might have drifted from their posts. I was out there a half hour or so when I noticed Danielle waving me in—a little frantically, if you must know—and by the time I got to her she was doubled up in pain.

And she was pissed. All of a sudden, I was a selfish fucking idiot, for wanting to surf while Danielle was in full-blown labor—and I guess she had a point. (Forget that she'd been into it; it was my fault for bringing it up.) So I got her in the backseat of the car and started hauling ass to Mission Hospital. Earned ourselves a police escort on the way, and once we got to the emergency room and they wheeled her inside, Isaiah made an appearance just a short while later. Elah had taken her sweet time, but her brother arrived in less than twenty minutes.

Here again, we hadn't found out about the gender, so when the doctor held the baby out and I peeked between his legs I was probably the happiest father in all of California. To see that little tally-whacker... man, I don't think I'd ever been that excited. Felt like my head was about to burst. My heart, too.

Isaiah was an absolutely beautiful baby. He was big and thick, with almond eyes and a full head of hair. Looked a lot like me in my baby pictures, only a little on the chubby side, which should have tipped us off to the kind of giant he'd become. He didn't have the same easy disposition as his big sister, didn't sleep as long or as soundly, but he was easy enough; it's just that they were on completely different schedules, so it wasn't long before Danielle and I were completely exhausted.

This time around, Danielle was in no rush to get back to work, which was just as well because Isaiah was born about a month ahead of the tournament season, so as soon as the first rush of fascination over the new baby wore off I was back at it. In between tournaments, I was hustling up to Newport Beach, to work with John on his boats, because Danielle and I knew money was going to be tight.

Elah was psyched to have a baby brother. She called him Prince, which she got from watching *Bambi* over and over. And it wasn't just a name with her; she treated Isaiah's arrival like he was the new prince of our little forest. She had the cutest baby-talk voice—high and gentle and sweet. She'd wake up in the morning and stand herself up in her crib and the first words out of her mouth were always, "Where's Prince?"

It was an amazing time in our lives. Our kids were healthy and happy. I was still ripping on the tour, still squeezing as much money as possible out of a sport that was never really about money, still feeling completely on top of my game. And Danielle was happy to be at home with our beautiful babies.

Life was good.

⊚

Might as well finish up with the last of our childbirth stories, long as I'm on it, before doubling back and telling the rest.

Eli, our third, was a classic surprise. He was what a less enlightened parent would call a mistake, but "surprise" sounds a whole lot better—and, really, it's way more accurate. Gets to the heart of how he arrived, what his arrival meant to our little family. Yeah, "mistake" works, too, but I've made a ton of mistakes in my life that didn't work out like this. *Like this* was a godsend—another blessing to round out the set. But before Eli came along and surprised us, we certainly weren't thinking of having another kid. Elah and Isaiah were about all we could handle. In fact, Isaiah all by himself was about all we could handle, because at about a year he started exhibiting symptoms of autism. We didn't know what it was just yet, only that his behavior was off. Way off. This, too, was a surprise, because up until this time he'd been developmentally on point. Crawled when he was supposed to. Said his first "maa maa, daa daa"–type words when he was supposed to. Made good and appropriate eye contact and seemed as plugged in and engaged as any other toddler—certainly, as plugged in and engaged as his sister had been. He even started walking before his first birthday, which everybody said was a big deal.

With Isaiah, the changes were subtle at first—the kind only a mother would notice. The kind a clueless, head-in-the-clouds father would choose to miss. Danielle was around way more than I was during this period, but even more than that, she was attuned to this type of thing. As a parent, she was superattentive and supervigilant about the health and welfare of our children. Me, I was more about hanging out and having fun with them, so for a couple years I was in complete denial about Isaiah. I didn't see what Danielle was seeing—because, hey, when it came to my kids, they were *just right,* pretty damn perfect, straight out of a fairy tale. Whenever Danielle would get all anxious about some Isaiah behavior or other, I'd remind her that I had been a quiet kid; I'd tell her how there was so much noise and nonsense in our camper household, I became shy and reserved, and that maybe that's what was going on here. Whatever her concerns, I'd explain them away, or tell her she was all wrong.

After a while, it got harder to explain away Isaiah's behavior. He started flapping his arms and doing this screeching-yelling thing he still does, tends to spook people out when they hear it for the first time. All of these little tics and mannerisms and idiosyncrasies started to turn up, but slowly, subtly, softly. They'd get bigger and louder and more pronounced over time, and as they did we'd see less and less of Isaiah. He was in there, somewhere, we felt sure, but however connected and plugged in he'd been as a toddler, however "normal" and by-the-book, it began to slip away, to where even I had to admit that something was terribly, terribly wrong.

We started taking Isaiah to a bunch of doctors. We did MRIs, and EEGs, and all these different tests. One doctor thought Isaiah might have some sort of brain tumor, and we were actually hoping this was the case because it would be something we could fix, so we didn't know how to feel when all those scans checked out clean. Every doctor said something different...until they all started saying the same thing: autism. We heard it like some dreaded diagnosis, because we didn't know what it meant. We didn't know where it came from, or how to handle it, so right away Danielle started doing all this research, trying to learn as much as she could, quick as she could. I went the other way. I shut down. I checked out. I simply refused to accept that there could be something so wrong with my son, my perfect little boy, so I brushed it aside. Danielle was terrified; I was more thrown. Wasn't what I was expecting, not at all, so I took my time processing it, ran from confused to pissed, mystified to sad, and all the way back to confused. Told myself whatever I needed to tell myself to get through my days. And, worst of all, I doubled down on my tournament schedule and started looking for reasons to travel to all these remote beaches, all over the world.

Basically, I shut my eyes and covered my ears and went surfing. Left it to Danielle to hold things together at home. Not exactly the most mature or loving or responsible approach, but all I could do was wish myself away, away, away.

More on my chickenshit response to Isaiah's diagnosis a bit later on; for now, I want to get back to Eli. Poor Danielle had nightmares the whole time she was pregnant with Eli. And she wasn't *just* worried this next kid would be autistic. Everything was on the table: she thought the baby would be deformed or unhealthy in some other way; in one recurring dream, the baby was born with a cleft palate, so she let her mind run. Whatever headline or TV movie-of-the-week she came across, describing some tragedy or other, that's what she'd worry about; it was really tough on her, and I was no help.

The week before Eli was born, I did something stupid that only added to Danielle's anxiety: I gave Isaiah a haircut. This alone wasn't so bad, I'd given him haircuts before, but this time I gave him a Mohawk—I think because he'd pointed to a picture in a magazine and I thought he'd like it. Big mistake. Plus, it was a shitty, home-made, uneven Mohawk. My little guy looked ridiculous, so I gave myself a bad Mohawk to match, and it would have been no big deal except Danielle was all hormonal and she was already worried about the baby, already beside herself about Isaiah, and now every time she looked at her two men we struck her like a still frame out of *One Flew Over the Cuckoo's Nest,* like we belonged in some mental institution. She actually cried a couple times, looking at us, so I felt like I'd really screwed up.

The other stupid thing I did was stop for a burger on the way to the hospital when Danielle went into labor with Eli. It was early in the morning, but we passed a Carl's Jr. and I realized I hadn't eaten, so I pulled into the drive-thru. Danielle was ripshit. And then, when I started wolfing down my burger as I drove, she started to retch from the smell. Clearly, it was a bonehead, piggish move.

Eli popped out in no time at all, just like his brother—and this last development kept the worry alive in Danielle. He was super-healthy, bigger than the other two, and there was nothing wrong with him, he was just a perfect, perfect baby, but all through his first year or two Danielle was completely on top of Eli, hovering over every little milestone. She measured everything against how old Elah had been, and what the books said, and what Isaiah had been doing at that same age.

And she measured my behavior against what it had been for Elah and Isaiah, back when I was fully engaged and present, when things were easy, when life was good, when the specter of autism didn't hang over our house like a dark cloud. And as I set these thoughts to paper, now, I'm realizing that Eli got screwed. In a lot of ways, big and small, the kid caught a raw deal. He didn't do anything but show up and smile, and all around him there was this shit storm of worry and weirdness. Ended up, Eli got gypped. Absolutely, he got gypped. Danielle and I were so focused on Isaiah, on everything it meant to have a young child with autism, that Eli never got the attention he deserved—Elah, too, but at least in her case she got a year or so of our full attention before Isaiah was born. Before I turned tail and hid out on the tour.

Even now that he's a teenager, Eli is always taking a backseat to his brother's needs. And in some ways, he probably always will. There's no avoiding it, but it kills me just the same. It kills me because Eli's such a tough, resilient kid. Smart. Funny. A little wise beyond his years. He's like an old soul, because he sees everything that goes on in our semi-functional family and he weighs in with a kind of uncanny wisdom. He knows all, he sees all . . . but he doesn't get to be a garden-variety kid. Sometimes, I watch him go about his business and it feels to me like he's some intelligent alien being, sent to live among us nut job Paskowitzes to set us straight.

And here's another thing: Eli doesn't surf. It's not that he doesn't surf at all, just that he doesn't care to surf. Don't get me wrong, he knows *how* to surf. He's actually got the stuff to be a strong surfer, if he wanted. But he doesn't want it. He doesn't live to surf, the way his dad, his grandfather, his uncles lived to surf. The way his sister lived to surf, for a time. I'm not such a complete ass that I attach any great significance to this, but I'd be less than honest if I said it didn't break my heart, at least a little. It does. It's like a sweet sadness that follows me around, whenever I stop to think about it, because I used to dream about having a little boy who'd follow me into the water. Same way my father had all *his* little boys following him into the water. Same way a lot of my surfing buddies are now watching their own kids become strong, competitive, champion surfers. It's a selfish take, I know. And it pains me to admit it. But there it is.

These selfish dreams didn't die with Eli, of course. When Isaiah was born, back before he was diagnosed, back before any of us had the first idea what we were facing, I held those same hopes and dreams for him. I'd wanted my firstborn son to know the joy and thrill of surfing, but that was not meant to be, so I guess I probably attached even more importance to this idea when Eli turned up.

But Eli had something else in mind, and I've learned to embrace his hopes and dreams and set my own aside. Lately, he's shown some serious chops as a musician—perhaps drawing on the other sides of his gene pool. He's got my mother's tremendous ear for music, and on Danielle's side he's got my father-in-law's sense of rhythm and timing. Eli's actually a gifted and accomplished drummer, just like his grandfather and his uncle Damian, so I'm grateful that he's got his own blend of silent fuel to drive his days. Doesn't have to be *my* thing. Just has to be *his* thing, right? Took me a while to realize that, but I got to it eventually.

11

Winding Up,
Winding Down

My **move was to hit the road** when things got tough at home. I gave myself an out. I would pretend to lose myself in my "work" and ignore the fact that the only one doing any real work in our household was my beautiful and tolerant and put-upon wife.

I had it good, hiding out on the professional tour, avoiding whatever was going on with Isaiah. Not as good as I thought, not as good as it had been, but far better than I deserved. Danielle was struggling to hold it together, dealing with Isaiah's tantrums and impossible-to-predict behavior, while I was traveling the globe, surfing, having a big old time. And it's not like I was earning a real living: I surfed, partied, drank myself stupid; next day, I'd go at it again; at the end of each road trip, I'd empty my pockets and see I'd spent almost every dollar I'd made, so it's like I was treading water. Doesn't seem fair, looking back, and I wish like hell I could reclaim some of that time and do a better job holding up my end, but that's not how it works. How it works is you learn to live with the choices you made and do what you can to fix the damage you caused by those choices.

Don't know that I'm quite there yet, but I'm still working on it.

For a professional surfer, life on the road can be a wild, heinous ride and I made sure to wring the most out of it. Even when I'd fallen off the lip of the wave and stopped competing at the top, top level, I found ways to justify each trip—like the time I flew to Bordeaux when the kids were little for an Oxbow tournament in the south of France. I had no business going, not really, but I went anyway. The world champion phase of my career had come and gone, but I was still competitive, still high-profile enough to attract a couple sponsors. I was riding my own line of boards at the time, which were shaped by Timmy Patterson, although my main sponsor was Hang Ten; the way it worked was we'd come up with a budget for my travel and expenses and they'd cut me a check. Back then, we had to book our own flights and make our own arrangements on the ground, but the check was meant to cover our costs. Our sponsors wouldn't put us up in high-end, luxury accommodations, but they'd find some middle-of-the-road hotel and use that as the standard; then they'd come up with a reasonable pier diem to cover our food and rental cars and whatever else we'd need for the run of the tournament. Of course, their standards tended to be much higher-end than mine, so I'd stay at crappy hotels, or maybe bunk with a couple buddies, and pocket the difference; then I'd be sure to eat and drink on the cheap, wherever possible. (In France, this meant lots of wine and cheese and canned sardines.) This way, I'd be guaranteed to take home *something*, no matter if the waves were with me or against me.

That's basically what happened in Bordeaux. Wound up making some money, but only in this lame, passive-aggressive way, selling my own damn surfboards and pinching my expenses. Wasn't exactly the point of the whole trip—aw, hell, it was a bottom-scraping move!—but I was keeping up a not-so-proud Paskowitz family tradition, grabbing at what I could.

Here's how that one trip went down: I ran into my buddy Jeff Kramer at the de Gaulle airport and we decided to throw in together. You never knew who you'd see on the way to these tournaments, but you'd always run into someone. Jeff and I spotted each other across the terminal; we were each hauling four or five longboards, which we used to carry in these superheavy boxes. That's how we made our way through the world's airports, lugging these giant coffins in our wake. People used to ask me what was in the box, which really did look like a coffin, and I'd tell them it was my father. I'd say I was flying his body to his favorite beach so he could be buried at sea, and folks would look at me funny and start to back away.

In those days, I didn't have a credit card, so I couldn't rent a car. Don't know that I would have sprung for the expense, but I didn't even have the option, so wherever I went I'd just take buses or walk or bum rides—not so easy with a coffin full of boards. I can still remember dragging those boards through the airport with Jeff, figuring how to get where we were going. For some reason, the airport in Bordeaux was covered with dog shit. It was the filthiest airport I'd ever seen, and we were dragging these boxes through these piles of dog shit, because you couldn't even lift them, so it was just a huge, disgusting pain in the ass—a sick metaphor, I thought, for what my career had become.

Finally, we were lugging our gear across the parking lot when we saw Josh Baxter, another surfer from back home. He was driving a big, minivan-type vehicle. I thought, *Yeah, Team California! Sweet!* We flagged him down, but he didn't seem too keen to help us out. He was worried about his own Timmy board—this superfragile, superlight glass prototype he'd just gotten. Jeff and I offered to throw our boards up top, so they wouldn't damage his precious Timmy. Josh looked for a beat like he was trying to work something out, seeing if he could get all our boards to fit, but then he drove off and left us by the side of the road.

The contest was held in a small town just south of Biarritz. (We ended up hitching some other ride—no thanks to our homey, Josh Baxter.) A bunch of us ended up staying in a little shit-hole motel, had to drag our boards up a couple flights of stairs. I remember thinking this was a helluva long way to travel, just to stay in a shit-hole motel in a tiny seaside village, but as soon as I hit the beach I realized why we were there. The surf was absolutely gigantic. Really, it was a big, big wave—one of the scariest, ugliest waves I'd ever paddled into. The other surfers were all checking it out and they seemed pretty pumped, but to a guy like me, that stage in my career, this was only a little bit exciting; mostly, it was terrifying, because I'd never been a good big-wave rider. I was never comfortable staring down a massive swell, but when I was younger I'd suck it up and go for it; now that I was a bit older, I didn't see the point. In this way, I was cut like my father; I'd push myself to ride those beasts, but I was never too happy about it.

In all, there were about two hundred surfers competing in this one event. A lot of the Oxbow guys had come from Brazil and Japan, but there was a strong American contingent—a lot of Hawaiians, certainly, and a big crew from California. I saw a bunch of guys I knew from San Clemente, which was always great when you were so far from home. Some would treat you like family and do anything for you, and then there were others who'd just leave you by the side of the road; the trick came in knowing the difference before you got out past the break.

The idea was to arrive a couple days ahead to get comfortable with the wave, which worked well with the rest of my agenda, which was to duck out on the hassle and heartache back home. It helped if

I could hang on until the day of the finals and justify my absence, but that wasn't always how it worked out. At this Oxbow tournament, I made it past the first heat, but then I got disqualified, so once I was tossed I looked to sell my boards. I'd already busted two in competition, but then I met some folks who sparked to the two I had left. One, a tremendous big-wave board, I loaned to my buddy Joel Tudor, who ended up winning the championship with it, so that added a little bit of value.

Typically, when I traveled to an event, I wanted to bring along a whole bunch of options. It's good to have a board for all different types of surf; sometimes your alternate board winds up being your go-to board on the day of the tournament, or sometimes you just feel like riding an old-school longboard when the waves are breaking a certain way. You never know how things will go, and you want to be prepared, but once I was out of the competition there was no reason to keep slugging those boards around Europe, so I sold them. For good money, too.

The reason I was disqualified was weirdly ironic. The waves for the second heat were killer—fifteen feet, in spots. I thought I was in position on a kind of peaky wave, thought I could ride it in for a good score. I was on the inside, on the right, and I could have gone either way with it, but just as I was getting ready to commit, Josh Baxter started paddling into the same damn wave, a beat or two ahead of me. I was always mindful of the great Skip Frye and the lesson of his example, so I tried to clear a path for Josh, so he wouldn't be disqualified. Instead, I ended up making a sudden turn the opposite way, in front of Josh, and I ended up disqualified. What happened was Josh had stood up on his board first, so he rightfully had "possession" of the wave; any move I made at that point would have sent me packing. It was a selfless move, and it came from a good place, but it was also a bonehead, panicked move—and just like that, my tournament was done, all because I was trying to give a ride to a guy who couldn't even be bothered to give me a ride back at the airport a couple days earlier.

You travel all that way for a tournament, it's not like you're in a rush to leave. At least, *I* was in no rush to leave, so I tooled around Biarritz for a couple days with Jeff Kramer and another pal of ours from back home, Devon Howard, who'd also been knocked out early. Worked out great for me, because those were the only guys who'd drink wine and eat snails with me; everyone else was so provincial they'd only eat McDonald's. We hit the town a couple nights running, drank ourselves silly, spent a completely wild and crazy night listening to some unreal music and watching a bunch of gorgeous lesbians make out on the dance floor. Spent a bunch of money we didn't really have, which was when I decided to sell my two remaining boards; I sobered up and realized that way I'd at least come out ahead. I mean, it's not like I'd laid out the money for them in the first place; they came from my own line, which my brother Moses was helping me to market, and it didn't cost me all that much to replace them—so, yeah, those babies were gone.

(A word or two on the Izzy-designed boards I was pushing in those days. They were pretty cool, actually. Innovative, too. What I did was take my shortboard experience and marry it to my long-board chops and design a line of high-performance longboards that were unlike anything else on the market. They were ultralight. Plus, they had the shape and details—down to the rails and the design of the fin setup—that were more like you'd find on a modern short-board, so surfers were really diggin' them. They weren't your typi-cal classic longboard noseriders, but back when I weighed only 165 pounds I could noseride anything. We sold a whole bunch of them, made a whole bunch of money, and for a while it looked like we might have stumbled onto a nice sideline business. It was all fine and dandy until Moses ran off to the north shore of Oahu and treated himself to a winter vacation that stretched a little bit longer than our budget, and on top of that he'd left me behind with all the factory bills and very little inventory, so that was the end of the Israel Paskowitz Longboards line.)

Before the money could burn through my pockets on that "lost" trip to France, I loaded up on souvenirs for Danielle and the kids, but that didn't begin to make up for what I cost my family by being away. Or what I cost myself. It was shameful, really. Inexcusable. And yet I'd go through some version of these same motions for a good long while, tournament after tournament, before finally getting my priorities straight and setting things right.

For years after this pointless trip to the south of France I would pass Elah's room and notice the porcelain doll I brought back for her and each time it was like a kick to the stomach. Each time it reminded me of the selfish, gutless, clueless ways I responded to Isaiah's autism, disappearing for weeks at a stretch, chasing meaningless money in meaningless tournaments in what was fast becoming a meaningless career.

I should have been home. Absolutely, I should have been home.

⊚

Meanwhile, Danielle was filling up the spaces where I should have been, doing what she could to keep it together. Isaiah was in free fall. He went from having a perfectly normal vocabulary of forty or fifty words at two years old, to three or four words at the age of three, and it was downhill from there. He started having these wild and violent mood swings. The bigger he got, the harder it became to control him—and he was a big, big boy. Every once in a while, in a moment of calm, he'd point to himself and say, "Want to fix the little boy." *Want to fix the little boy!* Can you imagine, hearing something like that from your kid? Knowing full well that he knew full well that he was somehow broken inside?

It tore me up.

You never knew what would set Isaiah off—or, I should say, *I* never knew what would set him off, because I was never around, and even when I was around my head was someplace else.

There was never enough money. My professional career, which had never brought in a ton of money, was now a charade; I fooled myself into thinking I was earning a living by selling off sponsor surfboards and pocketing my per diem. But I couldn't fool Danielle. She knew the deal. She'd stopped working after Isaiah was born, which meant we were now without health insurance, too. We kept it going for about a year, through COBRA, but after a while the payments were out of reach.

Things were not good.

Without even telling me, Danielle tapped into all these different social service programs. She started getting food stamps and signed up for a WIC card, through a federally funded health and nutrition program for women, infants, and children. It must have been so hard for her, to have to stand in line with all these desperate, hurting people and ask for help. To have her hand out. To have *our* hand out. But she sucked it up and did what she had to do—basically, because I couldn't bring myself to hold up my end.

Just to be clear, it wasn't humiliating to have to ask for help. No, that was the brave and noble and responsible thing for Danielle to do. That's why those programs are in place, to help folks in need, and we were certainly in need. The humiliating part was on me, for putting my beautiful wife in the tough spot of having to go through these motions on her own. For checking out and leaving it to her to sort through how to deal with Isaiah, how to find the time to pay good and positive attention to Elah and Eli, how to put food on the table... and on and on.

I should have been working full-time with John Meade, instead of chasing some elusive wave, or some vague notion I still carried

about what it meant to be a champion surfer. There was a real opportunity with John, but I had to commit to it. I couldn't expect the
job to lead anywhere if I kept taking time off to surf, or to travel to
these out-of-the-way contests. As it was, I wasn't qualified to do
anything more than wash a boat, or polish the brass on some of the
gorgeous yachts John serviced, but I could have learned a related
business. I could have turned it into something more. A lot of John's
guys, they learned to skipper boats, they learned to buy and sell, they
learned their way around the marina.

Summers, when Danielle and I needed extra money, I could always drop in at the family surf camp, which was still going strong,
but that was my dad's gig—and, after a while, my brothers'. They'd
pay me ten, twenty, thirty bucks a day, depending on the enrollment
that week, depending on what they needed me to do, so there was
no real money to be made there, more like a tip than a salary. It's no
wonder Danielle had to swallow her pride—*our* pride!—and sign on
for all these entitlement programs. There's no other way we could
have made it, but what's amazing and crushing and upsetting was
that she never said anything to me about it. She just did what she had
to do, very quietly, with whatever dignity she could bring to it.

Maybe she tried to tell me what was going on and I couldn't hear
it, but it finally came clear to me one day when we went shopping
together. We'd filled our cart with whatever it was we absolutely
needed, and when we reached the checkout counter Danielle pulled
out this WIC card. I'd never seen it before, never heard of the program. I thought at first we'd somehow qualified for a credit card and
Danielle had been holding out on me, but then she explained what it
was and I was mortified, horrified. It had never occurred to me we
were in such bad shape. It should have, but it didn't.

Danielle looked at me like I was a difficult child. "Wake up, Izzy,"
she said.

There's a lot she didn't tell me, back then. A lot I refused to see or hear. For example, I never knew that Danielle put a bolt on the door to Eli's bedroom because she couldn't trust what Isaiah might do if he was alone with the baby. Can you imagine? To be running a household with three little kids and having to worry that one of them might do serious harm to another? To have a husband who'd checked out in such a way that he didn't even know you were getting food stamps?

Oh, man, it's embarrassing how unavailable I was for Danielle and the kids. I was in my own little world. I was in absolute denial, about everything. And I hated that I was so disconnected from what was going on at home, but at the same time I couldn't see how to plug back in. I didn't know how to be around Isaiah, how to be the parent of a child just out of reach. I didn't know how to provide.

Basically, I didn't know shit.

Surfing, that's all I knew.

Luckily, mercifully, a couple things happened to shake me awake about Isaiah. For years, I couldn't deal with the thought that there was something wrong with my beautiful boy. I refused to accept it. I'd see him playing with his Hot Wheel cars in this wildly inappropriate, totally *off* way (for example, lining the cars up on their sides) and think he was going through a phase. Or he'd run off and start flapping his arms and screeching, completely out of control, and I'd convince myself he was letting off steam. I'd listen to Danielle riding me that we needed to get Isaiah some help, and I'd just tune her out. It's like I thought I could wish him whole...you know, just make him normal by willing it so.

But instead I looked away. I disappeared into what was left of my surfing career—which, frankly, wasn't much. One day I found myself alone in a beautiful oceanfront suite at a Hawaiian resort. Somehow, I'd weaseled these great accommodations from my sponsor, and it would have been nothing to bring along Danielle and the kids, but it hadn't even occurred to me.

I hadn't surfed too well that day, got knocked out early, but ESPN was covering the event and it was part of my deal to do color commentary for the network if and when I was eliminated. So there I was, out on the beach, still relishing the surfing spotlight. Didn't matter that it was shining on someone else; it was close enough. But then the sun went down and I went to my room and wondered what the hell I was doing with my life. I turned on the television, started flipping through the channels. After a while, I landed on *Forrest Gump,* just as it was getting started, so I threw a couple pillows behind my head and settled in to watch. By the end of the movie, I was bawling my brains out. Caught myself thinking of Tom Hanks, playing Isaiah as an adult. Thinking that the best, best, best we could hope for Isaiah was that he'd grow up to be like Forrest Gump. And it just shattered my heart, to where I started bawling all over again, only this time I was crying for Isaiah, not for some fictional character. I was crying for what he'd miss, for the boy his brother and sister would never know, for Danielle.

For me.

Want to fix the little boy.

So what did I do? Well, I emptied out the minibar, for one thing. And when there was nothing left to drink I went down to the lobby bar, where I found a couple guys I knew on the tour. They could see I was distraught, slid over to talk, asked me what was up. So I told them. Don't think I'd ever told anybody on the tour about Isaiah to that point, at least not in such an explicit, emotional way. Don't know why I opened up to these guys, but it just came out. It's like I had all these bottled-up things to say and share and the pressure had been building up and building up and it all burst forth.

Of all the people I could have opened up to that night, I happened to land on these two sweet guys who listened to me rant and ramble with all the patience and kindness in the world. At the other end one of my buddies turned to me and started telling me about his nineteen-year-old sister. I'd known this guy for years and years, and I had no idea he had a disabled sister, in such a bad way. She still slept in a crib. Still wore diapers. Still didn't speak. And he wasn't telling me in a *can you top this?* sort of way, but to let me know that I wasn't alone. That folks find a way to deal, whatever it is they're dealing with. And it absolutely floored me, that this great surfer could move about with such grace and composure with everything that was going on back home. That he could still function and be a great human being, and a really nice guy.

It must have killed this poor guy, to see his sister suffer and struggle, to have to suffer and struggle through her...but at the same time, it didn't *kill* him.

It took another incident to get my head completely out of my ass, and this one found me at Huntington Beach, at the butt end of yet another tournament I didn't win. Danielle and the kids had come down for this one, and she was so fed up with me at this point that whenever Isaiah started to have one of his meltdowns she'd hand him off to me. Didn't matter if I was surfing, or giving interviews, or doing something for one of my sponsors. It was like a game of Isaiah tag and it was my turn to deal with him.

Well, Isaiah had a major, major fit, and Danielle threw up her hands to let me know this was happening on my watch, and next thing I knew there was this huge fucking spectacle, with my crazy-ass son running up and down the beach, flapping his arms and screaming, "Neeeeeeeee!" The entire professional surfing world was on that beach, from Kelly Slater on down, along with sponsors and fans and photographers, friends and family, and everyone seemed to stop whatever they were doing to check out Isaiah, and it just tore me up. To have to see his behavior through the eyes of these great, fear-less watermen, guys I'd looked up to my whole life...it felt like the worst wipeout ever, multiplied out by about a million. Knocked the wind completely out of me, and as I started chasing Isaiah, zipping all over the beach like he was on fire, I got a picture in my head of what we looked like to all these people. For the first time, I saw Isaiah through the eyes of the world; I saw the two of us, together, through the eyes of the world.

I caught up to Isaiah, finally, managed to pin him to the sand and hoped like crazy I could get him to calm down. And as I was holding him close, brushing back his hair, trying to talk to him in a soothing voice, I thought, *Enough of this shit, Israel. Might as well just deal with it.*

Still, I kept surfing.

Yeah, this thunderclap of clarity had come over me about Isaiah, and yeah, I realized I needed to be a more available parent and partner, but I couldn't bring myself to give up on my career just yet. In fact, it took a good long while for me to finally quit on the idea that I could compete at the top, top level. For years, each time a tournament showed up on my calendar, I'd do a quick gut check and convince myself I could win. I was like Christian Bale in *The Fighter*, desperate to prove I still had it.

The *Fighter* comparison works all the way around, because you could see everybody's role shift in our family each time someone moved up or down a rung on whatever ladders we were climbing. In the movie, the mother was out as manager and the brother was out as coach… and then they were back in place. The mother needed the ex-champ, Christian Bale, who needed his brother, the up-and-comer Mark Wahlberg. They all needed each other, even though they each would have done better on their own. In the Paskowitz version, one of us would be soaring and doing okay for a while, making decent money. And then, after another while, someone else would start to soar and we'd all line up behind him instead, finding ways to hold him back or hoping like crazy he'd take the rest of us along for the ride. For years, we'd relied on each other to set us right when we had some trouble making our own way.

Truth was, I was drinking and partying too much to be competitive. I didn't recognize this at the time, but looking back it's absolutely clear. Looking back, I had no business thinking I could win anything. On a good day, I could still bring it, but the good days didn't come around so much anymore, and there was less and less to bring. I talked to my father about my struggles on the tour, my worries back home, but his head was someplace else. He didn't really get what was going on with Isaiah, he didn't have a whole lot of tolerance for sickness or weakness or frailty of any kind, and money troubles, to him, were nothing. In his mind, surfing was all. Health, good nutrition, physical fitness...they were right up there, too. He'd made these things a priority, and he'd raised us kids to keep them a priority, and that was that.

But that wasn't really that, of course. Took me a while to realize my father's hard-line, narrow views as a kind of failing; took my siblings a while, too. In fact, most of us struggled as we settled into our adult lives. Not all at once, and not in the same ways, but we had our rough patches. We weren't trained to do anything but surf; we had no education, no viable prospects; we were like drowning rats, scrabbling onto any piece of dry land or opportunity, hoping to find some way to hang on and make a little bit of a living.

For a while, this meant trying to make money in the surf world, or in some related business. And from time to time, one of us would make a go at...something. Jonathan had some success early on: he'd had his run on the tour; then he jumped on a good opportunity working for a sunglasses company and rode it hard for as long as he could. I had my day in the sun, too, making okay money and winning championships and shooting commercials for Nike, until my sun started to set. Adam, a couple years later, had some big-time success of his own, as the lead singer of the grunge rock group The Flys. They had a couple hit singles, like "Got You (Where I Want You)" and "I Know What You Want," and for a while Josh toured with the group as well, but then that kind of unraveled, and it was time for another Paskowitz to shine.

And so it went.

It's like we were taking turns, only I started to notice that if one of us was doing well and making good money he tended to stay away—I guess because a big part of our dysfunction as a family was an inability to keep our hands out of each other's pockets, or to stay out of each other's way. We'd get together on the beach at San O from time to time, or maybe during the summer at Surf Camp, and there was an unspoken thing among us that anyone who had money was meant to share it—or, at least, to pick up the tab. And so, in the beginning, we didn't see a whole lot of Jonathan, who seemed to hide out behind the sunglasses he used to sell. After that, *I* kept my distance. And then Adam gave us a wide berth, too. I can still remember going to one of his shows and having to wait in line with all of his fans while he took a shower, just to see him backstage afterwards.

But even with what was going on with Isaiah, even with Danielle's struggles to hold it together at home, I wanted it to be my turn again; I wanted my sun to keep shining. I loved the juice of competition too, too much to give it up. It made no sense, but I kept at it. I knew I needed to find a way to make real, consistent money; I knew I needed to be present, and to start finding some points of connection with Isaiah, while somehow blocking out time to form meaningful relationships with Elah and Eli, too. In my bones, I knew all of these things...and yet...and yet...my comeback was always just around the corner. I'd been a rock star surfer, no shit, no lie; it was all I knew, so I thought I could be a rock star surfer again. Or still. Whatever. I'd put it out there to Danielle that I was feeling good and strong, and that I owed it to all of us to get back out there and compete. And I'd make such a good and convincing case—to Danielle, to myself—that I'd head out for the next tournament and have at it.

And it's not like I wasn't competitive. It's not like I didn't deserve to be on the same wave as all these other longboarders. It's just that the wave was no longer mine.

12

The Second Wave

I've heard one other story like mine. Just one. Lots of
surfers, they talk about these giant waves, killer swells that slap
the crap out of you and drive you down. They're like the tall tales
you hear from fishermen, when they're out swapping stories over
beers. There's a macho pride in sizing up these monsters and living
to tell about them, but if you surf you can tell the guys with a real
story from the guys who are full of shit.

I was at the butt end of my career, but I was still getting low-end
endorsements, still skimming off my per diem and my swag to put
a little something in my pockets. I still wore my hair long and died
it blue-black, to look like Elvis. Folks on the tour, they knew who I
was, the kind of surfer I'd been. They knew my family, my story.
And, lately, they knew the turns my story had taken. They knew
about Isaiah. They knew I'd been down, hadn't won a thing in a
long, long while, and that I was running from whatever was going
on at home. And keep in mind, this was when there was a whole lot

going on at home, when Isaiah was getting bigger, and more and more of a handful.

A part of me couldn't deal with the thought of having an autistic kid, but a bigger part couldn't *actually* deal with this *particular* autistic kid, and it was in the middle of this swirl of craziness and denial that this one enormous wave knocked me clear to forever, left me thinking I was about to die. And then, just when I thought I might claw back to the surface, gulp back another breath of cool, wet ocean air and live to mess with another day, a second monster came and nearly finished me off.

That's the short version.

Here's the way I tell it over beers: We were on Réunion Island, a tiny slip in the Indian Ocean, off Madagascar. That's where they held the world championships in 1996. The idea was to go looking for the best waves on the planet. Never the same beach twice, never the same party, which was how we wound up in such a remote spot; after a while, they ran out of beaches. Some years, like when the event was in Australia, there'd be reporters, parades, crowds.... But on a barren outpost like Réunion Island, there was none of that. Just a bunch of surfers doing our thing, no one to thrill but each other, ourselves.

What I remember most about this one tournament was the flight—twenty-one hours, not counting a brief stopover in South Africa to refuel. Man, I was dreading that flight. Had all my surfboards packed and ready and I was pacing and jittery and nervous about spending all that time in the air. I don't usually mind flying, but this was such a killer trip, getting out to this small island in the middle of the Indian Ocean, it messed with my head. It set up the whole tournament like a real grind, where you want to approach one of these events with a healthy, open perspective. That's the ideal, right?

Typically, there's a real feel-good element that attaches to an

ASP world championship event. (ASP—as in Association of Surfing Professionals, the sport's main governing body.) That's also part of the ideal, part of the deal. You surf as a team, but you're judged as individuals. You represent your country, and that year I was captain of the U.S. team. It was an honor I no longer deserved, but it wasn't so long ago I was riding high. The way it works is there's a separate team from Hawaii, which I always thought was messed up—but, hey, Hawaii is out there on its own and it's produced so many legendary surfers, it's like its own country. So there's this ritual where you get a jar of water from your break back home and bring it with you to the event. It fell to me as captain to take care of it for our group, so I was flying with this jar of water, making sure nothing happened to it. Before the tournament, everybody takes the water and mixes it in a big bowl, and then they do this ceremony that's meant to symbolize the coming together of all the world's best surfers. You say a bunch of prayers, and they put these leis around your neck. Leis, rosaries . . . whatever we could grab to dress up the ritual.

I walked out into the water with all these other surfers, and it was a real moment. We all took it seriously—like we were making an offering to the surf gods. There's a lot of superstition among surfers, so everyone was careful to get it right, but at the same time we all knew it was kind of screwy. Still, none of us wanted to be the one to screw it up; we were buying into it and playing along, both. I was carrying this big-ass jar and wearing two beautiful carnation leis around my neck—one white, one red—along with a set of rosaries and a tiny cross that technically belonged to my youngest son, Eli, who was still just a baby. I'd thought to take them along for good luck—and to connect me to whatever was going on back home, whatever it was I was running from, whatever it was I was supposed to be.

I was still sort of hungover from the flight, so there was a whole lot of surreal to the scene. In fact, the flight was so damn long, I was probably hungover twice, and here on the back end of this second drunk I was moving mostly on residual fumes. I looked around at all these other surfers, people I'd known most of my life, all of us dressed for this weird-ass ceremony on the edge of nowhere, taking it seriously but not too, too seriously, getting ready to face down these gruesome waves that looked more likely to swallow us whole than to lay out a carpet for us to ride.

Oxbow was the sponsor again this year; wasn't much to sponsor, because there weren't a whole lot of folks around to notice, but Oxbow had photographers in the water, trying to record the ceremony for their Web site; they were a French clothing company, so they were big into pictures of beautiful people in beautiful settings, and there was plenty of both. Still, half the surfers were half in the bag from the long flight, so it wasn't much of a photo opportunity. A bunch of us had come out directly from the airport, and we were all thrashed and greasy and smelling like shit. By the end of the flight, one of the toilets on the plane had been stopped up, so the cabin reeked like an outhouse by the time we landed, and now the smell was in our hair, on our clothes, all around.

Meanwhile, all of this pain-in-the-ass travel stuff was running completely counter to the beautiful scenery. Beautiful, eerie, intimidating as hell . . . it was all of that, really. Like nothing I'd ever seen, and I'd been all over. Surfed everywhere there was to surf. But I'd never seen a spot like this. If it was a movie, it would feel like some bullshit, computer-generated special effect; you could close your eyes and picture it and still come nowhere close to what was actually unfolding in your view.

Réunion Island is essentially an atoll, which means it's mostly coral and it mostly surrounds its own lagoon. For surfers, this can make for some monstrous waves, which I guess is why the ASP folks chose this spot. The water comes at you from all sides, from great distances, and when the deep water hits the shallow reef it creates a vicious current. Actually, "vicious" doesn't begin to cut it. Réunion Island in particular was a spooky surf spot—breathtaking to look at, but also kind of ominous and treacherous. I was terrified of those waters. Plus, there was a jagged reef, all along the coast, and you could tell from the color that it went from deep to shallow, every here and there, so you'd never know if you were about to be slapped against a floor of coral. I was psyched and terrified, all at once. Oh, I'd go out and ride, but I wasn't looking forward to it, not like some of these hot-shit younger guys who seemed to be looking forward to it, not like I used to look forward to getting wet on some of these other beaches around the world. Actually, it's not even accurate to call this spot a beach. More of a sick joke wired to a sick wave machine. Wasn't any kind of resort to speak of, just a stretch of jagged lava rock. No sand, really. There were only a couple nothing special places to stay, so in some ways I guess you could say it was all about the waves. Wasn't anything else. Just a bunch of hard-core warrior surfers perched on a volcano, a long fucking way from civilization, our boards the only thing separating us from the heinous surf.

Okay, so we did our little ceremony, and struck just the right reverent tone, and at the other end there was still a patch of daylight. If you looked out at the water the scene was framed in such a way that the deep blue waves were cresting with all this thick white foam, all of it lit by this fiery orange of the fading sun. Oh, man, it made a pretty picture! But underneath the shot was the dark, dangerous power of those killer waves. Also, it was ridiculously muggy. The kind of muggy that sapped your strength and got you thinking of sucking back a couple more cold ones before calling it a night. A lot of the guys came right back to shore after we did our thing with the leis and the rosaries, thinking to do just that, but a few of us decided to paddle out and catch a couple waves. You know, just grab a taste, acclimate, give ourselves an idea of what to expect the next morning. So I slid my board from its bag, put the fins in, and went to check it out. The rest of my shit was still in the car. I hadn't even unpacked.

On the way out, I could see the line of waves stretching into the fat of the horizon. There was wave after wave after wave. Usually, there's a lull between sets; depending on the strength of the swell, there could be three or four sets, or ten or twelve, and here there was just no letup. Just one wave after the next. No letup, no lull.

The idea, heading out like this the night before a tournament, is to see where the waves break, where the sets are, where you'll line up the next morning. Of course, the surf would be completely different by the next morning, but at least you'd have a baseline. You might want to pick out some markers along the shoreline, to triangulate where you are. A palm tree. A house. A bluff jutting out towards the water. Something. Only here there weren't really any markers, just a long stretch of creepy coastline.

To my left, I could see a couple lifeguards on Jet Skis. Réunion Island was a French territory, so I figured these guys were probably French and that they wouldn't be much help. I would have much preferred a couple burly, fearless Hawaiians on patrol, keeping me safe. Still, these French lifeguards were zipping around, keeping a French eye on things, and after a beat or two I turned my attention to the water. I could feel the concussion of the waves, coursing up through my board. The sun had dipped another notch, and it was starting to feel like dusk. The color of the water, which had been a deep, vivid blue, was now more like cobalt, like it was covered in shadow, and it occurred to me I'd have to turn back in soon enough.

Just then, I saw a serious set approaching. My one and only thought was, *Fuck!* That's all. Just, *Fuck!* I didn't care about catching it; I just wanted to get over it. I'd reached a spot where the water was suddenly deeper. You could tell from the grading of the saturation.

The deep water meant I wouldn't get slapped onto the reef, but it also meant I could be driven so far down by this thing I'd never fight my way back up.

At this point, a lot of the guys were getting hit. The height of these things was just impossible to navigate. I made it over one, barely, and then the crash of the wave almost sucked the air out of me. I could feel the ripping wind from the wave, like I was caught in a giant force field, all the air being pulled down, down, down.

I was above the surface, but for a long moment I couldn't breathe.

First time I looked back, I saw a bunch of scattered boards. The other guys were getting annihilated by these waves, and best I could tell nobody had even tried to catch one just yet. If I listened, I could hear a couple of these other surfers screaming, only they were shouts of joy, exhilaration. They were crying, "Woo hoo!" Or, "Yeah!" Or whatever they'd taken to shouting to get their juices going.

Me, I was flat terrified. I was getting a little too old for this shit. My buddies were all stoked, even though they were getting killed by these sets, and I was in survival mode. That's all. I just wanted to get through it, past it, over it. I wanted it to be tomorrow. Hadn't even started yet, and already I'd had enough.

Next thing I knew, the water at my belly started to roil and feather. I'd come upon the killer wave of all these killer waves, and I struggled against it. Wasn't any time to think, just react. My mind raced back over the thousands upon thousands of sets I'd seen, in all my years of surfing. A million waves, probably—maybe more. And so, against this endless frame of reference, a lifetime of rescue maneuvers kicked in, and I reached for one of the worst, in this particular scenario. Without really thinking about it, on instinct, I attempted to duck-dive.

Normally, that's not a bad strategy, but I was a long way from *normally*. In a duck-dive, you use your board like a scoop and you kind of stand up against the wave and push the board under and through, but it left me vulnerable in the middle of this mammoth set. What I should have done was rip off my cord and dive under the water, beneath the power of the wave. The duck-dive would have been cool, if I could have pulled it off, and if anybody was looking on at just the right moment and happened to catch it, but as soon as I committed to it I knew it was all wrong. At first, I thought I'd make it through, but then my board popped up just as the colossal wave started to crest, and I was thrown backwards.

The hit knocked all the air out of me, which made a bad situation worse, because what you want to do just before you go under is suck in one last breath. Then you're okay. Then you wait out the wave and pop back up, but here I was already out of air when I went down. Or just about. I was in the heart of the impact zone, where the full energy of the wave whiplashes the current, and as I fell over it felt like I was being sent over Niagara Falls. Backwards. With no fucking idea when I'd hit bottom. And then, when I did finally hit, it felt like I'd tumbled two stories onto a slab of concrete.

My lungs were empty. My eyes were closed, my bones rattled to shit. I started sinking beneath the immense power of the wave, and after another beat I felt myself lifting. I was being slapped around every which way, flipping and tumbling, up and down, over and over. I was like a rag doll. In fact, that's what they call it, when you're tossed and turned like that by a giant wave. You're rag-dolled, and it felt for a long, sick moment like I was in a washing machine, set on full tilt.

I tried to think. Wasn't so easy, thinking. At some point, I realized that if I could only reach to the bottom I could push back to the surface. At the spot where the wave hit, it wasn't so deep— maybe twenty feet. The first problem with this strategy, though, was I couldn't tell up from down. The second problem: I was still attached to my board, and as I was being rag-dolled by the momen-

tum of the wave the board was being pulled against the current and
I was being dragged down by the leash.

(Oh yeah…the leash. I know I wrote earlier that I tended to
avoid the leash in competition, but this was not yet a competition;
this was just me, getting a feel for the wave. And these were no or-
dinary sets, so a leash seemed like a good idea.)

I couldn't figure out what the hell was going on. Meanwhile,
from the beach, you could see my board kind of tombstoned in the
water. That's another great surfing phrase for when the shit hits the
fan—"tombstoning," which is what your board is doing when it's
straight up and bobbing, half in, half out of the water. It's not a good
sign, when your buddies on the beach see that, because it means
you're below the surface, pulling against the board with the strength
of the wave.

Ten seconds passed. Felt like twenty.

Then, ten seconds more. Felt like forty.

I started to panic. Big-time. I even started to scream. My mouth
was shut, but I unleashed a sick, anguished cry. Didn't know where
it came from, what it meant; it was almost primal. My eyes had
been shut, but by now I'd opened them. A lot of good that did me.
Still couldn't see for shit, only now I had to think what this might
mean, that I couldn't see, that the water was so black I couldn't spot
my own hand in front of my face.

I was deep into survival mode, but I couldn't do a single thing
to save myself. I could only flail about in a blind panic, and start to
think I might never see my kids again. Me, who kept ducking out
when things got tough. Me, who couldn't deal with whatever Isaiah
was dealing with, what Danielle was dealing with in dealing with
him. Me, who half the time couldn't tell which way was up at home
and now couldn't tell which way was up in the Indian Fucking
Ocean.

In my panic, I began to feel claustrophobic. Like the world was pressing down on me, closing in, choking me. I'd been in some tough spots in the water, but I'd never felt anything like ... *this.*

I was desperate to breathe. My lungs were ready to burst. I was screaming, certain I was about to die, bumming that I was about to die. (Oh, man, I was bumming!) And yet, somehow, in the middle of all that wild frenzy, I could feel the full force of that killing wave start to fade, and for a thin, small moment I thought the waters would still and I could clamber to the surface. But then, another thin, small moment later, another wave came crashing down to replace the first, and I went from thinking there was a way out and that the worst had passed to thinking I was totally, seismically, completely fucked.

☉

It's funny, the thoughts that run through your head the moment you realize you're about to die. People say their whole lives flash in front of them, like a sudden slide show, but that's not how it was for me. It was more like every relevant thought flashed through my brain, all of them piled on top of each other. I knew right away what that second wave meant. I'd actually talked about it with a surfing buddy of mine named Strider Wasilewski, who'd been through the same deal. His was that one other story I hinted at earlier. We talked about if it was better to black out or swallow. Basically, those are your only two options, when you're drowning, and as this second wave crashed over me I gave some swift, serious thought to each. I knew I was about to die. I was dead solid certain. Only thing left was to figure *how* I was about to die, and I tried to remember what Strider had said. For the life of me, I couldn't remember if he tried to black out or take in water. If he felt like he even had a choice. I wanted to give up, but at the same time I didn't. I wanted to go unconscious, but I couldn't think how.

That second wave, man ... that's what sets my story apart. I knew it as it was happening. If one wave is likely to kill you, then two will leave no doubt, and here it left me twisting, struggling, fighting. It started to freak me out that I couldn't see. A couple seconds earlier all I could see was blackness, and now it felt like the blackness had been dialed down a couple shades. Like I'd somehow fallen into an abyss of the deepest, darkest blackness known to man. Weird, huh? And all I could think was when to start sucking in water, when to give up.

If I had to put a clock on things, I'd say it was about forty-five, fifty seconds until the first wave quieted. Maybe as long as a minute. And it's not like I had a lungful of air to start out with, either, so I was operating on a half tank to begin with, and then the second wave hit, and the clock started all over again, and now I was tapped. Done. And as I realized this, one dark thought piled on top of another, the claustrophobia I'd been feeling started to slip away. The panic I'd been feeling, it started to quiet. I felt calm, warm, almost euphoric. Sounds like a big fat cliché, I know, but that's how it came over me. And then, in another cliché, that deep, allover blackness began to fade, and I could see light and color. And fish! All in brilliant Technicolor! It was like a whole new daydream burst forth and swallowed up the nightmare of a beat or two before.

Amazing.

All of a sudden, there was no more panic, no more urgency. Nothing. Just, a complete sense of allover, inexplicable calm. Then I must have blacked out, because I have no memory of what happened next. All I know is that a short time later I was coughing. Somehow, I must have floated back up to the surface. Floated, swum, scrambled, clawed…whatever I did, I found a way up and through. I was conscious. I was spitting up water. My neck was on fire, from where the leis had been whipped about, but at first I thought a jellyfish had wrapped itself around me. It was the only way I could think to explain it.

Little slivers of reality began to slip through my fog, and I think I drifted off again at this point. I went back underwater. I saw two white lights, and I knew enough to register what I was seeing, but somehow the lights left me thinking, *Oh, shit! Here we go. I'm going to see Jesus!* Me, a nice Jewish boy, being led into the light. And then, I felt about a million tiny bubbles floating around my face. I'd swallowed a bunch of water, apparently, but there was all this trapped air in the foam. That's the kind of shit you read about in all those science articles and you file it away, thinking it's kind of cool but knowing you'll never apply it to your real life, to your surfing life. But those tiny bits of air brought me back to consciousness, and as I came clear I saw that those two white lights weren't Baby Jesus. Don't know what the hell they were, actually, but they fell away soon enough and in their place I heard this swelling roll of thunder. My first thought here was that these were the French lifeguards, on their Jet Skis, and this thought was soon replaced by another, by me wishing like hell I'd been knocked out in Hawaii so I could at least get a decent rescue.

I coughed and coughed and coughed, and when I finally shook myself alert I could see all these red and white carnations, dancing on the water. As far as I could see, there were these fucking carnations, and as I realized what they were I reached to my neck and felt the hot red burn of a big-ass welt forming around my throat. The carnations were strewn across the water the length and width of a football field; that's how far I'd been dragged along by these wicked currents. That's how long I'd been under. Long enough for these flowers to decorate the ocean for what should have been my funeral.

Underneath the welt, I could feel Eli's rosaries, still hanging around my neck, and I remember feeling lifted by this. I took it as some sort of sign, that the pull of family was so strong it could drag me back from those giant waves. It was unbreakable.

I grabbed my board, which was still lashed to my foot, and got back on top of it. I thought about heading into shore, but then I thought about it some more and turned to check out the next killer set that was already coming my way.

I thought, *All right, Iz. You dodged a big fucking bullet right there. That's the worst wipeout you'll ever have, and here you are. Still.*

I thought, *Shit, there's probably only ten minutes of daylight left in this sky.*

Then I pointed my board back out to sea and started scratching like crazy for the horizon.

13

Blobber Beach

It was one thing to shake myself awake about Isaiah, and another one thing to try to be more involved with the getting and spending and running of our upside-down household, and still another one thing to recognize that my career was passing me by... but I was a long way from following through on these realizations all at once.

One thing at a time was hard enough.

Like I said, my father was no real help on this. He could see I was on the downward face of my career. He could see I was struggling to keep ahead of my bills and get a handle on what was going on with Isaiah, but he never once took me aside and told me to get my house in order. If anything, the message I got from Doc was just the opposite. It was: *Keep surfing.* It was: *It's nothing a day at the beach can't fix.* It was: *You're a world champion, Israel. Remember that.* That's what it was all about with him, what it had always been about, but it wasn't working for me and Danielle and the kids. There was no money in surfing, only juice and glory—and I was pretty much tapped on these last two. What might have been right and good and true for my folks and *their* family was no longer right and good and true for me and *my* family.

And yet I kept at it. Been riding those waves for so long I couldn't step off. So I didn't. Got myself a new sponsor, in Glenn Minami of Blue Hawaii; Glenn was a talented shaper with a sweet line of surfboards, and I was happy to throw in with him while I still could, while I still had enough of a name to get someone to pay my way. Got to thinking it would help ease myself off the professional circuit, to be able to ride into the sunset on my own terms, and it worked out that one of my trips for Blue Hawaii was a real game changer for us as a family—for me and Isaiah, especially. Eli was just a baby; Elah and Isaiah were still little, but Isaiah's symptoms were full-blown; he was already a handful, had lost almost all of his language and his ability to connect with people. We'd had his diagnosis for a couple years, which meant I'd been rejecting his diagnosis for a couple years. It was a heartbreaking thing to see, so I tried to look away and pretend he was still the bright-eyed, beautiful, engaged little boy he had been as an infant.

Shortly after that *Forrest Gump* trip to Oahu, I had another opportunity to return to Hawaii, and this time I found a way to take Danielle and the kids. Seemed like the right move. Plus, I didn't want to be holed up in another nice hotel room, alone, crying over another movie that reminded me of the life I was trying to avoid.

The irony of my sponsorship deal with Blue Hawaii was that Glenn Minami was the guy cutting me the check, based on a fair calculation of what everything would cost. This was great, because hotels were expensive on Oahu, rental cars were expensive, everything was expensive, so there was good money coming back. But it was doubly great because I arranged to stay with Glenn and borrow his car, so he was basically paying me to crash at his place with my family and pinch his ride; either way, I was ahead of the game before I even got in the water.

I always loved being back in Hawaii, and this was the first time I was getting to share it with my whole family. I was really, really stoked about this. Guess a part of me thought if my kids could come to know and love Hawaii they would come to know and love me; God knows, I hadn't been around enough for them to come to this on my own merits.

First thing Elah and I noticed, together, was the way the whole place smells like a nursery the moment you step outside. Even the airport, against all those exhaust fumes, manages to smell like an exotic greenhouse; we were blown away by the sights and sounds and smells. It all took me back. And the food, all that kimchi and poi... I wanted to turn Danielle on to all of it, so it was a wonderful homecoming—long overdue, and very much needed, I thought, to set my family back on a hopeful, healing course.

The contest was being held at Maelie Point, on the south and west side of the island. It was an interesting place to hold an event, because there wasn't a whole lot of sand on the beach; the wave was nice enough, but there was no place for the kids to play and splash around, so before my first heat I left from Glenn's house and dropped Danielle and the kids at Pokai Bay, in Makaha, near where we used to live on Makaha Point, when my older brothers and I were little. It's a popular, legendary surf spot, rich with tradition; basically, it's where you'll find the heartiest, most out-of-this-world/out-of-their-minds surfers on the island, and if you're not there as someone's "guest" you'll start to feel unwelcome by the time you paddle out. It's not that the locals aren't good or gracious hosts, but they can be particular; you need to know someone if you want to surf Makaha; you need to belong.

Happily, I had the right pedigree. I'd grown up on that beach, after all, and a lot of the old-timers still remembered Doc, so folks couldn't have been more welcoming. I helped Danielle and the kids get settled by a gorgeous little bay, with crystal clear water and beach grass and palm trees. It was like a sliver of paradise. A part of me wanted to hang back and spend the day with them, but Blue Hawaii was paying our way and I had a job to do, so I laid out a blanket for them and lit out for Maelie Point.

One thing, though: I didn't think to pack a cooler, and poor Danielle had to walk into town for lunch. She managed to find Isaiah a decent plate of chicken nuggets, which was pretty much the only thing he could eat that didn't make him gag and screech and hurl. Found something for Elah, too. (Eli was probably still breast-feeding.) And for herself, Danielle settled on an order of Rocky Mountain Oysters, which she was told was a local delicacy. Sounded good to her, so that's what she got—and she ate it happily, hungrily.

Wasn't until later that she learned she'd eaten bull calf testicles. (Actually, it might have been pig balls, which are also called Rocky Mountain Oysters in those parts.) I suppose I could have kept this information to myself when she told me the story later, but that would have been way less fun than seeing the look on Danielle's face when she put two and two together and started to retch.

Before I left for the tournament, I had spent some time with Elah, splashing around in the water. It was such a perfect, perfect day I couldn't bring myself to leave. We could see all these tiny, colorful fish, dashing around in these giant schools, in complete formation, and she was fascinated by them. She asked me what kind of fish they were, and I pretended to know. That's what dads do, right? When we're stumped, we offer up an answer with all the authority in the world, because we don't want our curious kids thinking we don't know absolutely everything there is to know.

So I said, "Those are blobbers, Elah."

Elah crinkled up her face like she was making a mental note, and we goofed around for a while longer, studying all the tiny fish, and as I finally made to leave she hollered after me. She said, "We'll be here at Blobber Beach, Dad. We'll be waiting for you."

And as I drove off I caught myself wondering why I hadn't been taking my family to every damn tournament all along.

◎

The road to Maelie Point was snarled with traffic. Wasn't built for so many cars, so many surfers, heading to the same place at the same time. Cars were parked along a red dirt road, going back about a mile, so I ditched Glenn's Nissan and hustled to the tournament table on foot. As I approached, I took time to notice the scenery—it was breathtaking, really. The water was spectacular, breaking over a coral bed. The only drag on this spot was there was no place to hang out. You had to walk very light-footed onto the reef as you entered the water. I was running late, so my head was all over the place. Guys were already on the outside, the contest had started, and I was still reaching for my board.

Not exactly the best way to get my tournament going.

And there was also this: on my light-footed way into the surf, I slipped in a kind of hole; somehow got my toe stuck in the mouth of a baby moray eel. Scraped the shit out of my foot, too. It was a freaky thing, and it set me back. Wasn't that it hurt so much, but I had to stop and find a way to shake off the eel and get my head back into this first heat. Left me feeling completely out of sync, where what you want is to be so focused that all you're thinking about is grabbing that first wave.

By the time I got out there, it's like the waves were on a completely different setting. They were decent enough, but they kept missing me—or guess I should say *I* kept missing *them*. They'd pop up wherever I wasn't, or break in a way or in a spot I wasn't expecting. I had to keep paddling back and forth, chasing the next set, working on a canvas that was way bigger than usual. I'd paddle to the right, and there'd be no waves. I'd paddle to the left...no waves.

In the meantime, everyone else was getting waves. It's like there was just enough surf for all the other guys in my heat and because I'd gotten there late, or because I'd been distracted by that eel or tearing up my foot on the jagged coral, or because my heart was back at Makaha with Danielle and the kids...well, there were no waves left for me.

Wasn't too, too upset about this, I'll admit—only bummed that I could have traded this disappointing heat for a day on the beach with my family. But I kept paddling, kept waiting. Finally, I saw a wave heading my way, and I took off on it late but somehow managed to ride it in for a good score. It was a cool wave, actually—a bowl that came together and created a fine peak, which left me a classic tube. Caught another couple waves after that, but it was this tube ride that got me to the next round, so I was happy about that. Hadn't been my best day, not by a long shot, but it was enough to see me through.

Some tournaments, you have to hang around to surf your next heat, but there were so many competitors in my division that this first day had been set aside for just the first round. All these years later, I can't even be sure I waited to see where I stood. Maybe, maybe not; either way, I had a good feeling I'd advanced, but I had an even better feeling about doubling back to Makaha, so I got out of there soon as I could. Trekked back to Glenn's car, and as it started up I noticed the cassette player was still playing the same Sarah McLachlan tape it had been playing on the way out, so I started fumbling through Glenn's stuff to see if I could find something else. Wasn't much but chick music, not the sort of stuff I listened to, and the radio was for shit, so I left the Sarah McLachlan tape in the dash and let it play.

Got back to Makaha just as Danielle was starting to pack up, but

I motioned her to leave everything where it was so I could hang for a bit with the kids. Wanted to squeeze the last few drops of sunlight from the day. Also, wanted to soak in the scene before it slipped away from me entirely: Elah was a total towhead back then, with long white hair and a little-kid belly that couldn't keep from spilling over her bikini bottom; Isaiah was a giant butterball, and the way he looked up at me and smiled just about shattered my road-weary heart; and Eli was such a sweet, easy baby Danielle and I sometimes worried he was too good to be true.

As I approached, I flashed on an image of Danielle, collecting our few things, corralling the kids from whatever they were doing, and I caught myself thinking I must have done something right, somewhere along the way, to be a part of something so beautiful, so magical. It was almost spiritual. No, it wasn't a picture-perfect scene; there was still the anguish and worry about Isaiah, the tension between me and Danielle for the way I kept checking out on her. But it was as close to perfect as I had any right to expect, so I caught myself wondering where I'd been all these years while this beautiful, magical, spiritual picture was coming into focus; I was washed over by a whole range of emotions that ran from happiness to regret.

Anyway, the kids were completely fried by this point, so there wasn't much I could do with them in terms of playing or splashing around. Danielle was fried, too, so we sat on the blanket while the little bit of sun faded from the sky, and then we started to move towards the car. The big kids were still in their bathing suits, still wet, so we threw some towels down on the backseat, got Eli into his car seat, and started heading back to Glenn's place in the middle of the island, about forty-five minutes away.

We talked back and forth for a while. Softly, lazily. Danielle told me the Rocky Mountain Oysters story. Elah told me about her Blobber Beach adventures. And Isaiah was so calm, so peaceful, he was mostly still and silent, which was completely out of character for him. We were used to hearing him screech and grunt and mumble, all day long. Whatever language he'd had as a toddler was long gone, so for the past few years he'd only communicated with sounds and pointing and temperament. He had a few words, like "more," and a few sounds, like *neeeee*. He was like a little caveman, just grunting and pointing to make himself understood; it would have been cute if it wasn't so sad, so tragic.

Soon, Elah and Danielle drifted off to sleep. Eli, too. And Isaiah was just staring peacefully out the window, lost in whatever thoughts he'd managed to collect that day.

And then the most remarkable thing happened. The Sarah McLachlan tape that had been running all along started to play "Adia," which was her big hit at the time. The song was everywhere back then, coming through every damn radio, every damn speaker; there was no escaping it. And as it played, I heard a child's voice singing along with the chorus—a voice I hadn't heard in years and years. At least, I hadn't heard it in such a sweet, sustained way, only in distress, in outbursts, in fits and starts. But here was Isaiah, my great big butterball of a son who'd been lost in the fog of autism since he was one or two years old, singing his great big heart out.

"We are born innocent.... It's easy, we all falter. Does it matter?"

I was totally stunned. At first, I thought maybe there was some ghost, some spirit with us in the car. Then I thought some other kid had snuck into the backseat before we drove off. But it was Isaiah, singing! I nudged Danielle awake, because I knew she wouldn't want to miss this, and as she opened her eyes she could hear Isaiah in the backseat, singing, "We are born innocent...."

Danielle and I both started to cry, but they were tears of joy, tears of astonishment. We couldn't believe what we were hearing. Isaiah knew all the words, and he just sang and sang, and soon as he finished I started pumping Danielle with questions. I wanted to know what they had done all day, how long Isaiah had been in the water, what he'd eaten for lunch...everything. I was scrambling for some way to connect whatever had gone on that day to Isaiah's calm, tranquil, *singing* behavior. And as we talked we started to think that whatever was going on with Isaiah had something to do with the beach, with the water, with the calming, therapeutic effects of floating, swimming, splashing, playing....

Wouldn't go so far as to say a lightbulb went off in my head as we drove the rest of the way to Glenn's place, but I could make a strong case that the bulb was in my hand. Now all that was left was for me to find a place to put it and flip the switch.

14

Surfers Healing

I've always thought of my life as a series of waves. There've been moments of calm and clarity, and moments of chaos and confusion, and in between and all around there've been wild, unpredictable swells, followed again by a kind of stillness. Not a bad metaphor, huh? And in my case it works, because my personal life has had as many ups and downs and sideways spills as my surfing life.

Heading home after that curiously wonderful Hawaiian trip, I was starting to think the surf was headed up, only up. Danielle and I were so blown away by Isaiah's transformation after that long day at the beach we looked to re-create it as soon as possible. As often as possible. He'd always loved the water, always seemed more relaxed and more comfortable splashing around than he did on dry land. More like himself. But we never thought about the calming, soothing effects all that time in the water might have on his overall personality. We never made the connection. Danielle had just been too busy shuttling back and forth between Elah and Eli, and I'd been too busy running away from anything that looked like heavy lifting or heavy-duty parenting of a special kid like Isaiah.

All along, I'd wanted no part of caring for Isaiah...but now I wanted in. I was ready to embrace my son, at long last. Danielle was thrilled to see me finally connect—and not in a going-through-the-motions way, but in my gut, deep down. I was changed, suddenly and profoundly changed. Danielle had been on her own for so long she'd forgotten what it was like to have a partner, and I wanted to make up for lost time.

The most obvious way to do this, I figured, was to take Isaiah surfing. It's what I knew, right? It was the one thing I had to share with my son, special needs or no. No, Isaiah would never take to the water the way me and my brothers had taken to the water. But surfing would be our lifeline. It would see us through, just like it had always seen us through.

We had *some* history in the water, I should mention: I'd paddled out with Isaiah on a board before; I'd stood him up for a tandem ride, or held him in my arms while I did my thing; he always seemed to spark to it, in his own way. I never spent the whole day or even a good long while with him at the beach; it was always just a one-and-done kind of deal. We'd catch a couple rides; then I'd hand him off to Danielle and go back out by myself. But the great take-away from this long, glorious day at Makaha was that the pacifying effects of an open-ended day at the beach, the kind I used to enjoy with my brothers every day of our little lives, were surely remarkable. And that Isaiah was totally up for it.

Soon as we got back to California, I started taking Isaiah out in the water, every chance. All I had to do was walk up to him and say, "Go surfing?" And he'd take my hand and off we'd go. We'd look for reasons to head out—and, once we were at the beach, we'd look for reasons to stay. It wasn't a cure-all for Isaiah, not by any stretch, but for the hours we were in the water he was a different kid. He was attuned to his environment. He was laughing and happy. Mostly, he was calm. And for a few hours afterwards he was more manageable, more at peace with himself and his environment. He wasn't singing along to Sarah McLachlan tunes—*that* was a freaky one-shot!—but he was better able to dial in and follow what was going on right in front of him.

In a short time, surfing became something for us to look forward to, something to enjoy, and something to look back on—so we kept at it. We made it a full-on family affair. Soon, I started meeting friends on the beach with their own kids on the spectrum, and they'd ask me to take their sons or daughters for a ride. We'd hit San O or Doheny or wherever, and folks would wander over to check us out, and before I knew it there were all these special kids lined up, waiting for their turn.

It's not like there was an unmanageable bunch of families, looking for a taste of whatever medicine Danielle and I had seemed to stumble on with Isaiah. Each time out, there were only one or two kids brave enough to give it a go—the kids of friends, or friends of friends. It grew over time, but in the beginning there was usually a common thread to knit us together, other than the fact that we had autistic children. After a while, word began to spread and there'd be two or three kids wanting in, and then three or four. I was always happy to accommodate, happy to bring a sliver of lightness and freedom into the lives of these good people. It was no longer about friends or friends of friends; the common thread of autism was enough.

Some of my pals came regularly. For a while, I fell into a routine with Cliff Rehrig, who played bass in the band Air Supply. Cliff was a bitchin' dude, with long hair down to his butt, and I would take his son out every Wednesday. The kid's name was Sonic Blue, and he was totally into surfing. Big waves or small, it felt to him like we were surfing Réunion Island. We hit on Wednesdays because that was always a half day at Paskowitz Surf Camp. In those days during the summers, I'd pitch in at camp, just to make some extra pocket money. As long as I was at the beach I'd have Danielle come down to meet me and I'd get Isaiah in the water, along with anyone else who wanted a turn.

Sometimes, it was a struggle to get these kids out past the break. In rough surf, I'd have to press them down against the board with my chest, to keep them from slipping off. Some of the kids would be scared; some would be stoked; you could never tell how it would go, but they'd usually calm down once we got on the outside. I'd try to talk to them, if they were verbal; hell, even if they weren't verbal I'd talk to them, because somewhere in there they were listening. And there was also this: I used to cry all the time for these kids. I'd feel their pain—*really* feel it. I ached for them, for their parents, for the whole raw deal. But then we'd set about it and for a few moments we'd lift each other from the anguish of autism. We could just surf and hang and have a big old time.

Don't know when or how or why Danielle and I hit on the idea of formalizing what I was doing with these kids. It just kind of happened, took on its own momentum, and grew and grew. Without really realizing it, without really meaning to, we'd tapped into something bigger than Isaiah ... bigger than our own little family ... bigger than any of us could have ever imagined.

It was one thing to get comfortable with Isaiah in the water and quite another to find a way to be with him on land. He was a tough nut to crack—especially for a dad like me, who'd been completely uninvolved in his care up until this point. If you must know, I was making it up as I went along with Elah and Eli, and that was hard enough, but to try to figure things out on the fly with a kid like Isaiah was way past impossible.

One of our turning point moments found us in Cabo. Isaiah was six or seven. He was going through a lot of tantrums. "A lot" is probably an understatement. It sometimes felt like tantrum was his baseline behavior, the most common wave. He wasn't sleeping. Danielle and I hadn't yet gotten a handle on how to deal with his mood swings, his temper. With *him*. That would come, but much, much later. Danielle would figure it out, and a couple months later I'd catch on. But at the time it was an evolving, uncertain hassle.

Despite my halfhearted (at first!) and now full-hearted efforts, I still couldn't quite come to terms with being a father to an autistic child. Hell, I had a tough-enough time just being a father, but this was a whole other handful. That's why I'd bugged out, in the beginning. Even when I was home, I wasn't fully there. I drank, a little more than I should; I stayed out of the house, a little more than I should; and in every other respect, I did a little less than I should.

I'd call in every once in a while when I was on the road and pretend to be involved. My thing was to play at being an active parent, instead of actually being one. I'd call home and hear some noise in the background, which I could convince myself was laughter, and say, "How's Isaiah?"

Just like any other dad, off on any other business trip, avoiding any other family drama, except the noise wasn't laughter but screaming. Isaiah, screaming. The bustle of activity I could hear through the phone wasn't fun, family high jinx, but havoc. Isaiah-made havoc. Danielle would listen to my half-assed attempt at plugging in and say, "Fuck! Why would you even ask me that?"

It was just horrible, what she was going through with him. And I was nowhere, man. Just, nowhere. Turning tail and chasing waves.

Jump-cut to 1997. Isaiah was wearing an Izzy-the-mascot T-shirt, from the 1996 Atlanta Olympics. For over a year, he wore that shirt, until he outgrew it. That's how the moment has rooted itself in my mind, through this odd, computer-generated character that I happened to share a name with, and in the freeze-frame picture I carry in my head of this one defining road trip with Isaiah, that's what he has on. Man, he wore that shirt so often Izzy the mascot became the mascot of this one road trip. It's like he was cheering us on.

Danielle had been having an especially rough time with Isaiah. Each day was bringing a whole new set of problems, a whole new batch of strange, difficult behavior. I'd been trying to make more of an effort, but I had no idea what I was doing. About the only thing I could do was be present, so that was my big thing. To just be there. Hadn't done such a good job of that early on, but I was getting better at it. I was trying.

Now, in fairness to me, Danielle was much better at this autism stuff than I was. She had a whole lot more practice with it, for one thing. Had a whole lot more patience, too. She was strong, that way. She was the one running Isaiah back and forth to doctors, dealing with his medication, his diet.... She knew the drill, but more than that, I don't think she really trusted me to take good care of him. But we'd just slogged through an especially difficult couple weeks and she was having her version of a nervous breakdown. She was crying, all the time. I'd never seen her so low, so despairing. It felt to me like she needed a break, so I switched into my wandering Paskowitz mode and figured a road trip was in order. That's one thing us Paskowitzes had always been good at, getting in the car and driving. Towards something, away from something...didn't really matter. The idea was just to go.

Turned out my parents were getting ready to head home from their annual pilgrimage to Cabo San Lucas, so I set it up so I would fly down to Cabo with Isaiah and help my father on the drive back to California. He and Mom were still living out of their vehicle; those days, they had a 1963 Chevy, with a cab-over sleeper compartment that slept two, uncomfortably. It was an absolute piece of shit, all rusted out, through and through. Don't know how these two gentle old souls managed—hey, Doc was in his late seventies!—but they managed.

Couldn't really drive around town in the Chevy, so my folks traveled with their crappy old Mitsubishi Galant, which was also in sorry shape. The shocks were gone, and you could really feel it on those roads down in Mexico. Any bump in the road, you'd hear, feel, *taste* the scrape of metal on metal. It drove okay, that car, but it wasn't the most comfortable ride. Mom wasn't interested in driving the Mitsubishi back to California on her own, so a plan took shape for me and Isaiah to fly down and caravan back with my dad, while she flew home ahead of us.

Danielle wasn't too thrilled with this plan, because Isaiah wasn't really equipped for this type of traveling, but she was so beaten down by this point she would have consented to anything just to grab some peace and quiet. Isaiah's doctor wasn't so sure it was a good idea, either, because Isaiah had started having these petit mal seizures—like, constantly. I'd been with Isaiah through enough of these little seizures to think I had a handle on them, but the doctor was worried my kid would throw a grand mal seizure, so he walked me through all these different scenarios to make sure I knew what to do, what to watch out for. It was a huge issue, me taking Isaiah from all these resources we had for him at home, from his routines, but I set it out like it would have been an even bigger issue if he stayed. Because I thought he and I desperately needed to spend this time together. Because I thought Danielle desperately needed a break. I was relentless, to where Danielle didn't have it in her to fight me on this, even as she didn't fully trust me on it. Eventually, I wore her down and she helped me throw together a couple things for Isaiah and sent us off, hoping for the best.

I steeled myself with a couple shots of tequila on the flight to Mexico, just to deal with all the weird looks people were flashing me and Isaiah. He wasn't the best traveler, and he was pulling out all his best, most full-blown autistic moves, flapping his arms, screaming, going nuts. Whenever he was in an unfamiliar environment, his behavior would just shoot off the charts. I'd given Isaiah whatever medication Danielle had set aside for him, to help calm him down, but it didn't seem to me like it was doing any good, and for a while I thought he'd be better off with the tequila.

Over time, I'd get used to being on the receiving end of the ignorant stares of ignorant people, unfamiliar with a kid like Isaiah, but back then it pissed me off. The tequila helped, but not much, and it came with the downside of having to look like a neglectful, absentee-type father, unable to deal with his own kid without drinking to tune him out, but all I cared about was getting us down to Mexico. About being there for Isaiah until each fit or tantrum passed. About helping him to get through each moment, each adventure, each day. No, I wasn't exactly the poster boy for how to parent an autistic child, but I was doing my best, putting my own spin on getting it done.

My parents had been staying down in Cabo on the same stretch of beach for as long as I could remember. For all their noise and fuss about lighting out for the open road and not being tied to any one place, they were now creatures of habit. We kids had all grown. One by one, we'd left the campers of our childhood, the absurdly close confines of our growing up, and lit out on our own. Now it was just Mom and Dad, left to each other, and the shards of the itinerant, surfer lifestyle they'd basically invented.

There was a shack on the beach, alongside the camper, so that's where Isaiah and I stayed. It was a woefully run-down place. There were scorpions crawling on the mattresses, which would have freaked out most little kids, but for whatever reason Isaiah was more bemused than terrified. To him, the scorpions were a new thing to consider, that's all. There were plenty of other terrors to keep him occupied—most of them having to do with the fact that I'd pulled him from his familiar surroundings.

Mom stayed on in the camper for a day or so with my father, helping him organize his things before she flew home ahead of us. That left me, Isaiah, and my dad—three generations of Paskowitz men, each of us completely unlike the other, cut from entirely different cloths. Put us together and we made one fucking crazy quilt.

The camper was parked by a stretch of beach that was part of a compound belonging to a guy named Don Hilario. He was a real local character. If you know Cabo at all, you know Don Hilario. He kept a pack of big-ass dogs on the compound for protection, and the dogs were a mixed blessing. They helped to keep our part of the beach safe from the local thugs and no-accounts, so I could get Isaiah into the water, but the barking was a huge problem. Isaiah was hypersensitive to it; he'd put his hands over his ears and start to scream and shake and sweat. If I didn't stay on top of it, Isaiah would lapse into a psychotic-type rage. He'd bite himself, bang his head against the wall... whatever he could think of to make it stop. He was still small enough that I could fold him into my arms and hold him close until the fit subsided, but it would always leave us both in such a whipped-up emotional state. It was draining, exhausting, constant.

As I held him, I kept thinking, *Man, Danielle. I don't know how you do it.* And I didn't. I truly didn't. Only explanation I could ever come up with was that she was some kind of angel, heaven-sent to guide our family over these rough waters.

Isaiah was on a bunch of different meds—then as now. The meds were unfamiliar territory for me, because I'd never really been Isaiah's one-to-one caregiver over an extended period. I'd never seen him come down from these wild mood swings and then get whipped up again into one of his frenzies. It was a real roller coaster. Better—and, certainly, more appropriate—it was like facing down a giant set on a wicked surf day. Yeah, there were moments of calm, but what you remember are the killer waves.

We gave Isaiah his meds in liquid form back then; he wouldn't take pills, although we experimented with the gummy bear–type squares that the pharmaceutical companies were just starting to put out. Anything to get the medication down. He wasn't crazy about the gummy squares, but they were better than the pills. He didn't like the liquid, either, but it was usually our best option.

Eating was a whole other adventure. Little smells would send Isaiah over the edge. If I took him into an Arby's, or some other fast-food place, he'd instantly puke. It was like pouring syrup of ipecac directly into his mouth. When we finally hit the road in the Mitsubishi for the long ride home, the hardest part was finding a place for Isaiah to eat. My father lagged behind in the camper, and I couldn't drive slow enough for him to keep up with me, so we fell into this routine where Isaiah and I would travel ahead, at our comfortable pace, and then we'd pull over at some designated place by the side of the road and wait for my father to catch up. We weren't traveling with cell phones, so we had to keep to our meeting points, but that still left us plenty of time to go off in search of something suitable for Isaiah to eat.

McDonald's turned out to be a safe haven. Yeah, it was no different from Arby's or some other fast-food chain, but for some reason my guy wasn't set off by McDonald's. Isaiah was big into nuggets. That was his thing. And he would only eat them with ranch dressing—and only if the dressing was at precisely the right temperature. If it was too hot or too cold, he'd throw a fit. It had to be just right. When it was too hot, he'd start screaming, "Bubbly ranch!

Bubbly ranch!" And if you knew what was good for you, you'd run for cover, because he'd go completely ape shit.

Sometimes, in some of the more remote parts of Mexico, Isaiah would almost starve, because I couldn't get him to try anything unfamiliar. I couldn't find a damn McDonald's anywhere. We'd pull into some tiny Mexican town, and the only things I could find for him were cookies, or maybe a taco stand where I could get him to keep down some deep-fried pork. He wouldn't eat any of the healthy stuff my dad kept in the camper and he wouldn't eat the typical stop-and-go stuff you could easily find by the side of the road, so eating became my front-and-center worry.

And right alongside this one worry was another: getting him to keep his medicine down. Especially the ones in liquid form. Oh, man, he hated that stuff, and every time I gave it to him he'd puke it right back up. I used to pull over to the side of the road and actually sit on the poor kid to keep him from squirming away and force a dose into his mouth and hope like hell it stayed there. He'd spit it out; it'd get in his hair, all over his clothes. Sometimes, in some spots, we'd be lying, struggling on the ground, so close to the road I'd worry a truck would swing wide and run us over. Or I'd be kneeling on the road, with the hot gravel poking through my knee, wondering how the fuck my life had come to this. How *our* lives had come to this.

But there we were . . . and do you know what? It was actually kind of cool. Even with all the tantrums and the throwing up and the hassle of finding something to eat, I started to look on this time with Isaiah as special. A real father-son-type moment—our first. It'd be supercorny to suggest we bonded or anything like that; really, there was no way to bond with Isaiah at that time in his life. And yet, I *was* bonding, only what I was bonding with was the idea of being a father. With the idea of a son I knew Isaiah could be, what we could be to each other. Underneath the ordeal of actually caring for Isaiah was a beautiful, simple truth: I was *actually caring* for Isaiah. I was being a dad.

Even Doc came around to the same place—or close to it. I can pinpoint the precise moment. We were driving to our designated meeting spot in a small town called Cien. Isaiah and I pulled in by the side of the road and got out of the car just as the sun was going down, and it looked like there were flames licking up to the sky, the whole scene bathed in orange and red. There were no streetlights, no stores, no other cars. Nothing to light the scene but the fading sun. And then, just before dark, my dad drove up in his shit-box all-white camper and crossed to where we were standing, waiting.

Up until this one moment, my father had never really acknowledged Isaiah. Not just on this one trip but ever, ever, ever. It's a painful thing to have to admit now, looking back, but at the time it didn't really register as any kind of big deal—probably because it had taken me so damn long to find my own way to Isaiah. Best I could figure it, my dad had always had a hard time finding room in his heart, in his life, in his head, for folks who fell short of his vision of perfect health and wellness. In his own bizarre way, he saw illness or infirmity as a kind of weakness. He couldn't accept it, even as it related to his own children or grandchildren. It's not that my dad was a bad, unfeeling person; it's just that Isaiah was a hard kid to know; if you didn't have a handle on his situation or his mood swings it was sometimes easier to look straight past him. That's all. But here, on a small shoulder of bad road in a tiny Mexican town on the Baja Peninsula, something happened to change all of that. Might have been the beautiful sunset. Might have been the thrill of traveling with three generations of Paskowitz men. Whatever it was, I wasn't about to question it.

I reached for my camera and through the viewfinder I could see my father holding Isaiah's hand. Nothing like that had ever happened before, between those two, and it struck me just then as the most remarkable connection—a sight just as fucking beautiful as the fiery sunset. It almost felt like I was cheapening the moment, to be taking its picture, but it was something to cherish—the first time, really, that my father reached out to my son as a fellow human being, walking this same planet, along this same plane, at this same time. And, on the back of all that, it was the first time, really, that I didn't hate Isaiah for being who he was, how he was. Or hate myself for how I was with him.

I used to beat myself up all the time about Isaiah's autism. I used to think it came from me. I still feel this way, sometimes. Like I'm somehow responsible. But here was this unexpectedly human moment between my father and my son, and it made me want to live for all the other human moments that lay in wait. It made me realize I had to get back home, and get with Danielle, and look at how I'd been as a father. *Really* look at it.

And, while I was at it, look at how I'd be, going forward.

Not too long after Isaiah and I got back from Cabo, we were met at the beach by my pal John Shestack, a wacky Hollywood producer who happened to have an autistic son, named Dov. John and I had a whole bunch of friends in common, and we covered a whole bunch of common ground. John kept coming up as someone who might help Danielle and me get a kind of foundation going, maybe find a way to formalize what I was trying to do, surfing with all these autistic kids on the beach. It was just a loose thought at the time. Wasn't even sure it made sense to do this in any kind of structured way, but I couldn't shake thinking that whatever light or lift I'd been able to give to these kids and their parents could be shared with hundreds and hundreds of families...if I could just find a way to do it right.

John and I talked back and forth on this for a while. And I talked to other folks, too. I needed to raise money, raise awareness...and, mostly, raise a posse of world-class surfers willing to donate their time and help me out in the water.

That afternoon, John came out to San O with his son, just to hang. Dov must have been about five years old, maybe six, and the waves were a little much that day for me to think about going out with Isaiah, or any of the other kids on the beach. The waves looked to be about fifteen feet, about twice the height I was comfortable riding tandem.

Dov was a spirited kid. He was wearing a pair of Wal-Mart water booties, and trunks. He'd never been out on a board before, but as his dad and I talked back and forth Dov was drawn to the water. The rough surf didn't seem to bother him, and at some point his father turned to me and said, "What the hell, Izzy. Why don't you take him out?"

I looked at John like he was plain crazy. I mean, this was a sick, sick wave—bigger, even, than I liked to surf all by myself. I said, "You shitting me?"

John pointed to his kid and said, "Looks like he's up for it. Let's just go for it."

Well, the little guy was certainly up for it, but he had an excuse; he didn't know any better—and I guess his dad didn't, either. Me, I had no such excuse; I certainly knew better, but I grabbed my board and took Dov by the hand and headed for the water. It was a stupid-ass-crazy-screw-loose kind of move, but this was something John seemed to really, really want for his kid.

In my defense, let me just state for the record that I'm a huge fucking idiot. It's no defense, really, but most surfers will tell you there's something dangerously seductive about a big wave; even if you're scared shitless, you're drawn to it; even if you should know better, the wave tells you that you don't. And in John's defense, he couldn't really gauge how rough the surf was that day; to him, surfing was surfing; he trusted me.

Big mistake.

Before Dov and I even hit the water, one of the lifeguards pulled up in his Jeep, took me aside, and said, "You really want to do this, man?"

I just shrugged. Didn't really have a good answer, except "yes and no."

Must have stood on the top of the sand leading down to the water for twenty minutes, trying to time the sets. There was a short window for us to paddle out. The waves were breaking so far offshore, a little tide pool had formed in the shorebreak, so we were able to plant ourselves there and then time the lull and scratch for the outside.

Soon as we set out I started to have second thoughts, and after that some third and fourth thoughts, too. Dov wasn't even wearing a life vest, I was first realizing, so my damn fool move was becoming more damn foolish by the minute. And that cool, calm, collected demeanor Dov seemed to show on the beach was washed away soon enough. He panicked, once we got out there. Started to scream and kick, but at this point we were committed. Couldn't really blame him, but to turn back would have been senseless; the best move at this point—the *only* move, really—was to keep paddling to the outside, and then to hope like hell I could catch a do-able wave and ride it back in.

Dov was on his belly, facing out. I was on my belly on top of him, trying to pin him to the board so he couldn't squirm off. As I was paddling, I could see the lines start to form and the waves begin to come at us harder and harder, faster and faster—and so I paddled harder and harder, faster and faster. I tried to get a good momentum going, but on that wave I needed to be like a freight train to power past the break.

I'd been in this wave before, of course. I knew where and how it would break, but at the same time I had no idea. I was completely confident and completely unsure of myself, both. I could see the waves coming, but they were still swells, which meant they would hit the sandbar below us and pop in such a way they could wipe us out. And so I kept paddling...through the first wave...through the second wave...and then we barely, barely made it through the third. I thought about *turtling,* flipping us over to give the wave some room to pass, but the break was so massive I didn't want to lose the board. Instead, I sat up and wrapped my legs tight around Dov and the surfboard, but as I did the full force of the wave broke just in front of us and hit us both right in the face.

Poor Dov was flipping out. Screaming his little head off. But then, as we passed through the wave and I had a chance to catch my breath and my bearings, I looked down to try to read the kid's expression. He was just about hugging the board, facedown, and all I could see was the back of his head. We were now all the way outside and bobbing in the water, and we'd gone from chaos to calm, so I started talking to Dov in a soothing voice, told him we were past the worst of it. Told him that here on in we'd have a blast. Told him these things like I really, really meant them.

Somehow, I got Dov to lift his head and look back at me, so I could get a read on his expression, and as he did I could see blood dripping off his chin. This concerned me, of course. This was not supposed to happen. Then I checked the rest of him, and I saw that his Wal-Mart water booties were gone; the wave had just ripped them right off his feet. This also concerned me, because I knew how attached Isaiah could be over his material possessions; he could fix on a thing and become a total nut job if he lost it or couldn't use it or had to part with it for some reason.

Then I leaned over and did a mouth check, saw that the kid

hadn't bitten his lip. Saw that he hadn't bitten his tongue. So I put my finger inside his mouth and determined the source of the blood; one of Dov's baby teeth had been knocked all but loose and was now about to come out, so I pushed it gently back and forth until it fell free, and before the tooth could slip into the ocean I tucked it in my mouth against my cheek for safekeeping.

The whole time, I kept talking to Dov in my most soothing voice. I kept stroking his hair. I kept telling myself that if I presented an aura of calm and confidence, these things would pass through me and attach to him, and just as he seemed to get comfortable the bomb set arrived at our backs and I started to paddle us into it.

Oh, man, this sucker was huge. The wave itself was about ten to twelve feet, but on its face it seemed to reach to fifteen feet, at least. It was killer. The good news was that the wave was so huge I had plenty of time to pop up, and after that I was able to just pick up Dov and hold him. He wasn't wearing a vest, so I couldn't grab him by the collar, the way I'd taken to doing; I had to collect him about the chest, the way you'd hold a puppy. I positioned my feet in a wide, wide stance, tried to make myself as stable as possible on the board, and as I set myself I took off on the left and brought us around so we were looking directly into this massive wall of water—the face of the wave. From there, we must have ridden that thing a half mile or more, until the wave closed up on us, and at that point I laid Dov back down, and I laid myself down just behind, and we rode the rest of the way on our bellies.

Rode that way right up onto the sand.

John Shestack came running up to us, all pumped and thrilled and jazzed. He'd been around surfers, but he had no real idea what it was to surf, what it meant to ride a wave like that with a kid like Dov in tow. John was just so charged by what he'd seen, and the look on his kid's face, which by this point had gone from the sheer terror his father had never seen to the pure adrenaline joy that now washed over him.

As John raced over to us, he noticed that Dov's water booties were no longer on his feet. And just then, to John, this seemed like an important detail. He said, "Hey, his booties! What'd you do with his booties?"

A part of me wanted to turn to John and say, "Fuck his booties, man! Here's your kid. Safe and in one piece. And happier than he's ever been!" But I didn't. I was too energized by our wild ride to cheapen it with any dark thoughts, so instead I made one of the grandest gestures of my surfing career. I rolled from the board and stood to shake John's hand. Then I reached theatrically into my mouth with my fist and…(wait for it!)…pulled Dov's tooth from my cheek and handed it to his dad.

Said, "You might want to hold on to this."

Even as I said it, I knew it was an over-the-top, Clint Eastwood–type line—that is, if Clint Eastwood made movies about surfing with autistic kids in treacherous conditions.

But John was deliriously happy, because his kid was deliriously happy. Because his kid had just lost his first tooth, and ridden his first wave, and seemed to come out of the shell of his autism and brighten…even if it would only last these few moments. Dov was so psyched he wanted to go out again, but I told him it would have to wait for another day. Told him he'd just had the thrill ride to end all thrill rides and we should probably quit while we were ahead.

And it was in that moment, in handing this little guy's tooth to his father, after riding one of the wildest waves I'd ever seen at San O, that the idea of Surfers Healing finally and fully came into focus. It's when the phrase "extreme special ed" first popped into my head—a phrase I'd use over and over, explaining our mission. And it's when I realized that what Isaiah and I needed was for me to dedicate myself to taking autistic kids out surfing, to making them smile, to making their hearts leap, to making them realize what it felt like to soar.

Anyway, it's what I needed.

◎

By the following summer, Danielle and I had kicked things up a notch. We worked it together, decided this was something we should be doing for each other, for Isaiah, for Elah and Eli, for the autistic community in our area.

On my end, I recruited some of the guys who'd been working as surf camp instructors, off and on. Guys with huge surfing pedigrees—like Puna Moller, Josh Froley, Josh Tracy, Nick Hernandez, and Skippy Slater, Kelly Slater's brother. (In later years, Kelly would help us out, too.) These guys had been around Isaiah; they weren't freaked by his behavior, and they had the chops to ride tandem with a little kid, or even a big kid—no easy thing, by the way. Danielle and I set it up so the instructors knew this was a form of mandatory volunteerism. We basically guilted these guys into helping us out, told them it was their ticket to heaven to throw in on such as this. But it wasn't such a hard sell, after all; soon as they rode their first wave with their first kid they were hooked.

Our idea was to take advantage of the half-day schedule we ran on Wednesdays and spend the afternoon surfing with dozens of kids at San O. We didn't advertise what we were doing, just put the word out that we'd be on the beach and available to take these kids on the ride of their little lives; Danielle went about it like it was a grassroots campaign. For example, Cliff Rehrig was always talking about Sonic's surfing adventures to other parents at Sonic's school, so we pulled a lot of those folks down for a look. First time out, we started with six or seven families; each of us spent about an hour or two with each kid, and it was just incredible. Exceeded our expectations by, like, a mile. The next week, there were maybe eight or ten families, so each kid got a little less time, but we were able to touch that many more.

At some point, I came up with the name Surfers Healing, in part because it emphasized the healing aspect of what we were trying to do, but here's what I didn't tell people at the time: the "Healing" part of the name had as much to do with me as it did with these kids.

At some other point, we decided to do some fund-raising. In addition to being a world-class surfer, Nick Hernandez was also a great musician; he played in a band called Common Sense that was pretty popular in the San Clemente area, so he got his guys to do a benefit for us at The Coach House in town, ended up raising over ten thousand dollars. It was more money than we'd imagined—and a great, great start. We'd been pinching boards and other equipment from Surf Camp, but this allowed us to purchase some vests and other gear. It allowed us to get all our paperwork in order and set us up with insurance and all that good stuff.

It even allowed us to think about taking our show on the road and bringing a Surfers Healing event to Hawaii, which we were able to do in 2000. We decided to hold it on Waikiki Beach, right in front of the Duke Kahanamoku statue, which had become a real surfing landmark. Folks would travel from halfway across the globe just to drape a lei over Duke's neck, so it seemed like a fine and fitting spot. And it turned out to be such a validating moment for us, for me. Why? Because I'd put the word out to everyone I knew in the surfing world, looking for volunteers. We didn't have the budget to fly in our San O volunteers to help run the event, so I tried to recruit all my old Hawaiian friends, guys I used to compete against. Guys my father used to surf with as a young man. I was really diligent about it, working the phones, sending e-mails. I put it out there that this was something I was doing for my son, and for other families with kids like Isaiah, and that I needed their help. My goal was to get about ten guys, because we were told there might be as many as fifty kids turning out for our event. Ended up bringing all these amazing, dedicated guys to the beach that day, from all over the island—seventy-five volunteers in all! Seventy-five! It was just incredible, and a lot of these guys hadn't seen each other in years and years. Some of them, their fathers used to surf together, and now they were able to reunite over this good, good cause and re-connect.

Danielle came out with all three kids, and it was a hugely reward-ing, affirming experience for all of us. Told us we were moving in the right direction. There were hundreds and hundreds of people out on the beach. There were reporters, sponsors, extended families. We even had my buddy Zane Aikau and some of his cousins and uncles, renowned Hawaiian watermen, taking our special kids out on these kick-ass ocean canoe rides, so there was a real sense of island lore and legend that attached to what we were doing.

(Zane's late uncle, Eddie Aikau, is probably the most famous waterman to ever surf Hawaii's big, big waves, and as a lifeguard he was credited with making some of the most epic saves in Hawaii's surfing history, so having Zane and his family join our effort was a huge validation for us.)

The thing about Oahu is it's very territorial. It's a supersmall is-land, but folks are so dug-in to their routines and customs a lot of these guys could live and surf within twenty miles of each other and still never see each other. For years, they'd never see each other. That's why it was so amazing to see guys like Eddie Rothman, from the north shore, turning up on the south shore for our event. And Rusty Keaulana and his west side crowd…they were out in force, too, so it was a great big deal.

What we were doing really seemed to mean something to these good people. *We* seemed to mean something to these good people.

Really, it was magic—and the most amazing piece was we didn't have to tell a single one of these great Hawaiian watermen how to communicate with an autistic child. I didn't need to show them what to do, or give them the benefit of my experience. It was instinctive. And it all flowed from Oahu to now: as I write this, we're looking ahead to our fourteenth Surfers Healing season, surfing with over twenty-five hundred autistic kids, spread over seventeen camps throughout the summer, in Rhode Island, New York, New Jersey, South Carolina, Maryland, North Carolina, Virginia, Hawaii, Puerto Rico, up and down the California coast—and this year, for the first time, in Canada.

Kind of amazing to think it all connects to that fateful day on Blobber Beach with Isaiah. To that ever-present Sarah McLachlan song "Adia." To those first few wild rides with kids like Dov and Sonic Blue. To the simple notion that a child with autism should be encouraged to reach for *all* that life has to offer—and that a washed-up pro surfer who took way too long to connect to his own autistic child is just the guy to help with the reaching.

15

The Family Biz

I suppose I have Isaiah to thank for pushing me towards the next phase of my career. And it's not just because I finally realized I needed to step away from the tour and find a way to make a real living and a real difference at home, although that was definitely a part of it. More than that, it was through Isaiah and some of the special friendships he developed that I was introduced to new people, new ideas, new ways of building on whatever was left of my surfing career.

Specifically, it was through Isaiah's best bud, Jacob Antoci, that we met our good friends Jeff and Natalie Antoci. (Or, I should say, *the late, great Jeff Antoci,* because our pal is no longer with us.)

You have to realize, to even be able to use a phrase like "best bud" in regard to Isaiah was itself a major blessing, because it's not like he had any friends. He didn't really connect with people. Even people in my own family. It still pisses me off to think how some of my brothers would react, the few times we'd visit; they'd trail Isaiah with a bottle of Windex, wiping down everything my kid touched; it's like they thought they could somehow *catch* his autism.

This disconnect was especially true when it came to other kids, even other kids who were cut the same way. But for some reason Isaiah formed a real bond with Jakey. Their teacher called us in one day to talk about it, to suggest the boys get together outside of school. Apparently, Jakey would have the same kinds of meltdowns in school and then de-escalate and lapse into a kind of comatose zone, same as Isaiah. The teacher would look up, and Jakey would be laying on Isaiah's lap, decompressing, and Isaiah would be stroking his hair or petting him, and I heard that and thought, *Whoa.* It was pretty heavy.

Danielle got together with Jakey's mom, Natalie, first, and after a couple visits Jeff and I joined in. We all got along great. Jeff was a good, good guy, and soon as we got to talking the floodgates kind of opened for each of us. We'd been down the same road, carrying the same heartache, so we had a lot to talk about. That's how it's been over the years, when I meet families through Surfers Healing. You learn someone has an autistic child, you know exactly how they live their lives. You know their days. You know the kind of shit they have to deal with, the stares from strangers, the hassles, the meltdowns, the constant attention they need to devote to their kid. We have a different look about us, I think, a different way of seeing the world—because our world is nothing like everybody else's world.

Isaiah and Jakey, they were simpatico. They'd follow each other around. Even when they were apart, they seemed to be on each other's minds, to where Isaiah would sometimes say Jakey's name, from out of nowhere. Or he'd hear one of us mention the Antocis and he'd brighten. So it was a great, full-on family friendship, and it really blossomed. Jeff and I got along so well we started taking the boys on trips. Eli came with us on one trip, Elah came on one trip, and Jakey's brother, Joey, came, too. We always had a blast. We'd mix it up, depending on what was going on at home, on who was around. We'd hop into Jeff's van and head to Palm Springs, or wherever, mostly just to give Danielle and Natalie a break.

After a while, Jeff and I got to talking. He had a great business mind. He worked in commercial real estate, and he'd managed to build this network of connections, all over the country. He knew how to work a situation to advantage—not in a shark-like, cutthroat way, but in a chill and decent way. People really responded to him. Whatever new business idea or venture we talked about, he knew someone connected to it, at some high level or other, so he became an important mentor to me. And he had my back. I had no background for this type of thing, so I was looking for someone I could trust who would talk me through these new twists and turns, maybe point me in the right direction—and Jeff emerged as that someone, before long.

In the water, I knew what I was doing; out of the water, I had no fucking clue.

◎

Jeff was an incredible friend to the entire Paskowitz family, helping us navigate a landgrab that took place over control of the Paskowitz Surf Camp. Can't think how else to explain the mess my brothers and I nearly made of what was essentially our only asset as a family; best way to tell it is to just tell it.

What started back in the early 1970s as an informal, thrown-together way to bring in some money and spread the joy of surfing had become an important part of our Paskowitz legacy. My father knew a good thing when he stumbled across it, but he also knew the power and poetry of the Hawaiian spirit. He knew what it meant for an islander to extend a warm welcome to any haole. It was considered an honor, even an obligation, to teach people to surf—like you were sharing a profound gift, so that was a big, big part of what he was up to here. He even came up with a line to express this thought, which we still use in our camp advertising—"Share the aloha!"

The money was good, too. Not great, but good enough for him to keep at it, year after year.

As we got older, Doc put us to work. We'd hang with the campers who matched up with us in age, and eventually we learned how to be instructors, and as we left "home" and disappeared into our own, separate lives we kept coming back to San O on our own each summer to help out at camp. It was what we knew, who we were. And it was a way for us to keep tabs on each other, to reconnect as a family. Even when I was on the professional circuit and surfing out of my mind, I enjoyed being a part of it. I'd pass up certain tournaments, if it meant I'd miss a whole summer of camp... that's how much the tradition had come to mean to me. And my brothers and sister all made their own sacrifices to be there, too, whenever they could.

At some point, my father couldn't keep running it the way he always had. He and my mom wanted to move to Hawaii, where the water was warm and he could surf every day and stop moving around, from beach to beach. He was getting too old for this shit, he said. But he wanted the camp to continue, and to be a kind of anchor for our family, so he handed the reins over to Abraham. Don't know how or why Abraham got the nod, but he was happy for the gig—and he did a good job with it, for a while. Basically, he ran it the way my father had always run it. He took out ads in all the surf magazines. He reached out to past campers. And that was that.

After a while Moses took a crack at it, and then David ran the show for a couple years, but towards the end of the millennium his focus seemed to be elsewhere. David had all these crazy ideas about Y2K and the end of the world as we knew it, and he seemed to check out on running the camp, so my father looked to me. I'd finally ended my surfing career, and I was kind of floundering, struggling to find something to do, so my father came to me one day and said, "Israel, I've been waiting for this moment for a long time. This is something you've earned. If you want it, it's yours."

I was touched that he put it just this way, but at the same time I wasn't surprised. He was very particular about surfing, my old man. He placed great weight on what I'd been able to accomplish on the tour. He respected the kind of surfer I'd become, that I'd faced down the big waves he could never handle as a young man, that I'd almost drowned off Réunion Island, that I'd tamed all these monster waves and out-dueled all these surfing giants and helped to put a shine on the Paskowitz name throughout the sport. It's like it meant more to him than anything my other siblings had done—and I don't mean to suggest that I agreed with him on this, or that it was any kind of fair assessment, but this was how he'd always looked out at the world.

With him, surfing was all.

I grabbed at the opportunity like it was a lifeline, but I had no idea what I was doing. I had zero business skills. I'd never heard of a business plan—wouldn't have recognized one if you rolled it up and hit me over the head with it. But I told myself I was the right guy for the job because I'd earned my chops as a surfer, so where David and Moses and Abraham hadn't been able to make a go of it, I'd have a shot.

It's like I was starting from scratch, though. David had done such a loose job of it, he didn't even have a database. There were no files, no spreadsheets, just some handwritten notes on four or five pages of a legal pad, with the names and addresses of past campers. That was it.

(Don't know that a spreadsheet would have been all that much help to me, back then, because I was completely computer illiterate. I could turn one on, but that was about the extent of my technical skills.)

This was where Jeff Antoci was incredibly helpful—at least, this was his first piece of incredible help. He had a lot of strong ideas. He told me to focus on what I had, not on what I was missing, and what I had was a lot of experience chasing sponsors. I knew that world, knew how to play that game, so I went at it hard. I started making a bunch of calls. I reached out to all these different surfboard makers and accessory companies, trying to create something out of nothing. Somehow, I managed to get the Roxy/Quiksilver folks interested in starting an all-girls camp with us; we'd had a ton of girls surf with us over the years, but we'd never run a dedicated all-girls session, and here we got Roxy to kick in some money and some product and support from their pros. It was a huge success, too. They cut a check to us for forty-five hundred dollars and on top of that they donated a neat gift bag for each camper, filled with about a hundred bucks' worth of stuff—T-shirts, sunglasses, wax... whatever. They even helped convert one of our buses and dress it out with the Roxy logo. It was totally bad-ass, and they got a lot of nice coverage out of the deal, but then when I went to pitch them on the men's side the following summer it was slow going. I was dealing with a bunch of different suits, but they worked in the same damn company; they saw what we were doing with Roxy and had a good idea what we were capable of doing for the Quiksilver line, at relatively little cost, but I couldn't get them to buy in. And it's not like I was asking for a ton of money.

My pitch was that we were bringing authenticity to their brand. We had some authentic surfers in the water with our campers, and we were creating dozens of new surfers each week, so I thought if a company like Quiksilver could start making an impression on these campers at the outset they'd be customers forever. That's how it was with me, back when I started out. Whatever boards I surfed first, that's what I reach for now. Whatever gear I wore as a kid, that's what I wear now. For example, I'm big into Billabong; it's such a great product, and they've made such a mark, it's the only wet suit I'll use. There might be other great wet suits out there, but Billabong has made me a customer for life, and that's what I was selling here, with Quiksilver—a way to build customers for life.

But they weren't buying. Even for the low, low price of fifteen thousand dollars, which would have bought them a full season of signage and sponsorship and prominent mention in all of our camp advertising, they weren't buying.

So Jeff and I tried to think of other companies we could approach with the same pitch. At around this same time, I was talking with Kevin O'Malley, publisher of *Men's Journal*, who'd just done a tremendous story on us, and through him I met a bunch of influential designers and fashion folks, who were just starting to operate on the fringes of the surf apparel industry. They were dipping their toes in our waters, guess you could say, so Jeff and I started to realize it made all kinds of sense to target some of these mainstream companies, where promotional budgets were beyond ridiculous. To a company like Quiksilver, for example, a fifteen-thousand-dollar sponsorship deal was a big item; to a company like Tommy Hilfiger, it was a speck, so I made a quick side trip with Danielle to the MAGIC men's apparel show in Las Vegas, to chase down some high-end sponsors.

Now, it's no accident that Jeff and I were thinking in Tommy Hilfiger terms, because Kevin O'Malley had introduced us to one of their Macy's buyers, so we had an in. Ended up meeting with Andy Hilfiger, who was in charge of the jeans line, and we started talking about this new line of board shorts the company was introducing that year. Andy was all excited to show them to us, and completely bummed that we didn't seem to share his excitement. I had to be honest. The shorts were total bullshit to a real surfer, completely lame, and I said as much to Andy. The colors, the styling, the functionality were all wrong. Told him how the whale net they'd sewn into the crotch—the mesh nut sack you see in department store swim trunks—had no place in a true board short. Told him how real surfers like to ride commando, but these guys didn't know that. They knew fashion. They knew design. And here they were coming out with this nothing line that surfers and wannabe surfers just wouldn't wear, so I figured I'd give it to him straight, figured I had nothing to lose. And to Andy's great credit, he listened to me on this. He recognized that if he wanted to break from the mainstream and find a way to get hard-core surfers to wear his shorts and whatever else he was putting out, he'd need a little bit of *cred;* he'd have to throw in with someone who could lend some genuineness to the brand.

Out of all this we signed a fifteen-thousand-dollar one-year deal with Tommy Hilfiger, which was all the money in the world to us—enough to help us purchase some new equipment and enhance the camp in a bunch of ways. Wasn't game-changing money, but it certainly got our year off to a nice start. Don't know how we hit on that figure, because I imagine these guys wouldn't have blinked if I'd asked for twenty or thirty thousand dollars, but I wanted to build a long-term relationship with the company; I didn't want to scare them off, so I got them to make us a bunch of shorts without the whale net in the crotch, which we gave to our campers and instructors, and they cut us a check, and we were in business.

The following year, we went at them again, only this time we were operating from a position of real strength. There'd been a bunch of high-profile newspaper and magazine articles about me, about the Paskowitz family, about our camp … and in each case you could spot the Tommy Hilfiger logo on one of our boards or somewhere in the background. It was pretty prominent, so they'd definitely gotten a lot of bang for their few bucks. I knew what ads in these publications tended to run, so I was able to attach a value to the exposure—and at fifteen thousand dollars it was a huge bargain. My thinking, as we looked to roll over this first sponsorship deal into a second, was to ask for way more money this time around—maybe as much as one hundred thousand dollars—but at this level I was starting to feel like I was in over my head. I'd never been a good negotiator. I was never comfortable talking dollars and cents, so I thought about taking Jeff along to help me out, but then I had another idea; my brother Jonathan had started doing some work for us and he was a natural salesman, so I sent him to meet with the Hilfiger folks instead.

Best-case scenario, I thought, was we'd re-up at some number in between the previous year's fifteen thousand and our pie-in-the-sky figure of one hundred thousand, so I wasn't prepared for the deal Jonathan brought back—three years, one million dollars. I heard those numbers and had to sit down. Then I had to scream. One million dollars! It was so far off the map of my thinking, I had no frame of reference for it. Take all of us Paskowitz kids, add up everything we'd earned on our own since we left the camper, all the prize money we'd won, the sponsorship deals we'd signed, the record deals, the sunglass deals . . . and I don't think we'd have gotten anywhere close to one million dollars.

It's not like the Hilfiger folks were planning to cut us a check and leave it at that. It was a complicated deal, with all kinds of bonuses and out clauses and the formation of a sub-division of our own line of Paskowitz-branded apparel, but I didn't pay attention to any of that stuff at first. I just saw those seven figures. In my head, it's like the numbers were lit with neon, like a sign on the Vegas Strip. Like a fantasy. I'd never even considered that kind of money, but there it was. Not yet, mind you . . . but still.

◎

The initial check was for $115,000, but we couldn't cash it. This was the first I knew that our deal was going off the rails, the first whiff of the mess I mentioned earlier. The news of our sponsorship and licensing deal made such a splash in the industry, it almost derailed our partnership with Tommy Hilfiger before it got going; it also caused a rift in my own family, and for a while it appeared it might even cost me the camp.

On the industry front, the deal created a stir among traditional surf companies, because they knew they couldn't compete with the big-name designers. The Tommy Hilfigers of the fashion industry were making billions, while the Quiksilvers and Hurleys and Billabongs were making *only* millions, so the little guys started to think the big guys would swallow up their sliver of the surf market. They worried that if Tommy Hilfiger got any kind of traction with its Paskowitz Apparel line, they'd be followed by Nike and Adidas and any number of giant action sportswear companies and they'd be squeezed out. And the thing of it is, I'd come to know a lot of these guys over the years, guys like Bob Hurley and Dick Baker of Ocean Pacific. They were talking shit about our deal; a bunch of them had thrown in together and formed a group called SIMA—the Surf Industry Manufacturers Association—just to get a firmer toehold in the marketplace. I was broken up about this, but not too, too broken up, because these guys had all had their shot with us. I went to them first, but they laughed at me; they didn't want anything to do with Paskowitz Surf Camp. They didn't want to sponsor us for five, or ten, or fifteen thousand . . . so they certainly didn't want to sponsor us for one million dollars.

What this meant, for us Paskowitzes, was that for the first time in our lives our name had a bit of a stain on it in some parts of the surf world. For forty years, whenever a surfer came across my dad, or his name came up in connection to the sport, it was always attached to a positive vibe. Same for the rest of us, as we made our own way, on our own waves. Folks would hear the Paskowitz name and spark to it, but now there were some influential people within the surf industry—guys who'd sponsored me or Jonathan over the years, guys who used to surf with Doc—who were probably think-ing, *Aw, that Paskowitz kid is such a greedy motherfucker!*

It would all shake out to the good, over time, but for a while there wasn't a whole lot of aloha spirit coming our way.

The Hilfiger folks, they took us in with open arms. Sent us a whole bunch of gear. Had us looking like a real professional outfit, instead of the ragtag group we'd always been. They sent a box of promotional goodies for each instructor, filled with gear and swag worth about one thousand dollars. And they overloaded us with banners and stickers and signage, which we plastered all over camp, all over the beach, wherever we went. We ended up getting so much attention for Hilfiger, and becoming so closely associated with their brand, that my brother David couldn't help but notice. He hadn't been a part of Surf Camp since he handed over those few scraps of legal pad paper and I guess he started thinking he was missing out, so he started maneuvering to claw his way back in.

He had some encouragement in this, we later learned. He'd been hanging with a group of aggressive MBA types, who kept filling his head with talk about turning Paskowitz Surf Camp into a thriving national entity, convincing David he'd been squeezed from his birthright as Doc's oldest son, telling him they could make him rich if he'd throw in with them on a kind of hostile takeover—and even making the case that there'd be enough profits to spread among the other eight siblings, in such a way that all of us would be rich and fat and happy. These suits had David thinking he could take care of all of us, if only he'd step up and take control.

The first I heard of David's renewed interest was when I went to deposit that first check. I took it to the bank and asked for seventy-five thousand dollars back in cash. My idea was to distribute a little something to my father and then to put the rest of it to work on equipment and various improvements we were hoping to make that summer. I even brought an empty briefcase with me, to help me carry all those bills. I was like Ralph Kramden on *The Honeymooners,* counting the money in my head.

But then the teller came back and told me there was a stop payment on the check.

"Excuse me," I said. Wasn't sure I'd heard right.

"I'm terribly sorry, Mr. Paskowitz," the teller said, "but these funds are not available. There's been a stop payment order placed on your check."

Here I'd never seen that kind of money in my life, never even contemplated that kind of money, and it was gone before I had it in hand.

Apparently, David and his team of "advisors" had pulled an end-around move and gone to New York to meet with Tommy Hilfiger himself—presumably to demonstrate that he was the rightful owner of the Paskowitz Surf Camp and to show that he was the Paskowitz named under our current permit with San Onofre State Beach. This last was in fact true, because we were operating under a long-term permit David had signed while he was still running the camp. I guess it didn't matter to David that he was no longer involved with the camp or that he'd stepped away from it on his own. It wasn't even his deal; he hadn't negotiated it; he hadn't been a part of it in any way.

I was devastated, floored. And out-of-my-mind mad. I couldn't believe that my own brother would be behind such a despicable act. And it wasn't only an attack on me; I saw it as an attack on the whole family, so I switched into desperation mode. I rallied the troops, in what ways I could. I scrambled to secure space for the camp at Campland, an RV park and campgrounds where my family used to park the rig when we were kids, and to obtain permits with the City of San Diego to allow us to run the camp at Mission Beach. Then I flew to Hawaii and laid it all out for my father. He knew about the Hilfiger deal, of course, but he had no idea of the infighting going on with his sons, so I filled him in. Told him what David was trying to do. Told him how Jonathan and Abraham had been working with me and how Joshua and Salvador were on board to help with the designs. Told him there was even room in what we were doing for David in our apparel deal, if he wanted in, and if he backed off on this grubby-ass move to take back the camp. Spent a couple hours going through the whole sad ordeal, and at the other end Doc formally signed the camp over to me, and then I had those documents notarized.

What was mine on a handshake was now mine on paper.

Within two weeks, we were back in business—but not until Jeff and I attended a meeting with my siblings and our various advisors. David actually called the meeting, to explain his actions and to offer what he thought was an olive branch, to smooth things over. He wanted peace in the family, he said. He wanted all of us to do well. Then he showed us this slick document he'd prepared, which talked about his background as a world-renowned surfer and the standard-bearer of the Paskowitz family legacy as the oldest son; he'd made himself sound like he'd been touched by Tahitian royalty, and blessed by the Hawaiian surf gods, and somehow anointed as a kind of *surf whisperer*. It was total crap, and nobody was buying it.

Out of that meeting, our mess got even messier...and I came away thinking our entire Hilfiger deal was about to collapse. Going in, I'd thought we could somehow salvage that relationship, but there was so much poison in that room, I couldn't see how these guys would want to stay in business with us, even if we could find a way to settle our differences. Plus, my other brothers had been running up all kinds of expenses, which they were charging to Hilfiger's Paskowitz Apparel clothing line—limos, flights, bar tabs, hotel rooms... whatever they could justify in their own cockaroaching heads. Don't know what the hell they were thinking, but this was how we were wired; this was what we knew. We'd read in the papers that Hilfiger stock was at an all-time high; we'd see the company's urban line all over the place, the preppy line all over the place, the business casual line all over the place. The company was hot, hot, hot, so it must have seemed to my brothers that we'd tapped into this bottomless well of money.

Ah, but that's not exactly how it shook out.

How it shook out was this: David attempted to operate his own version of the Paskowitz Surf Camp. He took out ads in *Surfer* magazine, but hardly anybody responded to them. Nobody cared, I guess. I was eventually able to win back the camp name with the help of a camper who just happened to be a trademark attorney, and after that David had to call his operation the David Paskowitz Surf Camp, which made it even tougher for him to generate any business. We went from an average of sixty or seventy student weeks each summer when David was running the camp to over three hundred student weeks once we got going, so we were really able to invigorate the business in just a few years, while David's camp fizzled.

The bank finally released that $115,000 check, but by the time I paid off all of our legal bills and reimbursed the Hilfiger folks for the bogus expenses they identified on our account there wasn't a whole lot left—just enough to give my brothers and sister a few thousand dollars apiece, as a kind of goodwill gesture, and to throw a few thousand more at my parents, to help set them up for the next while.

That was the end of our sponsorship deal, but by some miracle of blind faith the Paskowitz Apparel line lived on for another couple months. The way the contracts were written, it was treated as a separate entity from our Surf Camp deal, and I guess the company wasn't entirely put off by our backstabbing nonsense. Yeah, they were put off enough to pay good and close attention to our expenses, but they must have had a lot invested in their surf line and wanted to see it through, so we installed Jeff Antoci as CEO of Paskowitz Apparel and got Hilfiger to hire Jonathan to lead the sales effort, and Abraham, Salvador, and Joshua were put on salary, too. We really wanted to make this thing work, and ended up producing a sweet line of merchandise—beautiful stuff, really, made with high-end, vintage fabrics. But that was as far as it ever went. Most of the line sat in a warehouse and was never distributed, although some of it was dumped into the discount bins at low-end outlets like Ross and Filene's.

Guess us Paskowitzes were a little more trouble than we were worth, after all.

⊙

A final few words on the Paskowitz Surf Camp—which, after all, was at the heart of this heartless landgrab that nearly tore my family apart. After forty years, we still run it the way my father imagined it in 1972: good surf, good folks, good food, good times. We remain a small, family-run operation, totally committed to capturing the warmth and good feeling that seem to find us on the beach, in the water, at the campsite at the end of a long, magical day.

It's the longest-running surf camp in the United States and the first of its kind, and what sets us apart from other surf schools and clinics is that we live with our campers for the full week and help them soak up the whole of surf culture. Any experienced surfer can *teach* a beginner how to get up on a board, how to paddle out, how to time a wave, but our goal is a bit bigger. We're out for something more. We're out to create surfers. It's like our version of that old *give a man a fish* adage. You know, *Give a man a fish, and he'll eat for one day. Teach a man to fish, and he'll eat for a lifetime.* That's how we look at surfing. Get a student up on a board, put him into a wave, and he'll ride it into shore. But create a true surfer, expose him to the rich history of the sport, share the aloha spirit that attaches to it, and he'll surf for a lifetime.

That's our thing, and folks seem to respond to it—some have been coming back for years and years. Hey, we've been at it so long, we're seeing the second and third generations of the same family come back each summer, giving these next generations a chance to build on what we started with their parents and grandparents.

It doesn't hurt that we bring in some of the world's best surfers as instructors and that each one seems to find a piece of joy in passing on the sport. And it doesn't suck that we've created a welcoming, nourishing camp environment, where we can sit around the campfire at night and swap surf stories and strum our ukuleles and look ahead to the next day's adventures.

Learning to surf can be an intimidating, daunting experience for a lot of folks, but our instructors keep this in mind. They consider it a profound gift, to be able to share what they know, to invite our campers into their world.

In a way, it's like a mini-, weeklong version of the way we lived in the family camper, for most of our growing up. We spill out of our sleeping bags and hit the beach. We break for lunch. We surf until the sun hangs low and we can hardly move, we're so sore from all that paddling. We light a great bonfire and sing and eat and drink our fill. Some nights, maybe Doc Paskowitz himself will stop by for a visit, to share some insight or other. Then we wake up the next morning and do it all over again.

No, it doesn't suck. Not at all.

EPILOGUE

Another Good Day
(Only This One Didn't
Start Out So Hot)

May 18, 2003.

It was meant to be a celebration for my fortieth birthday. Danielle was actually at San Onofre with friends and a great big cake, but I never made it back from Mexico, where I'd been running a couple weeks of Surf Camp.

In my head, I almost didn't make it back it all.

Since taking over Surf Camp, I'd gotten into the habit of holding two weeklong sessions in Cabo to start the season in the Spring and then another two to close it out in the Fall. It meant three days driving down and another three driving back, so I was usually gone about three weeks at a stretch, but it was a good moneymaker for us. We were able to keep costs to a minimum and still do it up right for our campers, with a nice place to camp and good, authentic food. Really, we gave a ton of value on these trips; we were able to introduce our campers to a bunch of off-the-beaten-path surf spots and offer a real taste of Mexico; the only hassle was the back-and-forth, because we had to haul absolutely everything we'd need from California. It meant loading up all our boards and wet suits and other supplies in the truck, which was packed tight, and then a bunch of spillover gear into the van we'd need to ferry our campers to all these great waves we'd line up for them in and around Cabo. It was a bit of a grind for us, but we always had a blast—and the campers did, too. Most sessions were filled with repeat customers, guys who kept coming back year after year, so we all kind of looked forward to it.

This one year, second session of the camp had been a bust. There was a sick tropical storm, unusual for that time of year in that part of the world. It rained for days and days, hard. Still managed to show our campers a good time, out of the water; we were down there to surf, but we tried to make the best of it. Turned out *the best of it* ate away at our bottom line, because we had to scrap our usual digs on the beach and spring for hotel rooms, to keep safe and dry. It was just one of those things, nothing we could do about it, so I decided not to let it stress me out or bring me down. Told myself I'd never been good at making money, anyway, so this week would be no different.

Another one of those things: during this washout storm week, more than half our campers were named Bob. Weird, how it worked out. I had my buddies Nick Hernandez and Caleb Wilborn with me, working the camp, and we had some trouble telling all these Bobs apart, so we came up with handles for them. There was Big Bob and Little Bob, natch. There was Little Big Bob. There was one Bob who looked like Tony from *The Sopranos,* so he was Tony Bob. There was Religious Bob and Gay Bob—not exactly the most politically correct nicknames, but they got the job done. Basically, there were a whole lot of Bobs, and a couple non-Bobs, and everybody got along great.

We were all bummed about the weather, of course, but we found our kicks where we could. One highlight: running into Chad Smith, the drummer from the Red Hot Chili Peppers. His bandmates Flea Balzary and Anthony Kiedis were longtime friends and supporters of Surfers Healing, so we'd gotten to know Chad over the years, and he was in Cabo sitting in with Sammy Hagar on an Alice in Chains gig, so he hooked us up with tickets.

Didn't exactly make up for the storm, but it certainly didn't suck.

We were all a little off our game, because of the weather. Got a late start headed home, but we were determined to take our time. You could do the drive straight through, takes maybe twenty-five hours, but it's a killer, draining drive. You're on high alert the whole way, on a two-lane road with no barrier and some serious drop-offs. So our thing this year was to take it slow, and it worked out that once the weather broke we were itching to get back in the water, to make up for all those lost surfing days.

The Bobs and non-Bobs had gone home at this point, so it was just me and Caleb and Nick, who we all called Nick-I. On a whim, we decided to take a detour, ducked off the "main" road and took a long, winding side road we knew that would take us to a spot we'd surfed in the past. Took us over an hour out of our way, but we didn't care. By the time we got to the beach, the sun was hanging low. There was about a half hour of daylight left in the sky, but the waves were absolutely beautiful. Intoxicating.

I knew Danielle had gathered a few pals for a mini-celebration back home, but I'd called ahead and told her we couldn't make it. Just wasn't happening. Felt bad about it, but it's not like we were running a couple hours late; we were going to miss it by a couple days, so I figured I might as well get in the water on my birthday. Something about turning forty and wanting to have that touchstone to remind you what you're about... what you've *always* been about. So we scrambled to get the boards off the truck before the sun dipped below the horizon. Couldn't find my board shorts in our mess of gear, so I slipped out of my jeans and thought I'd surf in my briefs, but then I thought better of it and left my shirt on—a funky, buttoned-down dickey-type shirt, with a collar, no sleeves, which left me looking a little like a crocodile. It was a lot of effort and silliness just to catch a couple waves, but it was totally worth it. Felt supervalidating, sustaining, to be able to ride on my fortieth birthday, even for just these few moments. Felt like it's what I was meant to be doing all along, for always and always.

We decided to camp right on the beach. We had no money for anything else; even if we did, there was no place to stay; anyway, we were long past hurrying, or worrying. We had tents and sleeping bags. We had some canned food. Most important, we had a giant cooler we'd just filled with ice, and about four cases of Pacifico. The ice could be a precious commodity in remote Mexico, so those cold beers were a luxury.

Couldn't really find any wood for a fire, so we burned some cholla cactus, which did the trick well enough—then, to feed the fire, we'd add little scraps of driftwood we took turns collecting by flashlight. When my turn came, I reached for a piece of cactus and caught a quick glimpse of a tiny black scorpion tail. I don't think I saw it fully enough in my sliver of flashlight for it to register, but as the tail swung around to hit the tip of my finger it came clear. Didn't really hurt—just kind of *stung*—but it scared the shit out of me. I screamed like a girl. (Also not the most politically correct choice of words, but it makes my point.) Then I pulled my hand back, stuck it under my flashlight. Couldn't really see any blood, any redness, any swelling. I tried to shake it off, put it out of my mind, but I hung back after that, left it to Nick-I and Caleb to finish foraging for stuff to burn.

I was completely creeped out, but I wasn't in any pain. Just nervous and jittery. We sat around the fire for a while, eating canned beans, drinking our icy cold beers, remembering all the Bobs and the misadventures of the past couple weeks. In almost every way, it was a pleasant, perfect way to spend a milestone birthday, other than the back-of-my-mind worry about that scorpion sting. But then the worry went from the back of my mind to front and center. My finger started to numb. After that, my whole hand went numb. And after that, my thoughts started running all the way away from me.

Nick-I could see I was freaking out, so he tried to calm me down with whatever bullshit scorpion facts he could come up with. "Don't think the ones in Mexico are poisonous, Iz," he said.

This might have been helpful, if I had reason to believe Nick-I knew what the hell he was talking about. Best I could tell, he was just talking.

Caleb, too. "'S all good, man," he said, between pulls of Pacifico. "No worries."

Essentially, these guys had no useful information on scorpion stings, which I could add to whatever I thought I knew on my own, and at the other end we all had absolutely no fucking idea what we were talking about.

Meanwhile, the numbness crept towards my upper arm, ever so slowly, and by now I was absolutely convinced I was about to die— and not a quick, easy death, but an agonizingly slow, painful one. I started imagining every worst-case scenario, and I'd put them out there for Nick-I and Caleb to consider, and they'd take turns laughing and dismissing each one, telling me to just have another beer and chill. The back-and-forth felt a little bit like Beavis and Butt-head discussing nuclear physics; we were clueless on top of clueless, and underneath I was trying to figure an appropriate next move. I thought about driving back to La Paz, but it would have taken two hours just to get back to the two-lane dirt road, and then another couple hours from there.

Instead, we took turns talking me out of the idea that scorpions were poisonous. In this, the beers surely helped. Drink enough Pacifico, you can convince yourself of anything. The numbness I was feeling, we all decided, was just some type of allergic reaction. Wasn't any kind of sign that I was shutting down, and yet even as I tried to convince myself of these things the numbness seemed to take a turn at my shoulder and move towards my chest, where a part of me felt certain it would give me a heart attack.

After a while, I decided to step away from the fire and crawl into the truck, to wait out my fate. Nick-I and Caleb stayed by the fire. Don't think they even bothered setting up a tent; they just slept on cots, while I stayed by myself in the truck—a Ford Crew Cab, where I threw down some pillows and made myself comfortable in the backseat. Before settling in for the night, we lifted the cooler into the bed and set it up so I could reach it from the backseat, through the little slider window in the back of the cab.

Would have been a nice little setup if I wasn't half out of my mind.

⊙

Didn't sleep that whole night. I was afraid if I drifted off I wouldn't wake up, so I kept sipping beers and thinking. Sipping and thinking, that's all. Nick-I and Caleb, those guys were out. Don't think they came by to check on me even once. Or maybe they did and I was too deep into my own thoughts to notice.

At some point in the middle of that long, long night, I went from going quietly insane to feeling washed over by an absolute calm and clarity. I went from being afraid to die to being absolutely okay with it, to thinking I'd lived a rich, full life and was leaving behind a meaningful footprint. I thought back over my childhood, to when we were in Hawaii, going to school barefoot; to moving from house to house in California; to finally lighting out for the open road and living by our wits on beach after beach.

I thought of my parents, living in an apartment on the beach in Hawaii—still surfing, still fucking like teenagers—and the wild, wacky lives they'd built for us kids. No, they hadn't done *absolutely* right by us, keeping us out of school, leaving us dreadfully unprepared to face the wide, wide world, but they'd done right enough; their hearts were right, at least.

I thought of the Paskowitz Surf Camp, which I'd been running for the past couple years, after taking it over from my brothers, and reimagining it, and then wresting it back from my oldest brother, David, and reimagining it all over again.

I thought of all those unopened boxes of Paskowitz Apparel merchandise, sitting in some warehouse or gathering dust in a storage shed at my Auntie Grandma's place in Paris, California.

I thought of the rift that nearly derailed my family over that $1 million Tommy Hilfiger deal, and how we'd each found our own way to get past it and settle into a kind of groove in and around San Clemente, in each other's midsts.

Mostly, I thought of Danielle and the kids, and the time I'd wasted on the tour after Isaiah was born, the good thing we were starting with Surfers Healing. I thought of the ranch Danielle and I had managed to build, on that beautiful spread in the hills of San Juan Capistrano where we'd lived like settlers back when Elah was born; I thought back to how the gods had finally smiled on one of our business deals and allowed us to catch a break, when we bought a nothing-special house in San Clemente at the bottom of the real estate market and flipped it a couple years later when the market was hot, and how with the proceeds we bought the land from Danielle's folks and put up a comfortable house, a stable for Danielle's horses, a foundation for our future.

I thought of Isaiah, and the way we'd almost lost him just the year before. It was February 2, 2002. I'll never forget the date: 02-02-02. He was crossing the street with his great pal Jennifer Tracy when a catering wagon happened by and caught his attention. We used to call those wagons roach coaches, and Isaiah knew there'd be something good to eat inside, so he kind of spun on his feet and moved towards it. Somehow, he let go of Jennifer's hand, just as a young marine driving a Mustang came careening down the street. Ran right into Isaiah, who rolled over the hood and landed on his back on the pavement.

Jennifer raced to Isaiah's side as she called 911. Gave the dispatcher her location, told him the situation. Then she called me. All she could say was Isaiah had been hit by a car. She couldn't tell me if he was okay. She was too hysterical to talk, so I got their location and raced over there like a madman. I was four exits away on the interstate—Estrella, Hermosa, Pico, and Presidio. Must have been going a hundred twenty miles an hour. Got there ahead of the EMS guys, and the whole time I had no idea if my boy was dead or alive. I was flat-out frantic.

I double-parked the car as close as I could to the scene, swung the door open, and ran the rest of the way on foot. For whatever reason, I was barefoot, and as I raced over to Isaiah I could see he was completely still. Completely cute and chubby and silent and still. When I got to him, I could see there was some head trauma. There was blood at the back of his head, but there wasn't any pooling, so it wasn't supersevere. And he was breathing! Thank God, he was breathing. I sat down on the street next to him and stroked his hair, talked to him, tried to soothe him, comfort him, however I could. At that point, I didn't know if he was going to be okay. I didn't know if I was saying good-bye to him or helping him to hold on.

I wanted to cry, but I didn't want Isaiah to hear me crying. I didn't want him to worry.

Seemed like an eternity before the EMS guys rolled up, but once they did they kind of took over. One of them tried to talk to Isaiah, and I tried to explain to him that he wasn't going to respond—because he was autistic, not because he was injured. This confused the EMS guys mightily. You'd think they would have come across an autistic patient in some distress or other, once they'd been on the job for any stretch of time, but I had to try and explain it—and just then I couldn't find the words.

"He's autistic," I finally shouted. "He's wired a little differently, that's all."

In my blind panic and frustration, that's all I could come up with, but now that I think back, it wasn't such a bad description. That about covered it.

Somewhere in there, Isaiah started screaming. Like a banshee, he started screaming. Like bloody murder. And underneath his wailing and kicking and screaming, I knew he'd be okay.

Danielle met us at the hospital, but not before I had to climb on board the gurney and sit on Isaiah's chest to pin him down so the doctors could work on him. It was a freaky scene. They tried to get a needle in him, to start a catheter, and he was just going completely ape shit. Finally, they had to intubate him, which was pretty horrifying—me straddling his chest the whole time. They had to inject him with some drug that shut down his system, stopped his breathing for a moment so they could take some pictures, run some tests, and once again I thought we'd lost him. Nobody had thought to tell me what they were doing, what to expect, so I started going a little ape shit myself.

After a long while, things seemed to calm down. Isaiah came back around and started to breathe normally. Danielle showed up in time to hear he'd suffered a concussion, that's all. No broken bones. No internal bleeding. No long-term damage. He'd have to stay the night in the hospital, for observation, but he was going to be fine.

And so there I was, backseat of the truck, trying not to drift off into sleep, thinking back on these terrifying moments—me standing in the hospital, listening to the doctor's good prognosis, staring at the ID bracelet some nurse had slapped on my wrist when we rolled into the emergency room, with my name, Isaiah's name, and the date: 02-02-02.

It's like it was burned into me, like a tattoo.

◎

At some point, fighting off sleep, I started talking to myself, just to give voice to all these different thoughts flying through my head. Actually, I wasn't talking *just* to myself but to Isaiah as well, as if he was some kind of spirit guide with the power to see me through. I was getting loopy, I guess, but I have a distinct memory of this, of asking Isaiah for strength. And—get this!—of feeling strengthened by my special, special boy.

With each beer, it became more and more of a celebration. If this scorpion was meant to kill me, it didn't seem like such a bad way to go. I wasn't in pain. My house was in order. My relationships were all in good shape. I'd go out on a high note, with my cooler full of Pacifico.

I was a good son, after all; I was a good brother, after all; I was a good husband, after all; I was a good father, after all.

No regrets.

There was no cell service out by the beach, otherwise I might have called Danielle and invited her into my racing thoughts. There was no way to record what I was thinking. I was lost in the stillness of my mind, alone, but in those loose, lost moments I looked back at the whole of my life—where I'd been, where I was—and it made me smile. Really, I would not have traded a single thing about my life at just that moment, all the way down to the still-real prospect that I might not make it through the night.

Soon, the morning sun started to brighten the sky, and I knew I'd be okay. The slow creep of numbness seemed to retreat back down my arm, back towards my hand, back towards my finger. Whatever it was, it wasn't about to kill me. It would take about a year for the numbness to completely leave the tip of my finger, but by then I'd gotten used to it. By then it was a warm reminder of this loopy night on the beach in Mexico, when I ran through the stuff of my life and came back whole.

When I could greet the sun and down the last of my beer and think, *Fuck, I'm good. Really, I'm good.*

THANKS AND SUCH . . .

A giant *Mahalo Nui* to the folks who helped me set my thoughts to paper. First and foremost, I should probably thank my parents, Dorian and Juliette Paskowitz, for sending us off on the mad adventure of our lives, and to my brothers and sister for sharing in that adventure. Doc also helped shake loose a couple of memories and share some stories that made their way into these pages. My lifelong pals Ian Reeder, BK Reynolds, Moe Tracy, and Michael Tracy also sat with me and reminisced about the good ole days, and Kevin O'Sullivan, Arty Tan, Jeff Ekberg, and David Buss read over my shoulder and helped make sure I was getting it right. A nod, too, to the coolest literary agent in New York, "Uncle" Mel Berger of William Morris Endeavor, for thinking there might be a book in here somewhere. And to Nichole Argyres at St. Martin's Press, who's pretty cool herself, for thinking the same and for taking such good care of my story. Also at St. Martin's, big props to Olga Grlic for designing the sweet cover, Kathie Parise for the kick-ass page design, Nadea Mina for getting the word out, and Laura Chasen for helping with the pics.

Also, a tip of the pen to my buddy John Pike, who first thought to push me to write a book. He even put me in touch with Dan Paisner, who helped with the heavy lifting on the writing front. I'd say more nice things about Dan, like he's brutally talented and disarmingly handsome, but he's writing these acknowledgments on my behalf, so it'd be kind of awkward for him to blow too much smoke up his own ass. Not cool.

On the home front, I want to thank Jennifer Tracy for helping out with Isaiah so I can have a life and find time to actually write a book, and to my in-laws, Danny and Sharon Brawner, for eventually deciding that they didn't hate me and that I might be good for their daughter. (Or, not too bad.)

In the water, an *Aloha Nui* to all of our Hawaiian, Californian, and East Coast surf warrior volunteers for making and keeping Surfers Healing a reality, especially the "original six" who helped Danielle and me get this effort started—Joshua Froley, Puna Moller, Josh Tracy, Nick-I Hernandez, Skippy Slater...and, I can't quite think who the sixth one was. (Oh, crap...it was me!) Also, can't forget my buddies Scott Ruedy and Roy Gonzalez, Renaldo Lopezy, Bob Bueno, and John Meade, who've been real diehards. And the dozens and dozens of big-hearted, world-class surfers who've thrown in with us over the years.

On the beach, I want to honor some of my personal heroes and great buddies from the world of surfing—"Tubesteak" Tracy (and his wife, Phyllis); Dale Velzy; Joel Tudor; Skip Frye; Uncle Herbie Fletcher (even though I kind of trash him in the book, but I'm hoping he won't read that part); the Keaulana, Froiseth, Downing, Hobie Alter, and de Soto families; the Aikau *ohana;* Chris, Keith, and Dan Malloy; Makua and Eddie Rothman; Glen and Noel Minami; and, *natch,* Kelly Slater.

In the media, thanks to our pals Kevin O'Malley at *Elle,* Graydon Carter, Edward Menachesky, and Sara Marks at *Vanity Fair,* Stephen Jacoby at *Esquire,* Armen Keteyian of CBS News, Lisa Bennett of HBO, Oprah Winfrey, Peter Liguori, Ted Skillman and Balisa Balban at Snackaholic, Tom Sacks, Paul Colliton, and Kelly Cutrone at People's Revolution for shining good and positive light on Surfers Healing. Thanks to you, folks know who we are and what we're about—at least a little bit.

On the trail, a fine *hey* and *howdy* to my Tortuga riding brothers, Brent, K.W., and Mr. Beans.

On dry land, I'm grateful to Miriam Buhl for taking care of business on behalf of Surfers Healing, along with her colleagues at Weil Gotshal and Manges, including Steven and Richard.

I'm also sending love and thanks to Andy Irons, Sion Milosky, Garrett McNamara, Tim McCabe, Anthony Kiedes, Flea, Jimmy Buffet, Russ Kunkel, Perry Farrell, Sarah McLachlan, Eddie Vedder, Common Sense Band (Jeff Antoci, Lois Pilot, Lorie Enryod . . . RIP), Pat Notaro III, John Shestack and Portia Iverson, Miguel "El Campion" Rojas, Farmer Dean Carlson, Mark Anderson, and Scott Caan for various good and solid turns along the way.

And finally, a heartfelt, heart-filled thanks to my family—my children, Elah, Isaiah, and Eli, and my beautiful wife, Danielle. You've put up with my crazy shit at home for years and years, and now you have to put up with it in book form for all the world to see. Sorry about that.

Oh, and almost forgot—a shout-out to Hot Cop.